SEÁN MOYLAN

AIDEEN CARROLL

SEÁN MOYLAN

REBEL LEADER

MERCIER PRESS

Irish Publisher – Irish Story

MERCIER PRESS
Cork
www.mercierpress.ie

Trade enquiries to CMD BookSource,
55a Spruce Avenue, Stillorgan Industrial Park,
Blackrock, County Dublin

© Aideen Carroll, 2010

ISBN: 978 1 85635 669 5

10 9 8 7 6 5 4 3 2 1

A CIP record for this title is available from the British Library

Printed and bound by ScandBook AB, Sweden.

Contents

Acknowledgements		9
Introduction		13
1	The Ties that Bind	15
2	1919	28
3	The Road to Recovery	39
4	The General Lucas Affair	47
5	Getting Guns	56
6	Spiral of Violence	62
7	Meelin	72
8	Meenegorman	77
9	Tureengarriffe	80
10	February 1921	89
11	Clonbanin	97
12	The Gun and Promotion	109
13	Cork No. 2 Brigade O/C	115
14	The Arrival of the Gloucestershire Regiment	120
15	Capture	129
16	A Writ of Habeas Corpus	138
17	The Court-Martial	145
18	Spike Island	159
19	The Truce and the Treaty	166
20	On the Edge of Anarchy	178
21	The Slide to War	183

22	The Civil War	186
23	Overseas	196
24	In the Wilderness	208
25	Dáil Career 1932–1937	218
26	The Bothy Fire	228
27	World's Fair – Seán Keating	232
28	Director of Air Raid Precautions 1939–1942	241
29	Dáil Career 1943–1957	247
Appendix I	Martin Savage – A Memory	268
Appendix II	Transcript of Voice Recording for the Bureau of Military History	271
Appendix III	Speech at Spike Island to commemorate Patrick White	275
Notes		280
Bibliography		307
Index		313

Dedicated with affection and respect
to Rick Moylan, who started the book
but failed to finish for the best of reasons.

ACKNOWLEDGEMENTS

The research and completion of this book would not have been possible without the dedicated support and assistance of a number of willing people. In the first instance I would like to pay tribute to the work of the late Rick Moylan, whose unfinished biography of his father was an invaluable reference for this project. A special word of recognition is also due to my mother, the late Peig O'Brien (née Moylan), who left an evocative voice recording of her Moylan relatives. I acknowledge with sincere thanks the contribution of Carmel Enright (née Moylan) and Eileen Bryan Brown (née Moylan) to the family history and the stories of their lives growing up in the Moylan household. A debt of thanks is also due to the late Stephanie O'Callaghan (née Moylan), who facilitated research on this subject which ultimately shed light on Moylan's parliamentary career.

A particular thank you is also extended to John Moylan, Rory Moylan and Joni Moylan, who generously provided access to relevant documents. I would also like to acknowledge the influence of the historian Dorothy Macardle and pay tribute to Richard Abbott, whose work on RIC casualties during the 1919 to 1921 period proved immensely valuable. To Michael Moynihan, TD, my thanks for access to the commemoration material displayed at the Seán Moylan fiftieth anniversary celebration in 2007, and a very special word of thanks to Ronan Burke for his skill in preparing and transferring the photographs and images to disk.

The blessings of an extended family were manifest in the numbers who came forward to search for material in obscure corners, to track down books and reports and to make pertinent suggestions along the way. To all those who were persuaded to read through newspaper archives and Dáil debates, and to search out photographic and other material, thank you – your efforts were above and beyond the call of duty. My thanks to Jack Enright for his many corrections and suggestions, to John Healy for his work in Kerry, to Jane Bryan Brown for her research at Kew and to Mary O'Brien for taking on numerous time-consuming tasks. Also to Tom Carroll, J. P. Enright, David Enright, Olwen Van Woerkom, Isabel Van Woerkom, Ethan Van Woerkom, Éamonn Ó Scolláin, Conor O'Brien, Mary Kelly, Rosemary Boran and Muireann Carroll, my sincere gratitude.

I would like to thank Father J. J. Ó Ríordáin, CSsR, who generously shared his memories and correspondence, not to mention his encouragement and support along the way, and to Katty Sheahan (of Newmarket) for the photograph of Seán Moylan in uniform and for identification of her aunt, K. T. Murphy, NT.

To Commandant Victor Laing O/C and the staff at the Irish Military Archives, Cathal Brugha Barracks, Dublin, thank you for your willingness to produce copies of the many witness statements used in the researching of this book. A particular thank you also to Tom Desmond at the National Library of Ireland manuscript department, who gave me invaluable direction in the early stages of my research. My thanks to Dr Peter Hart, who directed me to the Moss Twomey papers at University College Dublin Archives, and to Dr Éimear O'Connor of the Irish Art Research Centre, Trinity College, Dublin, who generously provided a newspaper cutting of Keating and Moylan at the 1939 World's Fair in New York. I am also obliged to George Streatfeild at the Soldiers of the Gloucestershire Museum for permission to use the Grazebrook material and related photographs.

I would like to acknowledge the assistance of Suzanne Mitchell at the Minister of State's Office, Office of Public Works, for providing the image of '1921, An IRA Column', and to Fiona White at the Department of the Taoiseach, who willingly dug into the 1937 archive to retrieve a copy of the report on seasonal migration. Sincere

SEÁN MOYLAN: REBEL LEADER

appreciation is extended to Donal Keating for permission to use the Seán Keating images reproduced in this book.

I am grateful to the following libraries, institutions and newspapers for permission to quote from their collections or newspaper archives: National Library of Ireland, National Archives of Ireland, National Archives (Kew), University College Dublin's Department of Archives, Dublin City Library and Archive, *The Irish Times, Irish Independent, The Times* (London), the Essex Regiment and the Queen's Royal Lancers Museums. My particular thanks to the *Irish Examiner* for permission to reproduce the transcript of Seán Moylan's trial, which appeared in the *Cork Examiner* on 31 May 1921. I would like to acknowledge the balanced and objective reporting conducted by that newspaper during the critical years of 1919 to 1921.

Every effort has been made to trace the copyright holders of the collection of Major General Sir Peter Strickland; I and the Imperial War Museum would be grateful for any information that might help to trace those whose identities or addresses are not currently known. Finally to George Murphy, who, despite my best efforts, I was unable to locate, thank you for your teenage memories of the air raid precautions in Wexford during the Emergency.

To Tom and Muireann, who suffered months of neglect while this book was in progress, a huge thank you, and to all those whose kind words of encouragement spurred on the work, *go raibh míle maith agaibh*. Any errors or omissions that appear in this work are entirely my own.

Caricature of Seán Moylan by Pyke.
Copyright: Irish Press Plc

INTRODUCTION

Seán Moylan was my grandfather and the bond was a strong one. As no historian has come forward to write his biography and make use of the family archive, this book seeks to offer a fair and balanced account of his life. Moylan once said that a biographer should take care not to make the subject 'a whale among minnows' and I have tried to avoid that snare. He also said that 'history is better understood if one has a conception of the personalities of those who make it'. The story of modern Ireland is Moylan's story writ large. His life was crowded with the milestones of recent Irish history: the events of 1920–1921 and the Civil War are gripping examples, and this book remembers all who suffered in those painful years. History is important and there remains a compelling interest in how wars were fought, in the stories of the brave and of the less than heroic, in why conflicts started and in how they might be avoided.

Moylan's record as a guerrilla commander is remarkable. He was cautious with the lives of his men and he was successful: the place names of Tureengarriffe and Clonbanin still resonate in Cork. His court-martial for levying war against the King remains one of the most interesting stories to emerge from this period. He was fortunate to survive both the War of Independence and the Civil War, and from the 1930s onwards he played his part as a politician in moving Ireland towards peace and prosperity. His oft-used phrase to his children, colleagues and constituents was *'Ar scáth a chéile a mhaireann na daoine'* – 'In the shadow of each other the people live.' This thinking underpinned his lifelong commitment as a public representative.

Moylan joined the Gaelic League as a teenager. He spoke Irish with a natural fluency and did much in his later years to promote the Irish language and the Gaeltacht. In politics he was known for his breathtaking directness of speech and an intolerance of rhetoric. Those outside the political classes remember him for his kindness and charm. He was a mass of contradictions: a barnstorming orator who could be funny, difficult and taciturn all in the same afternoon. He was erudite, quick-witted and at ease in debate, as a colonel of the Gloucestershire Regiment learned to his cost. But his heart frequently ruled his powerful intellect and there were occasions when this passionate man was entirely lost for words and fell back on a powerful right hook. His personality had an enduring impact on friend and foe, and he formed friendships in the most unlikely quarters. The men who served with him remember his loyalty and courage. Éamon de Valera described him as the soul of integrity.

Moylan was also a controversial figure. Many believed that he and others like him – Liam Lynch, Ernie O'Malley and Frank Aiken to name a few – started the Civil War when it should never have been fought and continued the war when all hope of victory was gone. It has been argued that many lives were needlessly lost and much bitterness ensued. Moylan was also a Dáil Deputy and a government minister at a time when there was entrenched violence and abuse within the industrial schools system. This system destroyed many lives and looking back we wonder why that political generation and the many agencies of the state failed to root it out.

A forthright politician who never dodged the hard questions during his time in office, Moylan shared in the shaping of modern Ireland, first as a Volunteer, then as a brigade commander and much later as a TD and cabinet minister. This is his story.

I

The Ties that Bind

Just before dawn on 6 March 1867, the Fenian Rising reached Kilmallock near the border of Limerick and Cork. Several hundred attackers surrounded the Kilmallock Barracks of the Irish Constabulary. The building was no more than a substantial detached house set back from the main street at an angle. A few of the rebels were armed with guns and some had pikes, but most were unarmed. They demanded the surrender of the garrison, but this was refused. The attackers then tried to burn down the barracks and the fight started in earnest.

The defence of the barracks was led by Head Constable Richard Adams, with fourteen men of the Irish Constabulary and a number of their wives. From the smoke-blackened rooms the constables fired their rifles through the windows at shadowy figures. Their wives reloaded and helped prevent the roof catching fire. The constables fought with no way of knowing when reinforcements might come. The attack continued until mid-morning when the Fenians came under attack from a heavily armed rescue party.[1] Volley after volley was fired into the ranks of the Fenians, scattering them within minutes. Among the fleeing rebels were Ned Raleigh, Seán Moylan's maternal grandfather, and Batt Raleigh, his grand-uncle. Until that morning the Raleigh brothers had been shoemakers employed at the Kilmallock workhouse.

Ned Raleigh escaped detection and returned to make shoes at the workhouse. Batt had to go on the run, 'hiding out first in Tankardstown, then Mitchelstown and finally like many others before and since, he disappeared into the Glen of Aherlow'.[2] When an amnesty was announced he returned to Kilmallock, where he lived long enough to witness another storming of the barracks in 1920. But that was still a long way off. The 1867 Rising was suppressed. Head Constable Adams was decorated for the defence of the barracks and later that year the gallantry of the Irish Constabulary was recognised and the name was changed to the Royal Irish Constabulary (RIC).[3] Law and order was restored to Kilmallock, but the Fenian dispossessed continued to smoulder.

On the morning of the 1867 Rising, another grand-uncle of Moylan's, Patrick Pickett, had been given the task of capturing a police dispatch rider travelling between Bruff and Kilmallock. He seized the officer's horse and dispatches, and brought them to Captain Dunn, a leader of the Fenians. After the Rising was crushed Pickett was interned at Limerick Gaol. When he was released he heard that another man had been convicted of the attack on the dispatch rider and had received a sentence of five years transportation. Pickett went at once to the police and his confession secured the other man's return from Australia. In his witness statement, Moylan recalls Pickett's return from Australia in the late 1890s. When he saw his grandfather silently gripping Pickett's hand, he asked about Pickett and learned about 1867.

Seán Moylan was born in 1888 at his grandparents' home in Kilmallock. His mother, Nora, had endured a number of miscarriages and in the later stages of her pregnancy she had gone back to Kilmallock to stay with her family. Her son was born safely and was christened John, but commonly called Jack. Nora's health was poor and she stayed with her relatives for a few months after the birth before returning to her husband in Newmarket. Her infant son remained in Kilmallock where he was raised by his adoring aunts. It might seem odd now, but the arrangement was not unusual at that time. And so it came about that the formative influences in Jack Moylan's early years were the Raleighs and their acquaintances, men such as Batt Raleigh and

Patrick Pickett and a phalanx of formidable aunts including Mary Raleigh and her five sisters. Moylan later recalled that Batt Raleigh was a slight, religious man and he had difficulty reconciling this figure with armed rebellion against the greatest empire in the world. Patrick Pickett he admired for being too proud to let another man take his punishment.

Kilmallock heaved with a history that crowded into young Moylan's life. The walls of the town bore testament to a troubled past and everywhere there were echoes of its historical significance: the castle, the abbey and the monument to the unknown Fenian. Even the street names were redolent with nationalist history: Sarsfield Street, Wolfe Tone Street, Lord Edward Street and Sheares Street where the Raleighs lived. When the anniversary of 1798 came around, his schoolmaster gave fireside readings each week as episodes were published in the press. Moylan recalls the teacher sitting between a veteran of the American Civil War and a huge bearded survivor of the Crimea. He was entranced by the events at Ballinahinch, New Ross and Killala, and night-time brought vivid dreams: 'the pitchcap, the cat o' nine tails, the gallows, the Hessians, the burned homes and churches'.[4]

But the more immediate influences were the Fenians and on 6 March each year the Kilmallock men marched to remember the 1867 Rising. In November they also marched to remember the Manchester Martyrs, William Allen, Michael Larkin and Michael O'Brien.[5] This small dwindling band of elderly men who fought for Ireland continued to march each year under the watchful gaze of the RIC. They walked and sometimes shuffled. Beaten men, without influence or means. Moylan 'looked in awe and respect at old toil-worn men marching because [he] knew that they, unarmed and untrained, had faced the guns of the police in '67, that they had suffered'.[6]

While young Moylan daydreamed at his grandfather's house in Kilmallock, his father, Richard, ran a successful building business in Newmarket. In 1900 he won a contract in Kenmare but got a soaking one day and a cold turned to pneumonia and then to tuberculosis.

Nora had read about barrier nursing and moved her husband into his mother's house next door. Wearing protective clothing she nursed him until he died and then burned all his belongings and bedding to avoid infection. Jack was thirteen years old and he had four younger brothers and sisters: Ned, Joe, Mamie and Gret. The family's financial circumstances became uncertain and Nora turned her hand to millinery and got by running a grocery shop in Newmarket for many years.

After his father died, Moylan returned to live with his mother. The Moylans had been part of the Newmarket landscape for generations, moving from Church Street to the western end of the town in the latter part of the nineteenth century. At the time of the 1911 census this was an attractive town amounting to no more than a few intersecting streets. On one side of the wide main thoroughfare was a stone entrance to the Aldworth demesne, on the opposite pavement Jimmy Liddy's tree had stood for some 300 years. There was a substantial Church of Ireland in cut stone and a Catholic church which was built in the 1830s.[7] The only other buildings of note included a courthouse, the RIC barracks, two small schools and a fever hospital. It is a description that could answer for many towns in Munster. It had no particular claim to fame other than being the birthplace of John Philpot Curran and the final resting place of his daughter Sarah.

In 1904, a branch of the Gaelic League was established in Newmarket. Moylan joined shortly after and learned Irish.[8] His teachers were Dan Galvin of Glashakinleen and, much later, Seán na Cóta Kavanagh of Dunquin. The Moylan ladies were most hospitable; recognising his strengths, they overlooked Seán na Cóta's liking for strong drink and provided bed and board for the duration of his stay in Newmarket. Moylan developed a devotion to the Irish language and was a frequent visitor to Dunquin for the rest of his life.

A Christmas 1904 letter to his Aunt Maggie Raleigh in America captures the essence of life in a north Cork country town in the early years of the twentieth century. Moylan writes about his mother buying a consignment of toys, cakes and fruit for the shop, and getting a free silk umbrella from Musgrave's in Cork. He tells Aunt Maggie, 'there will be a ball here [upstairs in the workshop] on New Year's Day and I'm going to Kilmallock for Christmas'. His Uncle Daniel Moylan's clandestine fishing activities are also mentioned – 'we got a few salmon from Din and sent one to Kilmallock' – and more ominously 'there is a lot of fighting and moonlighting going on around here'.[9]

Unlike Kilmallock, where the nationalist tradition was strong, there had been no such tradition in Newmarket, where the unionists held the reins of power. They occupied all the key jobs: postmaster, bank manager, clerk of the sessions. The means by which power was controlled were unseen, subtle and pervasive. Moylan recalled a small but pivotal moment in the early years of the twentieth century that was the first faltering sign of dissatisfaction with the old order. It was the occasion of an annual fundraiser for the local hunt, an event organised by, and for the benefit of, the local ascendancy. It finished, as every concert then did, with everyone standing for the national anthem. As the first few words of 'God Save the Queen' rang out, a small voice from the back of the hall sang loud: it was Moylan's younger brother Joe and he was singing 'God Save Ireland'. The words were taken up by all those in the cheap seats and, as the closing bars hung in the air, the crowd poured out onto the streets cheering and laughing.[10] Nothing was ever quite the same again.

In the summer of 1905, Moylan left Drominarigle school and sat the exams for a clerkship with the Great Southern Railway. Passing the exams was one thing, but having influential contacts meant more. He failed to gain a position.

It is likely that Nora then decided her eldest son would train as a carpenter so that he could take up what remained of the family business and build on old contacts. He returned to his grandfather's house in Kilmallock and undertook an apprenticeship. His father had been an able builder and carpenter, employing a number of men to fashion wheels, carts, windows, ladders and doors. Richard and his brother Din had made the beautifully crafted pews in Newmarket church and were the third generation of Moylans to run a carpentry business in the town. But Séan Moylan was not an eager apprentice; he served his time from a sense of duty but faced with the choice of picking up a hammer or opening a book, he would always choose the book.

Moylan was an energetic young man of average height and sturdy build. He had thick, dark, unruly hair, a strong Roman nose and a wide engaging smile. He appears to have been a thoughtful young man with conventional aspirations and was inclined to keep the company of adults. He read Charles Dickens, William Makepeace Thackeray, George Eliot and Anthony Trollope, as well as any newspapers he could lay his hands on, although his grandfather Ned had the annoying habit of sitting on the *Limerick Leader* while he read the *Freeman's Journal*.

He was also a good athlete and joined the Gaelic Athletic Association (GAA) in his teens, at a time when hurling was still a cross-country affair. Hurling was the sport he loved most and it was a lifelong passion, but he was better at Gaelic football. He was a useful half-forward and was a member of the Kilmallock side that won the county championship in 1908 and 1909.[11] The Kilmallock GAA club also had a fine tradition in athletics and could claim connections to the Olympic successes of John Flanagan from Kilbreedy. It was that connection which brought the American team to Kilmallock for final training before going on to London for the 1908 Olympic Games. In July the entire town turned out to watch Tom Longboat, the legendary Indian distance runner, sail home, having run from Limerick to Kilmallock 'paced by horses, ponies, cyclists and sprinters'.[12] The Americans came and went and life returned to a slower beat.

In 1913, the final year of his apprenticeship in Kilmallock, Moylan joined the Irish Volunteer Force and changed his name to Seán, although to his family he would always be known as Jack. Inspired by a spirit of nationalism, many of his companions in the GAA and the Gaelic League did likewise. Twelve months later he was back in Newmarket. His grandmother, Mary Noonan Moylan, was an astute businesswoman. In her younger days she could look at a stand of trees and know what it would yield in profit. She had kept the Moylan workshop ticking over with the sale of ironmongery and agricultural implements and was well into her seventies when Seán took over the family business, dividing his time between carpentry and the Newmarket branch of the Volunteers. His mother Nora continued to run her grocery shop on New Street and his three redoubtable aunts, Maud, Kate and Annri, operated convivial refreshment rooms next door. For the Misses Moylan it was the ideal enterprise and provided hospitable surroundings for storytelling, playing cards and exchanging gossip.

On Easter Sunday, 23 April 1916, Moylan mobilised a mile outside the town at Barley Hill, along with the rest of the Newmarket Volunteers. He was twenty-seven years old. The Volunteers had little training, few guns and conflicting orders. They were sent home on the Sunday evening and in the days that followed they read about events that would later change their lives. For the first time since 1798, the capital city was in the hands of republican revolutionaries, but by 30 April it was all over. On 4 May the *Cork Examiner* reported that Dublin was returning to normal and Cork county was quiet, 'with the exception of an affray in the Fermoy district where a head constable was shot dead'. By July the papers had reverted to news on the First World War and life continued at a normal pace in Cork. That summer the Kilmallock senior football team won the county championship again, this time by a single point. Moylan played on the winning side and it was probably the last occasion he played in earnest.[13]

Moylan's links with the GAA and the Gaelic League had been strong for many years and this, coupled with his republican beliefs, meant his involvement as a Sinn Féin organiser was inevitable. The year 1917 was a momentous one for Sinn Féin. The election of Count Plunkett in Roscommon was followed by the election of Joe McGuinness in South Longford, Éamon de Valera in East Clare and William Cosgrave in Kilkenny. It also marked the reorganisation of the Volunteers in Cork, where Moylan attended the first meeting along with other notable figures such as Tom Hales, Seán Hegarty, Tomás MacCurtain and Terence MacSwiney. Moylan took over the Newmarket battalion and was convinced that the future of the country would be decided by military conflict. The main problem in Newmarket was that they had few guns, and only shotguns at that. It was a problem that resonated throughout the county. Paddy O'Brien of the Charleville company recalled that their battalion had only four shotguns.[14] The Millstreet company had thirty-five shotguns and little ammunition.[15] In the autumn of that year Moylan organised several attempts to steal rifles from the RIC. Each raid failed and it was not until March 1918 that he got his own weapon, when a rifle snatched from a policeman in Newmarket was passed to him.

In spring 1918, against the backdrop of the First World War and in particular the slaughter on the Western Front, the British parliament introduced a bill to impose conscription in Ireland. The subsequent protests generated a huge rise in the ranks of the Volunteers. For many Irish people of moderate opinion, Ireland's strategic value to Britain came into sharp focus. For centuries, and in particular throughout the nineteenth century, Ireland had been a source of troops to defend the British Empire – big, strong, healthy farmboys who contrasted greatly with the rickets-afflicted men from the inner-city slums of England. Taking the King's shilling was a route to survival in difficult times. They had fought with Wellington on the Peninsula, at Waterloo, in India, in the Crimea and against the Boers. But conscription was a step too far.

At that time Moylan was still living at home in Newmarket, but the carpentry business had collapsed; too much of his time was devoted to Sinn Féin. Meanwhile his brothers were leading strikingly different lives. Joe had won the King's scholarship and gone on to take a degree and write an MA dissertation on the poetry of Thomas Moore. Ned had emigrated to the United States and when America entered the war he joined the 69th Regiment, winning a commission in the field. In spring 1918 he was fighting with the Allies in France and leading a patrol to capture prisoners. His men had evaporated in the fog, some lost, some pretending to be lost, but Ned had captured a German soldier, wrapped a piece of barbed wire round his neck and pulled him back to the Allied lines. He finished the war as a captain in the infantry and was awarded the Croix de Guerre.

While Ned Moylan made his contribution to the Allies, and indirectly to the British Empire, the RIC and the army were rounding up known Sinn Féin leaders in connection with the 'German Plot' to overthrow the administration at Dublin Castle. Very little evidence of such a scheme has come to light, although with the war hanging in the balance British intelligence clearly feared such a plot. Seventy-three members of Sinn Féin were interned and shipped over to England, where they were held until March 1919.

Moylan evaded the initial sweep, but was forced to leave home and go on the run. He remained a full-time Sinn Féin organiser and commandant of the Newmarket battalion. However, he was facing a problem. Many of the Volunteers who joined as a result of the conscription crisis were men of moderate opinions and the thought of fighting was something they could not contemplate. Others simply enjoyed the company and some were even set on buying musical instruments and forming a band. Moylan recalled cycling thirty miles to Danny Martin Murphy's house in Glounakeel in cold, wet weather to persuade the Volunteers there not to waste money on band instruments. He describes what happened next:

The house was gradually filling. The settle was first occupied, then the chairs and stools, and finally the rooms were robbed of their scant furnishings to provide accommodation. And still the company came. The walls of the kitchen were now lined three deep. There was a low animated murmur of conversation. I was under a constant if covert survey. There was a watchful solemnity about the whole affair which reminded me that it might have been a wake and I the corpse but for the fact that no prayers were offered, at least publicly, on my behalf. The change from the penetrating cold and dampness of the outside world to the now steaming atmosphere of the kitchen was becoming oppressive and I was about to suggest that the conference with the officers in the upper room might begin when the matriarch spoke again. 'Danny,' says she, 'wouldn't ye play the band for the organiser.' Danny frowned and looked sheepishly at me ... shrugged his shoulders and smiled. I turned round. Two large men had a smaller man on their shoulders. He was handing down bright, new, gaily painted drums from the collars where they were resting to the reaching hands of the others. I counted a big drum and four side drums. A space was cleared in the centre of the floor, the big drum was braced, the smaller drums were screwed up and the drummers stood to line. Then it seemed as if all the others present buried their left hands in inner pockets and produced fifes. The big drummer gave a preliminary and encouraging tap and then while thirty fifes shrilled forth 'The Wearing of the Green' all the drummers, like demented semaphores, whirled their sticks as if their lives depended on their drowning all sound other than that of their own production. The windows rattled, cups danced on the dresser, the lamp flame jumped agitatedly, the sheep dog lifted his pointed nose in the chimney corner and howled mournfully. In sympathy and approval I scratched him between the ears. He expressed my viewpoint.[16]

A more pressing problem tested Moylan's mettle in the spring of 1918, as the threat of conscription sharpened the enthusiasm of others in the Volunteers. Jerry Scannell, the Kiskeam company O/C (officer commanding) decided to attack Newmarket Barracks. About 150 men turned out. Dan Flynn recalled that the company was armed with all kinds of weapons: 'shotguns, slashers, pikes, pick handles'. They marched for some time, building up a head of steam as they bore down on Newmarket Barracks and 'when we got to Coolagh bridge, about a mile from Newmarket – we met Seán Moylan'.[17] It seems that the War of Independence might have got off to an unplanned and chaotic start had Moylan not appeared, standing, arms folded, in the middle of the road. This stopped the men in their tracks and the march was aborted. Moylan was developing the habit of command and demonstrating the kind of hard-headed realism that would avoid combat except on ground of his choosing.

An unsuccessful attempt was made by the British to capture him in June 1918. It followed the election of Arthur Griffith in the Cavan by-election. The election was celebrated in Newmarket with a march around the town led by the Kiskeam Brass Band. All went well until the band reached the RIC barracks and the constabulary charged, smashing all the drums and brass instruments. Soldiers followed into the fray, with rifle butts used indiscriminately to clear the street.[18] At the time the blame was laid on the RIC inspector; it is now known that a memo sent out by Dublin Castle some weeks previously authorised the destruction of all disloyal bands.[19] It is fair to say that the Kiskeam Brass Band was thoroughly disloyal.

The following morning, at 5 a.m., Moylan was awakened by reports that the house in which he was lodged was surrounded by troops. He made his escape through a skylight, crawled along the roof and dropped some twenty feet into a neighbour's yard. He was next spotted by the police on 15 August, as Constable Thomas Driver reports:

On 15 August 1918, I was on duty with Sergeant Conlon at Newmarket in the county of Cork. About 2.45 p.m. on that day we saw some people from the West End on the road at the National School. We immediately went to where they were and on arrival we saw John Moylan of Newmarket standing on the wall at the gate leading into the school. There were about thirty-six people gathered around him. The accused was reading aloud from a paper which he held in his hand ...[20]

The words that he spoke do not survive but they can be guessed at! In any event, before the RIC could issue a warrant for his arrest for the offence of sedition, Moylan fell ill with Spanish flu and remained hidden for many weeks in the care of sympathetic friends. The epidemic had swept through the Western Front that summer and spread around Europe and Asia. It would claim the lives of tens of millions that coming winter. Moylan was in bed for a month and

SUMMARY OF EVIDENCE IN THE CASE OF JOHN MOYLAN OF

NEWMARKET, IN THE COUNTY OF CORK, CIVILIAN.

1st Witness.   Sergeant Eugene Conlon, R.I.C. stationed at Cullen, in the County of Cork, states :-

On the 15th day of August, 1918, I was on duty at Newmarket, in the County of Cork, and was accompanied by Constable Thomas Driver. At about 2-45 p.m. we were at the East End, Newmarket, and we saw a crowd of people on the public road outside the National Schools, and when approaching them I heard the voice of some one as if reading aloud. I heard the words "aeroplanes hovering over peaceful crowds" When I reached the crowd I saw John Moylan of Newmarket, the accused, whom I now identify, standing on the school wall. He had a document in his hand which he was reading to a crowd of about 36 men. I then took a paper from my pocket, which I had been previously supplied with and turned my back towards the crowd, and told Constable Driver to face the crowd, and I kept following the reading of the document with the one in my possession, now produced and initialled by me. The accused, John Moylan, had got as far as the part where I have marked with a red cross on the document produced, and the remainder of the document he read to the crowd corresponded word for word with the document I had in my possession.

When he got as far as the word compromise (on the 10th line from the end) the accused said "this means applying for permits but we will apply for none.

When the reading of the document finished he distributed about a dozen copies of it amongst the crowd. The crowd dispersed after cries of "up the rebels".

(Sd) Eugene Conlon.

The accused declines to cross-examine this witness.

2nd. Witness.   Constable Thomas Driver, R.I.C. stationed at Glenravel Street, Belfast, states :-

On the 15th day of August, 1918, I was on duty with Sgt. Conlon at Newmarket, in the County of Cork. About 2-45 p.m. on that day we saw some people from the West End, on the road at the National School. We immediately went to where they were and on arrival we saw John Moylan of Newmarket, the accused, whom I now identify, standing on the wall at the gate leading into the school. There were about 35 people gathered around him. The accused was reading aloud from a paper he held in his hand. I first caught the words "aeroplanes hovering peaceful crowds of men, women and children." The Sgt. took from his pocket the paper, now produced, and followed it as the accused continued to read. I had previously seen and read the paper in possession of the Sgt., and the paper the accused continued to read from appeared to be similar in language. When the accused finished reading the paper he distributed amongst the crowd about a dozen papers, which appeared to be similar to the one he had read. Some of the crowd shouted "up the rebels" and after a speech made by another member of the crowd they dispersed.

Summary of evidence prepared under the Defence of the Realm Act for the arrest of John Moylan of Newmarket for the offence of sedition.

spent another month recovering. The after-effects of this debilitating illness would plague him for years to come. While he was convalescing, the war in Europe ended and with it Westminster's urgent need to implement conscription.

On his recovery Moylan was involved in organising the Sinn Féin campaign for the general election of December 1918. His name was put up as a candidate for what would become the First Dáil. He declined to go forward and suggested Páidín O'Keeffe, whom he thought more qualified. O'Keeffe's opponent withdrew, so Moylan went up to help with electioneering for Joe Doherty in Donegal. Here the elections were keenly fought, although when the votes were counted Sinn Féin had won by a landslide.

2

1919

On 18 January 1919, the Versailles Peace Conference convened in Paris. On the diplomatic circuit there was behind-the-scenes jockeying to allow Irish representation at the conference, but Britain blocked access on the grounds that events in Ireland were an internal matter. In addition to maintaining the British Empire, which had started to creak even before President Wilson's doctrine of self-determination had been transmitted around the world, the British were concerned with other strategic issues connected with their rule in Ireland: manpower for the armed forces, control of the Atlantic ports and the links forged by centuries of union. And if the links with Ireland in general were close and strong, the links with Ulster in particular, which derived from shared religion, culture, tradition and military service, were stronger still.

On 21 January, the First Dáil convened at the Mansion House in Dublin and the Declaration of Independence was issued. Only twenty-seven of the seventy-three Sinn Féin members elected were present, many of the others being in prison. That same day two other events took place which set the tone for the rest of the year. The first was the breakout of four Volunteers from Usk Prison in Wales; prisoner escapes were to become common in the following months. The second was the Soloheadbeg ambush, which took place when the South Tipperary Volunteers ambushed a group of RIC men who were escorting a consignment of gelignite to a quarry. The RIC men were ordered to drop their weapons, but they refused and raised their carbines. The Volunteers opened fire and Constables James McDonnell and Patrick O'Connell were killed. Their courageous resistance was typical of RIC men in the coming conflict. It is often said that Soloheadbeg marked the start of the War of Independence, although some historians argue that the war had endured for centuries: rebellions had been crushed from time to time but always re-emerged and this was simply another episode. Whatever position is accepted, the Soloheadbeg ambush is an identifiable moment that marked the re-opening of hostilities.

The killings were widely condemned and many sympathisers of the republican cause were openly dismayed by what had taken place; they had hoped and expected that the Irish would meet the British in open combat. The Volunteers had tried without success to import large quantities of arms; the ill-fated Casement affair is the best-known example of this. Had the guns promised by Roger Casement arrived, it is likely that the Volunteers would have fought a conventional battle against British troops, the notion of guerrilla warfare not yet having taken hold. In these circumstances, inferior in numbers, training and equipment, they would undoubtedly have lost and suffered devastating casualties. However, the failure to import large consignments of arms meant the Volunteers were compelled to take guns by stealth or by force. From these small ambushes and skirmishes a guerrilla campaign emerged that would continue until the summer of 1921.

Crucially, the Volunteers were an autonomous military force and not under the direction of Dáil Éireann. Local initiatives prevailed and they often took their lead from the Volunteer journal, *An t-Óglach*. In this unusual arrangement lay the future seeds of discontent over the terms of the Treaty, the Civil War that followed and the culture of using violence to achieve political ends which dogged Ireland for many years. The genie was out of the bottle.

Moylan was ready to play his part in the war, but he was arrested for sedition in mid-February and went to prison on the evidence of three RIC officers. He was taken to Cork Male Prison to await a court-martial under the Defence of the Realm Act (DORA) and was confined alone in a cell, locked down for twenty hours a day. Unlike other prisoners, he was not subject to active ill treatment by his gaolers, but otherwise his detention was typical:

> The cold, narrow, stone-floored cell was like a vault. The light from the small window, high on one wall, served only to emphasise the presence of the bars. On one corner stood a shelf, on which were a Bible, a small wooden box of salt and a comb, not over-clean. Against one wall was a narrow wooden platform standing on edge; on this neatly piled were several rough blankets. A slop pail completed the furnishings. At four p.m. supper was served. This consisted of a piece of soggy black bread and a tin of some kind of cocoa without milk or sugar, nauseous and bitter. With the delivery of this meal, business closed down for the night. Silence more profound descended on the prison ... Breakfast came at eight. Half a pint of cold and lumpy porridge and a few ounces of black bread.[1]

There is a record of the summary of evidence prepared for the court-martial by Lieutenant H. G. Jones of the Lancers. This procedure was the equivalent of committal for trial. The record shows that the preliminary hearing took place in the Cork Male Prison and Moylan's recollection suggests he was held in custody for some time awaiting trial. Constable Patrick Rynne, stationed at Cullen, County Cork, stated in evidence:

> On Sunday 2 February 1919, I was on duty with Sergeant Conlon in the village of Cullen in the County of Cork. On that morning we had noticed posters put up on the walls that there was a Sinn Féin meeting to be held there on that date. There was a meeting held at about twelve o'clock (after Mass) of about 300 people. Timothy Condon of Coalpits opened the proceedings and introduced to the meeting John Moylan as Sinn Féin organiser and soldier of the Irish Republican Army. John Moylan, of Newmarket, the accused who I now identify, got up on the side of the car and delivered a few sentences which I

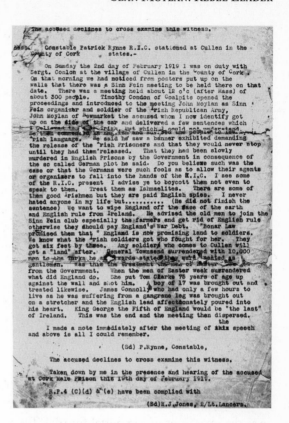

Evidence from Constable Patrick Rynne, RIC.

believed to be in Irish but which I could not understand. He then commenced in English. He said he saw a banner exhibited which demanded the release of the Irish prisoners and that they would never stop until they had them released. That they had been slowly murdered in English prisons by the government in consequence of the so-called German Plot he said. Do you believe such was the case or that the Germans were such fools as to allow their agents to fall into the hands of the RIC. I see some of the RIC present. I advise ye to boycott them. Not even to speak to them. Treat them as Ishmaelites. There are some of them good Irishmen but they are paid English spies. I never hated anyone in my life but ... (He did not finish the sentence). We want to wipe England off the face of the earth and English rule from Ireland. He advised the old men to join the Sinn Féin club especially

31

the farmers and get rid of English rule otherwise they should pay England's war debt. 'Bonar Law promised them that'. England is now promising land to soldiers. We know what the Irish soldiers got who fought for her. They got six feet by three. Any soldier who comes to Cullen will get a 'land' after. General Townsend [*sic*] surrendered with 10,000 men to the Turks, he afterwards stated they were treated as gentlemen. Was this the treatment the men of Easter week got from the government? When the men of Easter week surrendered what did England do? She put Tom Clarke, 75 years of age, up against the wall and shot him. A boy of 17 was brought out and treated likewise. James Connolly who had only a few hours to live as he was suffering from a gangrene leg was brought out on a stretcher and the English lead affectionately poured into his heart. King George the Fifth of England would be 'the last' of Ireland.[2]

The record shows that Moylan declined to cross-examine the witness. Some of the language Rynne attributed to Moylan is passionate and at times intemperate. We do not know for certain that he used such words but it is doubtful that Moylan ever had a desire 'to wipe England off the face of the earth'; he was a man who loved English writers and poets, often quoting Richard Lovelace, and who hoped one day to replicate British political institutions in Ireland.

Moylan was tried by district court-martial on 28 February. There is no record of the court-martial itself. Standing orders required Volunteers not to recognise the court and to take no part in the trial. However, a fleeting reference in Moylan's witness statement indicates that he was unable to resist having a tilt at the prosecuting officer: 'A small Welshman, a lieutenant, I argued with him over the precise meaning of certain words used by the witnesses not indeed of any hope of mitigation of my certain sentence. But just from sheer cussedness. I was satisfied when he lost his temper.'[3] The prison record shows that Moylan was sentenced to twelve months with hard labour. He made no complaint about the fairness of his trial or the length of his sentence; one suspects that it might have been shorter had he held his tongue.

Having been convicted, Moylan was returned to his cell where he collected his possessions and was moved to Wing 10 for political prisoners. The entry in the prison record – '19 March John Moylan (seditious speech) DORA ameliorations' – shows he was entitled to various privileges due to his political status under the Defence of the Realm Act.[4] The privileges were contingent on good behaviour, although this appears to be wishful thinking on the part of the Prison Board. Moylan recalls that the DORA prisoners were an unruly lot, 'refusing to work', 'intractable' or 'shouting and singing', while outside the prison there were demonstrations, stones were thrown and police were required to escort warders in and out. Describing his thoughts about imprisonment, he said: 'It was the penalty of achievement, the guinea stamp of accomplishment, but I felt it as a personal disaster.'[5] The regime was harsh: solitary confinement, poor food and bullying warders.

There were 138 such courts-martial in 1919 and there were many summary trials before resident magistrates and many other summary courts-martial in proclaimed areas.[6] While Moylan faced the prospect of twelve months in prison, some republican prisoners were more fortunate. For example, the remaining 'German Plot' internees were released in March; the flu epidemic raged throughout English prisons and it seems this factor may have moved the government to release them. In Ireland, Volunteer Robert Barrett escaped from Mountjoy leaving a note for the governor telling him that the accommodation was not what he had hoped for. On the other hand, an attempt to free Robert Byrne from Limerick Gaol ended with the killing of RIC Constable O'Brien, two other policemen and a warder; the prisoner was fatally wounded.

In April the most turbulent counties – Cork, Kerry, Limerick, Tipperary and Roscommon – were 'proclaimed' as being in a state of disturbance, triggering the use of special powers of arrest and detention under the Criminal Law and Procedure Act 1887. Notices were nailed up in public places setting out the fact of proclamation, the powers available to the police and the orders made. These powers included the right to declare organisations unlawful, prohibit markets, impose curfews, forbid transport by car, ban parades and extend powers of arrest and detention. In the months that followed Cumann na mBan and the Gaelic League were proclaimed and suppressed.

Around this time, the Dáil instituted a national loan to fund the work of government. Members of the public were invited to subscribe and did so in huge numbers. Newspapers advertising the new Dáil loan were raided by both the RIC and the army, and printing presses were seized.

Back in Cork Male Prison, Moylan was on hunger strike: 'Threatened, abused, ridiculed at first, later I was wooed with specially prepared delicacies. I refused to break. I was taken to the prison hospital and here I found the instrument for my swift release. I was weak, emaciated, with a ragged beard when taken to hospital'.[7] One of the other prisoners, Martin Beckett of Kilgarvan, hatched a plan to effect Moylan's escape by pretending he was insane. Moylan played his full part in this charade until notice had to be taken. Moylan's prison record shows that on 19 March he signed a note acknowledging his entitlement to special privileges as a DORA prisoner, which would be contingent on his good behaviour and just over two weeks later there is another entry: 'John Moylan certified insane 4 April and removed to Cork Lunatic Asylum.'[8] Moylan describes what happened:

> Early in the morning came the governor, the doctor and a mental specialist. I maintained my position and my silence. They departed, an hour passed and then came four warders. They dressed me while I lay passive on the bed, hauled me downstairs in their arms, put me in a cab and delivered me at a city hospital. Here I spent a day still speechless, still refusing food. Early the following day Tomás MacCurtain, the brigade O/C came to see me, looked at me without speaking. There was no need for speech, we understood each other.[9]

With the help of a rescue party, Moylan escaped in the late spring of 1919. His flight was marked by a small piece in a local newspaper:

What with escapes of prisoners from gaols, trains, workhouses, hospitals and now from asylums, people will soon imagine the Sinn Féiners must be direct descendants of those Tuatha De Danann whose necromancy so often assisted them in defeating their enemies. Seán O'Maoileáin of Ath Treasna (Newmarket) who was removed from Cork Gaol to the asylum a month or so ago bade a very sudden farewell to that institution on Tuesday. Without even saying 'Slán liv [*sic*] a cháirde' he turned his face to the Blarney road side of the exercise field, cleared over the fence and went off God knows where.[10]

Other prisoners were also escaping. In mid-May Seán Hogan, who had been involved in the Soloheadbeg ambush, escaped when his captors were ambushed at Knocklong railway station. After a desperate shoot-out that began in a train carriage and spread to a crowded platform, Sergeant Peter Wallace and Constable Michael Enright lay dead. Dan Breen, Seán Treacy, Jim Scanlon and Ned O'Brien were wounded, but all the Volunteers escaped.

Moylan was also free but his hunger strike and the effects of the Spanish flu that nearly killed him the year before had weakened his constitution far more than he had realised. His health was broken and he spent several months recuperating at Ring College near Dungarvan. While he rested he read about events on the international front and fulminated on President Wilson's announcement in Paris that no small nation would be permitted to be represented at the Peace Conference without the unanimous consent of the 'Big Four' (United States, Great Britain, France and Italy). In relation to Ireland, Britain was the sole dissenting member. It was an important moment, because access to the conference carried the chance of a peaceful resolution, whereas the Westminster government was inadvertently channelling the Dáil and the Volunteers towards a military campaign.

Meanwhile events were gathering pace in Ireland. In late June, District Inspector Michael Hunt, who had been involved in the capture of Seán Hogan, was shot dead in a crowded market square in Thurles, an event later identified in the 6th Division Record of the Rebellion as a key moment.[11] It was of particular importance because no witnesses came forward. Many ordinary people were now actively sympathetic with the rebels' cause, while many others were afraid of being labelled informants and the consequences that would bring. The following month the first DMP detective (a group commonly known as G men) was killed on the orders of Michael Collins. Detective Sergeant Patrick Smyth was shot many times by a five-strong ambush party. He was unarmed. He managed to stagger home, but died of his wounds in a Dublin hospital. A few days later Constables John Riordan and Michael Murphy were killed in an ambush in Clare.

At this crucial juncture RIC Inspector General Byrne was informed by the British Army that support for the RIC in outlying areas would start to be withdrawn at Christmas. These troops would be urgently redeployed to Britain, where it was feared that strikes by miners and railway staff could lead to widespread disorder. They were also needed in Russia to oppose the Bolsheviks; in the Rhine area; and in garrisons in Gibraltar, Malta and new territories acquired as a result of the Versailles Treaty. Nationalist feeling was also stirring in Egypt, Palestine, Mesopotamia (where there would be a rebellion in 1920) and India (where the Amritsar Massacre had fanned the flames of rebellion). The withdrawal of this military support proved calamitous for the RIC, as it left the lower ranks exposed in rural areas, and the Volunteers pursued every opportunity to take their guns and burn their barracks.

Stealing guns was the priority throughout 1919. In April Michael Fitzgerald led the Fermoy battalion in a raid on the Araglen RIC Barracks. The raid took place on a Sunday morning when most of the garrison were attending church. The Volunteers, who were unarmed, tricked their way in and captured four rifles, two revolvers and a quantity of ammunition. In early September Liam Lynch led a raid on a group of soldiers who were on their way to church in Fermoy.

SEÁN MOYLAN: REBEL LEADER

A few of the Volunteers were armed with revolvers. The 6th Division Record of the Rebellion records:

> A party of fifteen soldiers belonging to the King's Shropshire Light Infantry were proceeding to Divine service at the Wesleyan chapel, Fermoy. They were armed with rifles but no ammunition as was the custom at the time. Just as they were entering the church they were attacked by a party of forty rebels. These rebels fired on the troops with automatic pistols and revolvers, killing Private Jones and wounding others.[12]

According to Florrie O'Donoghue's account, Lynch blew a whistle and called on the soldiers to surrender. They made to resist and a struggle ensued. Lynch was wounded in the shoulder and his attacker was killed. Fifteen rifles were taken by the raiding party, which left by car, pursued by two lorries from the Fermoy garrison which found the road blocked by felled trees. These had been partially cut earlier in the day and were brought crashing down as soon as the raiding party passed. The East Kent Regiment, the Buffs, wreaked havoc in Fermoy the following day.[13]

Moylan was a member of the brigade that carried out the Wesleyan chapel raid, but he was unable to participate due to chronic bad health. Charlie O'Reilly took his place as battalion commandant. With no improvement in his condition, Moylan went to Dublin in search of treatment. He first sought out the TD for north Cork, Páidín O'Keeffe, who put him in touch with Senator Tom Foran, a leading trade unionist. Foran got him a job as a carpenter and with money in his pocket he rented digs and found specialist medical help. He was still weak but he was earning a wage. He spent any spare money on books and read late into the night. He recalled passing a day with Tomás MacCurtain, who was in Dublin for a meeting, and also spending time at Leinster College perfecting his Irish. Moylan attended lectures at Bolton Street, where one night Piaras Béaslaí, fresh from his escape from Strangeways prison, made a dramatic appearance. During this time Moylan did not participate in any political activity as his illness was debilitating and often painful, and he was barely able to hold down his job.

At about this time Dáil Éireann was proclaimed a dangerous organisation and suppressed under the special powers legislation. Arrest warrants were issued for many of the Deputies, including O'Keeffe, who was arrested for sedition and sentenced to two years in prison. Sinn Féin headquarters was raided and more arrests followed.

As autumn arrived the RIC started to withdraw from outlying barracks. These were quickly burned by the rebels and stood, as Moylan read in *The Times*, 'like tombstones to British supremacy in Ireland'.[14]

December was marked by another wave of arrests and deportations to England. On 19 December, at Ashtown near the Phoenix Park, there was an audacious ambush on the Lord Lieutenant's convoy. The ambush was beaten off and Lord French and his men were uninjured, although Volunteer Martin Savage was killed. Moylan was working in the Phoenix Park that day and noticed some excitement at a nearby RIC depot, where orders were being shouted and men were falling in. Acting on instinct he quickly left the park and only narrowly avoided being caught up in the army cordon that quickly surrounded the area.[15]

On Christmas Eve 1919 he caught a train to Millstreet and walked from there to Newmarket, arriving at his mother's house after nightfall. He was in a state of collapse; the medical treatment in Dublin had been unsuccessful and he remained bedridden until May 1920.

3

THE ROAD TO RECOVERY

The war against the RIC gathered pace and attacking police barracks to seize arms was the main strategy. A night raid was the usual method of attack: trees were felled across roads to impede reinforcements getting through, telephone wires were cut and petrol and oil were used to burn the roof and smoke the defenders out. This tactic was put to good effect at Kilmallock in 1920 when the barracks there was reduced to rubble. Where explosives were available, the strategy shifted to blowing out the gable wall. Occasionally raiders were able to trick their way in or attack when defences were weakened. The raid at Gortatlea, one of the first barracks to be attacked in 1918, took place when most of the garrison had gone to the railway station and a raid at Mallow Military Barracks in 1920, occurred when most of the garrison were out exercising their horses.

In the spring of 1920 the RIC evacuated a number of smaller barracks in Cork. Other larger and more centrally placed buildings were fortified with steel shutters, sandbags, barbed wire and external lighting. Firing slits and bomb holes were fashioned at many barracks. Another successful tactic was to line the roof space with a layer of soil that caused petrol and oil attacks to burn out ineffectually. Rabbit wire mesh was often fitted to the underside of the roof and this proved effective at catching Mills bombs (grenades) and allowing them to roll down the side wall to reduce the impact of the blast. Internal walls were also loopholed to allow defenders additional protection if the outside wall had been blown in. Dye was sprayed at attackers, marking them out for arrest. Senior army officers were recruited to fill posts in the upper echelons of the RIC and to stiffen leadership and resolve. The RIC received tactical training on the defence of barracks and there was a drive to install wireless equipment.

Sporadic shootings and minor ambushes continued. Constable Luke Finnegan was shot dead returning home from Thurles Barracks. Constable Timothy Scully, a sixty-four-year-old married man, was killed in an ambush; some homes in Cork were burned by way of reprisal. Some RIC men were shot dead leaving church, including Constables Healy and Rocke. There were nearly 10,000 raids conducted by the military searching for weapons or suspects.

In late March the policy of selective shooting of Irish Republican Army (IRA) suspects began to emerge. Tomás MacCurtain, Lord Mayor of Cork and Commandant of Cork No. 1 Brigade, was shot dead at his home in front of his wife and children. Terence MacSwiney took his place. In April a coroner's jury returned a notable verdict on the death of Tomás MacCurtain, namely that he was 'wilfully murdered under circumstances of the most callous brutality; that the murder was organised and carried out by the Royal Irish Constabulary, officially directed by the British government'.[1] It was the most famous of a number of such inquests.

The carnage was accompanied by pantomime and tragedy as the British government caved in to public pressure. On 15 April the *New York Times* carried a headline on the release of eighty-nine hunger strikers from Mountjoy jail. An administrative blunder saw all hunger strikers set free, including those who had been convicted; their release was greeted with wild celebrations and indiscriminate shootings of civilians by the military in other parts of the country.

In April the IRA burned nearly 300 evacuated RIC barracks. According to William Reardon of Millstreet this was the result of an order issued to all brigades.[2] It was followed by an order to destroy tax offices and nearly 100 were raided. Many were burned and all records were destroyed. In this way the apparatus of the state began to fall apart.

In May 1920 the cabinet at Westminster listened with approval as Lord Curzon advocated the imposition of 'Indian measures' in Ireland including collective fines on towns and blockading whole districts.[3] The special powers of the Defence of the Realm Act were mirrored in many important respects in the provisions of the Defence of India Act. Indian measures would soon come to pass: reprisals, official reprisals, internment and military courts were just around the corner. When these failed, tactics that had been used against the Boers would be considered. The reality was that Ireland had become ungovernable. When the first republican postage stamp appeared in Dublin it provoked a furious response at Westminster.[4]

Moylan followed events from his sick bed, where he had many visitors:

… no one expected me to recover and these were farewell visits … my mind was clear and eventually it became a habit with the local leaders to come and consult with me. Police barracks were being attacked in other districts. There had been no such attacks in ours. An attack was planned. It was discussed in all its details in my bedroom. It was carried out unsuccessfully. Again another action was planned and again without success; worse still, several Volunteers were wounded.[5]

Moylan was fortunate to have found an able doctor, Algie Verling, who had seen service on the Western Front and had extensive experience nursing the victims of Spanish flu. But before he had fully recovered and despite Verling's protests, Moylan decided he must take part in the next operation: 'I struggled out of bed and into my clothes which hung woefully about me. I got outside … was driven to the point of mobilisation and when all was ready marched a further four miles to the point of attack. It was a weary march for me. A dozen times I lay flat on the road in sheer weariness, but I arrived.'[6] The raid related to the capture of a civilian gang of armed robbers operating in the area, whose activities had been attributed to the IRA. This was essentially a policing operation and it was successful. Most of the robbers were caught and orders were made for their deportation. The bulk of the money they had stolen was recovered and returned to the bank. Liam Lynch arrived immediately after the raid and restored Moylan to the post of O/C of the Newmarket battalion.

Other notable activities beyond the borders of north Cork included the attack on Kilmallock RIC Barracks. Although Moylan himself was not involved, this was the town of his birth and his links with Kilmallock were strong. He took a keen interest in the events of 28 May 1920. In the early hours over 100 rebels gathered quietly and closed in on the barracks, which was fortified with barred windows and steel shutters. The attack began with an attempt to burn the roof, but shooting commenced soon after. On Wolfe Tone Street, and well within earshot, an old man stirred in his bed. He had taken part in the last attack on the barracks in 1867. His name was Batt Raleigh, Moylan's grand-uncle. The 6th Division Record of the Rebellion describes the attack:

> The defence was conducted by eight men under Sergeant Tobias Sullivan; the police held their barracks against several hundred rebels for over seven and a half hours, notwithstanding that under their very eyes two of their comrades were burned alive in the flames. The remainder had to continue the fight from room to room as the building collapsed bit by bit, and as more petrol was poured on it from the roof of a neighbouring house, not exposed to the fire or the police. Eventually when the whole of the building had collapsed, and when there was nothing left to defend, this gallant little band of policemen charged the rebels with fixed bayonets, and compelled them to retire hastily, but not before all but one of the RIC had been wounded.[7]

Moylan's account of the events does not differ significantly, except that according to family sources, the rebels simply ran out of ammunition.

The rebel party suffered a number of casualties and one fatality. Moylan did write many years later with admiration for the surviving RIC men advancing 'charred, wounded and weary but still defiant, and with bayonets fixed'.[8] His attitude to the RIC is revealing: 'They were of the people, intermarried among the people. They were generally men of exemplary lives and of a high level of intelligence. They did their oftimes unpleasant duty without rancour and oftimes with a maximum of tact.'[9]

The RIC had by then been detached from the community to whom they were formerly so close. The policy of ostracisation had begun to bite deeply. No social contact was permitted with RIC men and in many areas the shops and bars would not serve them. Hospitality could not be given or accepted, nor could one share a pew in church with an RIC man. A widow in Thurles who allowed the dead body of Inspector Hunt to be taken into her home was boycotted and elsewhere a hearse that had been used to bury an RIC man killed in an ambush was burned. The landlords of RIC men and the women who worked in the barracks were subjected to pressure to extend the boycott. In County Clare an RIC man and his family were turned out of the abandoned barracks where they had been living. The barracks was burned and the woman and children were denied shelter in the area. Threats were made to women who associated with RIC men and in some cases women had their hair cut for breaking the boycott. The 6th Division Record of the Rebellion alleges that the IRA was motivated by jealousy because 'they had to fall back on sour-faced and disaffected Old Maids, whom no decent person would be seen near'.[10]

By the spring of 1920 recruitment to the ranks of the RIC had dried up and the impact of resignations began to be acutely felt. This fuelled the need for more men, for the Black and Tans and in due course for the recruitment of the Auxiliary division. The RIC was at the frontline for most of the war and many of its members showed remarkable courage and exemplary conduct. In Listowel, a group of RIC officers, including Constable Jeremiah Mee, were told by

Divisional Commissioner Smyth and Major General Hugh Tudor that they could have a free hand to meet the IRA threat:

> If a police barracks is burned, or if the barracks, already occupied is not suitable, then the best house in the locality is to be commandeered and the occupants thrown out into the gutter. Let them die there. The more the merrier … if persons approaching carry their hands in their pockets or are in any way suspicious looking, shoot them down. You may make mistakes occasionally and innocent persons may be shot, but this cannot be helped. I assure you that no policeman will get into trouble for shooting any man.[11]

This was what British Prime Minister David Lloyd George would later privately term 'gunning'. In what became known as the Listowel Mutiny, Mee handed in his weapon at the end of the speech, which he described as 'incitement to murder'. The other men present were ordered to arrest him. None of the fourteen constables present complied. Two senior officers from Smyth's party dragged Mee to an adjoining room. A few minutes later the constables burst in and released him. Mee resigned. Smyth gave similar talks at Killarney, Tralee and Miltown Malbay; five officers at Killarney resigned after his speech. There are many well-documented instances of RIC men who resigned rather than take part in such operations.

Others were less scrupulous. Sergeant Tobias Sullivan, who led the defence of Kilmallock Barracks, was subsequently promoted and transferred, but the attack appeared to have scarred him and he returned to Kilmallock with a party of RIC, who burned a number of houses and mistreated people from the town. Moylan recalled how he had information that Sullivan passed between Cork and Limerick with a military party on a number of occasions and 'many times I lay on that road awaiting him and his party'.[12] They never met and the importance of Sullivan's conduct faded as other more pressing issues arose.

In June 1920, Moylan organised a raid on the mail train. The purpose of this was to discover the identity of those supplying information to the RIC and the military. A good deal of information was found and resulted in several people being warned or required to leave the area. This was the first of a series of raids on the mail that summer.

The destruction of RIC barracks meant that the mechanisms supporting the courts had fallen apart. It was no longer possible for the RIC to gather evidence freely, to make arrests or to serve a summons. The Republican Courts filled the gap and Moylan and his battalion provided the services that allowed these courts to flourish. He sometimes sat in judgment on cases and at other times organised the listing of the court that tried land disputes, assault cases, poaching and on one occasion an action by the wife of a British soldier against her landlord for wrongful eviction. She won her case and although the house that was the subject of the litigation was in the shadow of the military barracks, the decision was enforced. The courts were active, free from red tape and legal fees, and served the needs of the community. As the months wore on there were many outraged protests at Westminster about the new courts. For example: 'Captain Foxcroft asked the chief secretary for Ireland whether the County Council of Donegal granted the use of the courthouse in Ballyshannon for the holding of Republican Courts, and, if so, what action the government intend to take on the matter?'[13] Yet nothing was done and the new court system flourished.

Moylan's time was also taken up with other activities. He raised money for railway staff who had been dismissed for refusing to carry soldiers on the trains. In June he won a seat on the rural district council. The local elections proved a landslide victory for Sinn Féin and the nationalists and most local authorities started to declare their allegiance to Dáil Éireann. Moylan's commitment to council meetings was enthusiastic but time consuming. He was forced to resign when a series of army raids on the meetings exposed him to the possibility of being captured.

The main business in hand for the Volunteers was the campaign against the RIC and the acquisition of weapons. North Cork was a remote rural area and access to weapons was limited. The Newmarket battalion had a few rifles (stolen or captured from the RIC), some shotguns, revolvers and a little ammunition. The picture was much the same throughout the Cork No. 2 Brigade. This need for weapons dominated Moylan's thinking and led to the evolution of a plan to capture General Lucas.

4

THE GENERAL LUCAS AFFAIR

Heard early that Lucas and Danford were kidnapped yesterday from their
fishing cottage. Latter escaped from car later and got two bullets.
Major General E. P. Strickland, Commander 6th Division, personal
diary entry

On 26 June 1920, Brigadier General C. H. T. Lucas and Colonels
Tyrell and Danford left British Army headquarters in Fermoy to go
on a fishing trip on the River Blackwater. A small party of Volunteers
captured them. After an escape attempt which left Danford seriously
wounded, the two colonels were released, but Lucas was spirited away.
This led to one of the largest manhunts by British forces in Irish
history.

Moylan's witness statement claims that the operation had its
origins in a plan to steal guns, which were in short supply. They had
information that senior army officers were using a fishing lodge at
weekends near Fermoy and the plan evolved into an operation to kidnap
them: 'These officers were of the class that created and controlled an
empire … Why not pull them down and see what made them tick.
Why not prove to the Volunteers that they were not endowed with
any qualities denied to the rest of the human race?'[1]

Others, notably Liam Lynch, were motivated by the possibility of
a prisoner swap for Michael Fitzgerald of Fermoy, then in Cork Gaol.

As brigade commandant, Lynch's role was usually strategic, although it is clear he had a fine appreciation of when it was necessary to take an operational role. On this occasion he led from the front. Others in the raiding party included Moylan, Paddy Clancy and George Power. They were supported by Laurence Condon and a section of Volunteers and had at their disposal a single car borrowed from local man John B. Curtin. Moylan recalled the raid in his witness statement:

> The centre of the immediate operation was a small fishing lodge surrounded by a low stone wall and occupied, we were informed by the scouts, by a number of British soldiers, the officers' escort … Clancy and I were detailed to lead the charge on the house. My men and I crept through shrubbery and took cover outside the boundary wall at the front. My comrade with his section carried out the same manoeuvre at the back.[2]

At this time most IRA units depended on a whistle to signal an attack or withdrawal. The signal for this attack was to be a blast on Moylan's whistle:

> At the whistle both sections charged for the front and back doors, burst them in and swept through the house. There was nobody in possession but an old lady, the cook and housekeeper and a young girl … We lay in the shrubbery for about an hour and then three men approached the house coming from the river. Two were tall, athletic men, one smaller and lighter. The bigger men disappeared from my sight round an angle of the house. The smaller man came in my direction and I took him in charge. Driving him before me, I came to where the others were. Here those others had been held up by the brigade commandant and those with him.[3]

They now had Lucas' batman and the two colonels. George Power picked up General Lucas on the river bank shortly after. Power later wrote in his statement to the Bureau of Military History that Lynch introduced himself and his officers by name and rank. Lucas did likewise. The batman was then allowed to prepare a meal for his captured superiors. Moylan takes up the story:

> We had two cars; the car I had brought out and that of the British officers. It was decided that the assistant brigade commandant, George Power, would sit beside the driver of the leading car. He was familiar with the area ... I sat in the back with one of the prisoners. The brigade commandant sat with the driver of the next car and Clancy sat between the remaining prisoners at the back. We started. George Power kept an eye not merely on the road we were travelling but backwards to assure himself that the second car was following. Having travelled several miles, we rounded a bend. Power looked back but the car that was to follow did not appear. We turned at once and a quarter of a mile from our turning point we came upon a dogfight in the road. The second car was ditched. The driver had just extricated himself from behind the wheel and there was a life and death struggle between two pairs of men on the roadway.[4]

Lynch later recounted that Danford and Lucas had exchanged some words in Arabic and launched themselves on their captors. The car went off the road into a ditch, knocking the driver unconscious. Clancy and Danford grappled on the road. Lucas still in the car had grabbed Lynch's gun and pressed it to his chest. The safety catch was on and the impasse was broken when the car door suddenly snapped open and both men tumbled into the ditch. Lucas was then forty-one years old. Some years previously he had lost two fingers in a shooting accident but he was a big strong man, over six foot two in height. The struggle hung in the balance for some time before Lynch freed himself. He turned to see Danford throttling Clancy and shouted, 'Surrender or I'll shoot!'[5] Danford ignored the order and Lynch shot him.

Moylan recalled the incident slightly differently: 'I could not help in the struggle. I drove my prisoner out of the car and kept him covered ... A shot rang out and the struggle between the brigade commandant and his opponent was over. The British officer lay wounded on the road. The second combatant, seeing the game was up, threw in his hand.'[6]

Danford suffered a graze to the forearm and head and was unconscious for nearly four hours. Clancy was very badly shaken. A decision was made to release Tyrell to tend to his injured colleague. The car in the ditch was put beyond use, Lucas was handcuffed and the party crowded into the remaining car. They drove to the nearest village where a man was sent to find a doctor for the wounded Danford and George Power was dispatched to Dublin to brief IRA headquarters.

It was evening by the time British Army headquarters at Fermoy had been alerted. The *New York Times* gave the following account:

> Barracks and camp were immediately alarmed and all soldiers turned out of bed. Soldiers of an artillery battery mounted their horses, and numerous parties of fully equipped troops in motor lorries, and motor cars, accompanied by police scoured the country for miles around all night and all day today but their search proved unavailing. The general had vanished completely. The affair has created a sensation in military circles and the greatest reticence is being displayed.[7]

Lucas and his captors had slipped through the net and arrived at O'Connell's farm in Glantane near Mallow around 3 a.m. on Sunday. The following day, Moylan's sister Mamie was sent to buy pyjamas and a toothbrush for the general and young Patrick O'Connell arrived home from St Colman's College in Fermoy with the news that the military was going to blow up the town. His brother Jack takes up the story:

> He was unaware of the presence of General Lucas in the home … he did know Liam Lynch who was sitting at the kitchen fire reading a book … Lynch … went into the room where General Lucas was detained. In a short time he returned with a dispatch written by General Lucas to O/C British forces at Fermoy telling him to ensure that no reprisals were to take place … General Lucas was removed about 11 p.m. to Dan McCarthy's at Creggane and after three or four days … to West Limerick.[8]

By then the search parties were out in force. Arrangements were made with the West Limerick Brigade and the general was moved on. At some point during the tense but uneventful drive Lucas is said to have remarked: 'I was under the impression that we were in military occupation of this country.'[9]

The event made headlines in Dublin, London and New York. At Westminster the War Office was pressed for news. In reply to Sir H. Craik's request for information on the kidnapping, Sir A. Williamson, Parliamentary Under Secretary for War, replied, 'Brigadier General Lucas and Colonels Tyrell and Danford were arrested at Kilbarry, five miles from Fermoy, where they had been fishing … by twelve armed and masked men in a motor car bearing no number … a telegram received at 12 o'clock says no news of General Lucas'.[10]

Back in Fermoy, British troops had failed to find Lucas and were exacting revenge on the town. According to Florrie O'Donoghue the smashing and splintering of windows was accompanied by chants of 'We want our fucking general'.[11] The following day Winston Churchill, then Secretary of State for War, recounted to the House of Commons what had transpired: 'Plate glass and other windows in about fifty houses were broken last night by about 400 military men.'[12] Fermoy was a barracks' town and it is doubtful that the widespread damage carried out by troops took place without official sanction. Indeed, Churchill chooses his words carefully. He does not say 'soldiers' he says 'military men'. There was considerable damage to property but no injury or loss or life. It had the hallmark of a warning and it was not the last reprisal against Fermoy.

At British Army general headquarters, General Sir Nevil Macready pressed the government for permission to take hostages to secure the life of General Lucas. At Westminster, wiser heads prevailed. It is clear that there were no immediate fears for the life of General Lucas. The release of Colonel Tyrell to tend to the wounded Danford did not suggest the kidnappers were intent on killing Lucas. Major General Strickland's diary reads: 'Papers left behind said … done by Second Cork Brigade … He would be well treated.'[13]

It was already known that the kidnap of Lucas had not been authorised by IRA headquarters and Westminster decided to try to avoid inflaming the situation. Macready had to be content with 'a drive with all available troops'.[14] The drive involved thousands of troops combing the Cork and Limerick areas. But it was a very wet summer and army convoys were impeded by heavy rain and were often bogged down in mud. The search continued and was followed with glee by the press. On 28 June *The Irish Times* reported: 'All the roads are patrolled, and aeroplanes are scouting in every direction but up to this evening no trace had been found of the captured officer.'

The embarrassment to the British Army was considerable. The 6th Division Record of the Rebellion recalls the strenuous efforts of the military to track down their missing general. In Ireland, a ballad was written. In England, no musical hall show was complete without a joke at the expense of the unfortunate Lucas.

Lucas was permitted to send mail and receive it from his wife on an almost daily basis. The arrangement to receive mail seems to have impressed him most and was perhaps a further reminder that the power of British forces in the region was more tenuous than he had imagined. On 1 July an extract of a letter from Lucas appeared in *The Irish Times*:

I am being well and considerately treated. Letters will be delivered to me after being censored, provided they are done up and delivered at … in Fermoy. If you try to follow up the letters they will not be delivered. You will not, I am afraid, get anything out of it and I will not get the letters. I have nothing to complain about as to the consideration shown to me. They are doing all they can to provide me with everything I want. I want some money, about £10. I am very glad to know that Colonel Danford is not dead. He and I tried to escape and attacked the guard …

A photograph of Lucas in captivity survives. It shows the general seated, arms folded and frowning. It has the sense of a 'proof of life'

General Lucas (seated centre), Paddy Brennan and Joe Keane (front), Paddy and Michael Brennan (rear). Courtesy of the Rifles (Berkshire and Wiltshire) Museum

photograph. Some of the Volunteers, oblivious to the risk of capture but intuitively grasping the concept that everyone is famous for fifteen minutes, are also in the camera.

The search parties and raids continued, although the sense of urgency at British headquarters was not palpable. In Major General Strickland's personal diary, we discover that 'rain ruined tennis' on 5 July and the next day 'no tennis of course'. Lucas also enjoyed tennis and, the weather being rather better where he was, his captors arranged a tennis match for him. He was also promised a day's shooting. The opportunity for this would come about in an entirely unexpected manner at the end of his captivity.

Lucas was passed from the Limerick Brigade to Michael Brennan of the East Clare Brigade, who records: 'We kept Lucas at Cratloe at Ernest Corbett's, in Clonmoney at Brennan's, at Tullyrarriga at Hasting's, and in Doonass at Hartigan's.'[15] On one occasion Lucas was moved only hours before a raid. He is reported to have consumed a great deal of whiskey, which proved a drain on resources. Joe Moylan and other educated young men were called in to provide conversation and company. He played bridge until 2 a.m. and, when the weather was fine, he worked in the fields at his own request. When offered the chance to go salmon fishing in the Shannon, Lucas initially refused on the grounds that it would be poaching and therefore illegal. However, after some agonising the fishing trip did take place and late one night the general fished for salmon whilst the IRA guarded both sides of the river. It seems Lucas was more concerned with being caught poaching by the bailiffs, than he was with escaping. His mind was put to rest by one of the fishing party, who admitted that the head bailiff was one of his captors.

The months that followed were marked by mayhem and destruction by the British forces. The murder of civilians and burning of homes became commonplace. Meanwhile, the imprisonment of Lucas continued to be a huge drain on the resources of the East Clare Brigade. It was not just a matter of security but supplying bridge partners, ensuring his post was received and delivered, and keeping him comfortable. It also meant a suspension of operations in the area: raids brought counter-raids and the risk of discovery. The hoped for prisoner swap never materialised and the Lucas affair was becoming burdensome.

Major General Strickland's personal diary for 31 July reads: 'At Oola, mail cars attacked. 2 of our men killed 2 wounded. Lucas escaped!'[16]

The full story trickled out slowly. On 4 August *The Times* reported that his captors had left Lucas unattended while they organised the attack on the mail cars at Oola and that Lucas had removed the bars from his window and managed to slip away. Walking all night through torrential rain, he found his way to Pallas Green RIC Barracks where he was put on a Crossley tender, which was carrying military mail and was guarded by soldiers of the Oxford and Bucks Light Infantry. Almost immediately they ran into the ambush at Oola. According to *The Times*: 'During the fight at Oola he was as busy as the privates of the military with a rifle, and in his efforts to counter the attack of the raiding party he received two slight wounds, one under the nose and the other in the forehead.'

Michael Brennan, who was faced with the increasing difficulties of holding the general, offers another perspective:

> We took Lucas for long walks across the country and I noted with satisfaction that he studied the topography carefully from every hilltop. Up to this we had always left a man outside his bedroom window at night and when his room was on the ground floor we withdrew this man. At first nothing happened. He may have suspected a trap, but when we got up the second morning our prisoner was gone.[17]

There is no reason to discount Brennan's explanation. It is certainly unlikely that Lucas would have found his way across country without the tacit consent of local IRA units.

It was suggested at the time that the Oola ambush was a determined attempt to recapture Lucas. This theory can be rejected for two main reasons. First, the number of ambushers was said to be over fifty. The raid took place before the inception of the flying column system and no local IRA command could put fifty men into the field at such short notice. Second, the evidence later presented to the Bureau of Military History makes it clear that the Oola ambush was pre-planned and that Lucas was not the target. In any event, the General Lucas affair was over. But for most of those involved, it was a lighter moment in an otherwise bloody war. Curtin got his car back. Danford made a full recovery. Lucas returned to England, where his wife had just given birth, and wrote a briefing paper advising that the Volunteers were a much more formidable force than had been thought. He never spoke about the incident in public except to say that he had been treated as a gentleman by gentlemen.

5

GETTING GUNS

In Cork, the capture of General Lucas was played out in parody to the air of 'The Blarney Roses' and was sung by small boys and their fathers long after Lucas had returned to England. It was a brief moment of respite in what had become a bloody and bitter conflict throughout Munster. In June and July there were raids at Howes Strand, Skibbereen, Downdaniel, Rathmore, Dingle, Glengarriff and Bantry. An attack on Brosna Barracks on 5 June was beaten off as one of the Black and Tans in the barracks played a melodeon and sang throughout.[1] There were occasional shootings. The first Black and Tan to be shot dead was Alexander Will, who was killed during an incident at Rathmore. Another notable casualty was Divisional Commissioner Smyth, who was ambushed in the smoking-room of the Cork County Club. Smyth had lost an arm in the First World War and, finding himself surrounded by gunmen, struggled to free his sidearm. He was shot dead as he rose to his feet.

The intelligence war became especially bloody. In July 1920 two British intelligence officers were captured and shot by the Coachford company of the IRA. In the months that followed a number of intelligence officers met the same fate.

Also in July, Tom Hales and Pat Harte of the West Cork Brigade were captured by a party of soldiers led by Major Percival, intelligence officer of the Essex Regiment. They were tortured at the military barracks in Bandon and later hospitalised; Harte did not recover.

The Essex Regimental Diary records the capture of Hales and Harte but says nothing about their questioning. The diary summarises intelligence gathering in a bland manner: 'Reliable information was a matter of extreme difficulty. Very little could be elicited from the inhabitants; this, and scanty details pieced together from captured documents, had to suffice. Gradually, however, a fair knowledge of the area was obtained. Arrested men frequently gave false names but subsequently when cross-examined gave themselves away.'[2]

In August the Essex Regiment raided the post office at Clonakilty and found a note inviting a Volunteer to attend a brigade meeting at Cork City Hall. During the resulting raid on the City Hall they picked up Terence MacSwiney, most of his brigade staff and others including Liam Lynch. Most of the arrestees were released because the military failed to realise who they had captured. They held on to MacSwiney, who was tried and convicted by court-martial on a charge of possessing a police cipher.

Then there were the growing number of reprisals by Crown forces, who tried to undermine the Volunteers and reassert their control over the civilian population. Isolated instances of reprisals on civilians and properties in the spring had become routine by the summer of 1920. Creameries were burned or sometimes bombed, grain stores and homes were torched, and civilians were shot on suspicion of being Sinn Féiners. There were also attempts by the military to stifle the new republican police force. John O'Brien, a member of the fledging force, was shot dead on patrol in Cork. The army raided Bettystown Races and confronted members of the new force, confiscating their armbands and sending the would-be police officers on their way.

Back in north Cork, Moylan received a sum of money from a relative in the United States. He does not say who sent it, but most likely it came from his brother Ned, who had been serving in the Canadian Mounted Police. Ned received a substantial reward for the capture of a bank robber and used his windfall to help his family.[3] It was the first time Moylan had any significant amount of money and he decided to spend it on weapons. He travelled to Dublin and managed to buy a small quantity of guns: six pistols, two parabellums, a dozen hand grenades, a rifle and a quantity of ammunition. The deal was fixed over lunch at a hotel in the centre of Dublin. His lunch companions from IRA general headquarters (GHQ) were Liam Tobin, Tom Cullen and Fintan Murphy. These wanted men sat calmly amongst the other diners, some uniformed, some not. The guns were delivered to Moylan's hotel at night. Moylan never spoke of that journey to Dublin or of the dangers of a wanted man carrying weapons back to Newmarket, but luck was on his side and he evaded detection. The guns proved to be of poor quality, but they were useful for training and were a significant boost to the morale of the Newmarket battalion.

At a brigade meeting some weeks later, revolvers were distributed to battalion commanders but not to Moylan. Liam Lynch seems to have reasoned that Moylan had just bought guns and therefore the Newmarket battalion's need was less. The guns were parcelled up and the meeting commenced. Moylan was quietly seething. He slipped away, took two revolvers from a bag and put a piece of firewood and a stone in their place. Afterwards he agonised over what he had done, but the man whose bag he had raided was captured the next day and the guns were never missed. It seems that in the life of a revolutionary, tragedy and farce are never far apart. Moylan examined the revolvers with his friend Paddy Clancy. The guns, he later observed, were rough, badly finished and typical of 'the rubbish that is produced in certain European ports for sale to revolutionaries'.[4] There is a note of bitter experience here. Moylan and Clancy agreed that the only sure way to get good quality guns was to steal them from the military.

In the late summer of 1920, Clancy decided to join one of the newly formed flying columns. The flying columns were small, mobile active service units that had come about for a variety of reasons: the RIC and army were moving in larger convoys; there were more men on the run after the passing of the Restoration of Order in Ireland Act 1920; and it was reasoned that full-time rather than part-time Volunteers were necessary. A few days later Clancy and Battalion Commandant

Jack O'Connell were surprised by the army at O'Connell's farmhouse. There was a gunfight and they exhausted their ammunition and were shot dead making a dash for freedom. The death of his friend Paddy Clancy had a profound impact on Moylan. Among his papers almost forty years later was found a photograph of Clancy, an intelligent, good-looking man.

The conflict continued to escalate. The Auxiliaries were being recruited and the Restoration of Order in Ireland Act had begun to bite. This act provided powers to intern without a time limit and gave the army the power to try capital offences and other public order offences. Government funding was to be denied to local authorities that were not loyal. Coroner's courts were to be replaced by military courts of inquiry to consider deaths caused by the Crown forces: these quickly became known derisively as courts of acquittal. Terence MacSwiney joined Michael Fitzgerald and others on hunger strike. In Cork city there was a determined ambush on Major General Strickland; seven bullets lodged in his car but he escaped unhurt.

Moylan recalls being summoned to a brigade meeting in late September 1920. A staff captain from GHQ attended. Moylan describes the man: 'Red hair standing on end, blue eyes, with a scar on his keen face, he seemed to be clad in guns and fountain pens and surrounded by maps and notebooks.'[5] This was Ernie O'Malley, who was on a fact-finding mission to collate the names of all Volunteers in the district. All officers there were questioned and provided full answers, but Moylan's instincts were to put as little as possible in writing: 'I answered all questions with perfect inaccuracy. The brigade commandant knew I was lying. I knew he knew it and disapproved but he expressed neither commendation nor disapproval.'[6] O'Malley filled his notebook and though he and Moylan did not quite hit it off, Moylan later conceded he had 'tons of courage and ability of a high order'.[7]

After the meeting there were discussions about a raid on Mallow Barracks where the 17th Lancers were stationed. Information from Volunteer Dick Willis indicated that when the army horses were being exercised the number of men in the barracks was much reduced. The plan involved Paddy McCarthy tricking his way into the barracks on the pretext of being the clerk of works. Once inside he would team up with two other Volunteers, Dick Willis and Jack Bolster, who were working there as painters. One man would engage the sentry in discussions at the front gate, while a second would force his way in, allowing the others to follow. Moylan was kept off this high-risk operation by Liam Lynch, who sent him to what he regarded as a minor task on the far side of the county. It was a hugely frustrating moment for Moylan. Why was he kept off the raid?

The answer may be gleaned from Paddy O'Brien's witness statement. The raid would involve Lynch and his deputy George Power and many of the most senior Volunteers in the brigade. Ernie O'Malley would engage the sentry and Lynch, with typical unselfishness, intended to take the role of the second man, the most dangerous role, for himself. It was the biggest operation launched by Cork No. 2 Brigade and Lynch evidently thought that it was necessary for him to lead from the front. It is a logical inference that Lynch intended, should the operation go badly wrong, that Moylan would be available to take over the brigade.[8] The raid took place as planned, although some of the senior Volunteers decided they could not allow Lynch to put himself at risk and therefore Paddy O'Brien of Liscarroll and a few others forced their way in front of Lynch at the last moment. Inside the barracks McCarthy, Willis and Bolster produced guns and held up the men in the guardroom. Sergeant Gibbs of the Lancers was shot and, although O'Malley and others administered first aid, he later died of his wounds. Three cars were let into the barracks and guns, including a pair of Hotchkiss machine guns, were gathered together and piled into the waiting cars.

It was a day when clichés were stood on their head. The conduct of the rebels belied David Lloyd George's description of back-street assassins and murderers. In contrast, after the raid a large body of men from a British regiment, which had previously been a model of restraint, ran riot in the streets of Mallow. The town hall and ten houses were burned. Firemen working to douse the flames were shot at by the troops and 'a small group of Black and Tans gave sanctuary to some women and children' as the high street burned.[9] 'An expectant mother and a woman who had spent the night in a graveyard died of exposure.'[10] Many miles away, the raiders watched the night turn gold and then red as the flames reached towards the sky.

This phase of the war was coming to an end. Although the Volunteers would constantly be searching for arms, the emphasis was now shifting from seizing guns to attacking the military.

6

SPIRAL OF VIOLENCE

I had one and a half hours this evening with Lloyd George and Bonar Law. I told them what I thought of reprisals by the 'Black and Tans' and how this must lead to chaos and ruin. Lloyd George danced about and was angry, but I never budged, I pointed out that these reprisals were being carried out without anyone being responsible; men were murdered, houses burnt, villages wrecked …

Sir Henry Wilson, Chief of Imperial General Staff, personal
diary entry, 29 September 1920[1]

We have murder by the throat.

David Lloyd George, Guildhall banquet speech,
9 November 1920[2]

The second half of 1920 will always be remembered for atrocity and mayhem. Moylan recalled one incident involving a farmer from Liscarroll by the name of Noonan. The army raided the farm and beat Noonan and his son before dragging the youth outside and putting him against a wall, where an officer shot him in the head. Amazingly, the boy survived, but the scandal of the atrocity filled north Cork. Moylan also remembered watching a convoy of troops in the distance, unaware that they had just kidnapped a middle-aged man called Moynihan, whom they shot and dumped by the roadside. Such incidents were disturbingly common and not limited to the Black and Tans or the Auxiliaries. It is worth looking at the combatants.

By the autumn of 1920 there were over 40,000 regular troops in Ireland. Nearly every British regiment of distinction had a battalion in Cork. The roll call included the Green Howards, Cameron Highlanders, Welch Fusiliers, Lancers, Essex, South Staffordshire, Northamptonshire, Gloucestershire, East Lancashire, King's (Liverpool), Lincolnshire, East Kent and Hampshire Regiments. Many of the men were post-war recruits who had seen little or no action. Their quarters were cramped. Food was plentiful but of poor quality; there was always a choice on the menu: take it or leave it. These men had money but few places to spend it and although there were opportunities to drink outside barracks these became increasingly unsafe as the war dragged on. They rarely caught sight of the enemy and endured long periods confined to barracks, punctuated by raids on private homes or long patrols.

It had been common up to 1920 for the army to travel by train but early in that year this mode of transport had become hazardous for small parties of soldiers. Moreover, many railway staff simply refused to move the train with soldiers on board. Lorries became the usual method of military transport and allowed the army to travel long distances and carry heavy equipment. However, as the Essex Regimental Diary explains: 'They were very cold to sit in and also induced drowsiness, which rendered them more vulnerable to ambush. Road obstructions held them up and if in close fighting a hand grenade burst inside, the result was deadly.'[3] So the soldiers travelled in convoys – crowded in lorries or clinging to the back of a Crossley tender – on poor roads, often in wet and cold weather and always aware that they might suddenly find themselves caught in a murderous crossfire from an unseen enemy.

Many British Army regiments behaved with restraint in the most difficult of circumstances; for example, the King's (Liverpool) Regiment under the command of Colonel Hudson, who was described by Liam Deasy as 'an upright and humane man'.[4] On one occasion

Hudson intervened to save a group of Volunteers from summary execution by the RIC. Some regiments, notably the Gloucestershire and Northamptonshire Regiments, were tough but scrupulous. Others were not.

Army tactics became increasingly robust. The 6th Division Record of the Rebellion shows a variety of ruses adopted as the British forces got into their stride. 'Q lorries' were left apparently abandoned in the hope that Volunteers would try and burn them. When the Volunteers showed up the curtains were dropped to reveal machine gunners who started firing.[5] Some officers would pack ammunition with high explosives and leave it out to be stolen. The bullets, when used, would explode, destroying the rifle and wounding or killing the firer. There is an account of soldiers coming on a group of rebels demolishing an abandoned police station: 'Seven rebels who could not run fast enough were killed and others were wounded. The troops suffered no casualties.'[6]

Although British Army headquarters must have been aware of the allegations of beatings, robberies and unlawful killings that filled the pages of the newspapers and of Hansard (*the official report of parliamentary debates*) during this period, there is nothing in the 6th Division Record about the killings of civilians and only a single paragraph dealing with unauthorised reprisals by the military, which it said were quickly stamped out. The failure to refer to the atrocities or to steps taken to investigate these allegations and to prevent such occurrences indicates that the 6th Division Record is a flawed history. Clearly action should have been taken: there was a moral imperative and a strategic need for the army to be seen to act within the law.

The Black and Tans were well established in Ireland by the autumn of 1920. According to one RIC man: 'They had neither religion nor morals, they used foul language, they had the old soldier's talent for dodging and scrounging, they spoke in strange accents, called the Irish "natives", associated with low company, stole from one another, sneered at the customs of the country, drank to excess and put sugar on their porridge.'[7] They were distinguishable from the RIC by their uniform – the dark green caps and jackets and khaki trousers which gave them their name, their accents and their manners. They were ex-military men and so lacked training as police officers. Ireland was not their country and when they, as mercenaries, finished their tour of duty, others would be left with the consequences. It was always doubtful that they would ever achieve success as a policing force, even with close supervision. They were recruited in a hurry as the RIC was sustaining significant casualties and the boycott against it resulted in falling recruitment and increasing resignations. Meanwhile the level of the military threat posed by the IRA was escalating. Replacements were needed because the government at Westminster perceived the problem as primarily a policing issue and it was easier to obtain funding for a police force than for the army, which was already overstretched.

The Auxiliaries, or Auxies, were also recruited in a hurry. In total, just over 2,200 were mobilised. They were all ex-officers and many had been decorated in the First World War; three held the Victoria Cross. However, they had all the shortcomings of the Black and Tans. In addition they were not placed under the control of the army or the RIC. The historian Michael Hopkinson rightly points out that it is likely many of these men suffered psychological problems as a result of the First World War.[8] Field Marshal Sir Henry Wilson wrote in his diary:

... no discipline, no esprit de corps, no cohesion, no training, no musketry, no mess, no nothing ... then to make matters worse Macready proposes to draft these mobs over to Ireland at once and split them into lots of twenty-five to fifty men all over the country so there would be no hope of forming and disciplining this crowd of unknown men.[9]

The crucial absence of leadership and discipline in this volatile and difficult environment meant that Wilson's fears were fully justified.

The Black and Tans and the Auxiliaries served alongside the RIC and the regular army. The reputation of each was different; Seán O'Casey summed up his experience in *Inishfallen Fare Thee Well*:

A raid! … Which were they, the Tommies or the Tans? Tans … He guessed that a part of them were Auxies, the classic members of silent and sibilant raiders. The Tans alone would make more noise, slamming themselves into a room, shouting to shake off the fear that slashed many of their faces. The Auxies were too proud to show a sign of it. The Tommies would be warm, always hesitant at knocking a woman's room about; they would even be jocular in their funny English way, encouraging the women and even the children to grumble at being taken away from their proper sleep.[10]

The atrocities and reprisals carried out in late 1920 and early 1921 owe much to the weak leadership of these men and of the government in Westminster. In the House of Commons, Lloyd George and his cabinet rebutted allegations of wanton reprisals and shooting to kill unarmed men. Wilson's diaries, however, tell a different story: 'The Sinn Féiners were being shot by police without question or trial.'[11] The diaries make it plain that Lloyd George and senior cabinet ministers knew the scale of reprisals and knew about the selective assassination of suspects.

And so to the autumn of 1920 and a series of tit-for-tat attacks. The Mid-Clare Brigade carried out an ambush at Rineen, near Miltown Malbay, in which six RIC men were killed. The following day the RIC ran amok in Lahinch and Miltown Malbay in an orgy of burning and beating. At the end of the month Trim RIC Barracks was captured by the Meath Brigade. Immediately afterwards, a large number of houses in Meath were burned out and many civilians were badly treated. RIC barracks were attacked at Schull and ambushes were laid and fought at Toureen, Aherlow, Leary's Cross and Glencurrane.

In the remote areas of north Cork the main difficulty was finding the enemy in the open. The new flying column laid ambush after ambush without encountering the enemy. Moylan's view was that the flying column was not being well utilised; he had been scanning the available intelligence on local troop movements and had identified a pattern, which he took to Liam Lynch to make his case.

Moylan, Lynch and Ernie O'Malley travelled by trap through the back roads to the proposed site of the Ballydrocane ambush. Some remark of Moylan's found favour with O'Malley, who turned to Lynch and said, 'Do you know, these country fellows are coming on amazingly.'[12] Thirty years later the fact that O'Malley's comment still grated with Moylan was made clear in his witness statement. They waited at the proposed ambush site and sure enough two army lorries crowded with men passed at the appointed time. The site was a straight stretch of road between Kanturk and Newmarket. Halfway down was a gate. Once the lorries were clearly into the field of fire it was planned to push a cart out through the gate to block the road.

The preparations for the ambush included felling trees to block reinforcements and using billhooks to cut firing positions into the hedges. Moylan walked the ambush site with section leaders so that they would understand their duties. Late that night the flying column arrived, about thirty strong, and was billeted in the locality of Drominarigle. The Newmarket battalion had already turned out in force to provide flanking protection for the column, which set off at 3 a.m. marching across country to the scene and settling down in the hedgerows to wait. Moylan recalled the scene in his witness statement: 'The early morning workers passed on their way unsuspectingly, later came the children on their way to school. At eleven o'clock we were still crouching beneath the fence … Suddenly we heard the sound of a lorry.'[13] Paddy O'Brien, later commandant of the Charleville battalion, described what happened:

A single lorry approaching from Kanturk was signalled to the column. This lorry moved directly into the ambush position. A milk cart taking milk to a nearby creamery at Allensbridge was within the ambush position at this time. Fire was opened on the lorry, the driver was shot dead and the lorry collided with the milk cart coming to a halt in the middle of the ambush position. The enemy returned the fire and some of them jumped from the lorry and took cover underneath it. The fight lasted only about a minute, when the military intimated by shouting that they would surrender. A few members of the column immediately jumped over the fence and the military underneath the lorry again fired at them; none of them were wounded. A return blast was then given by the remainder of the column, inflicting slight wounds on the majority of the military.[14]

The driver of the lorry was dead. Moylan recalled looking at the body trapped in the wreckage and feeling for the man's mother. The guns and ammunition were gathered up and the column departed, leaving the disarmed soldiers at the roadside. It was a familiar scene in this part of Ireland and one not disputed by the 6th Division Record. The practice was to disarm troops and send them on their way, and this discipline survived in Cork until the end of the war.

After the Ballydrocane ambush the men returned to Drominarigle to rest before moving on that evening. George Power later wrote: 'Fearing reprisals by the British on the civil population, as had happened in Fermoy and Mallow, we moved into Kanturk with the column for three successive nights but the British did not retaliate'.[15] The absence of reprisals was greeted with surprise. It was the exception not the rule. That autumn there were reprisals and atrocities at Balbriggan, Ennistymon, Trim, Boyle, Listowel, Granard, Nenagh, Littleton, Athlone, Thurles, Longford, Tralee and many other towns. This policy would culminate in an orgy of burning, looting and killing in Cork city in December.

Also in December, two men claiming to be army deserters were found on the road near Buttevant. They were brought to Moylan for interrogation and were held overnight. There had been a number of episodes of such supposed deserters later returning to the area they had reconnoitred with a large raiding party. Moylan sent the men back to Buttevant Barracks with a message for the intelligence officer. He believed they were spies and threatened that if any more spies were sent out they would be shot. Later that day the 'deserters' returned with a large raiding party but Moylan and his party were long gone. The episode, which shows Moylan refusing, not for the first or last time, to execute men, was later recounted by prosecuting counsel during Moylan's court-martial.

The treatment of intelligence officers in other areas was a great deal more ruthless. Captain Thompson of the Manchester Regiment was killed while on intelligence duties. Two other officers, Rutherford and Brown, were kidnapped and killed. The 6th Division Record states they had been engaged in intelligence duties but were not so engaged at the time of their death. The Charleville battalion captured two more. When informed of the decision to execute them one was said to have replied, 'We die for the Empire.'[16]

The British Army had few available intelligence-gathering options and men in plain clothes were easily identified and picked up. Other ruses had to be adopted. According to the 6th Division Record, the army arranged for a fake letter to be captured purporting to be from a Volunteer requesting payment for information given; the Volunteer then had to leave Ireland to escape retribution from his own brigade.[17] In general the army was forced to rely on intelligence gained by raids and interrogations. In this climate, mistreatment of suspects became common.

The war was becoming increasingly bloody and bitter. The ambushes were stepped up. The number of RIC casualties continued to grow. In late October Michael Fitzgerald died on hunger strike. Terence MacSwiney and Joseph Murphy died soon after. In November Kevin Barry was hanged. There followed a series of callous military killings of civilians. A few of the more notorious include Ellen Quinn, a young housewife from Galway, who was shot dead on her doorstep; Annie O'Neill, aged eight, was shot and killed in Dublin; Father Michael Griffin, who was abducted from his home at Montpelier Terrace in Galway, was found dead a week later in a bog in Barna; and Tim Crowley and seventy-year-old Canon Magner, who were shot dead in Dunmanway. The killing of British intelligence officers in Dublin was followed by the killing of civilians at a Sunday afternoon football match in Croke Park.

In an ambush at Kilmichael at the end of November, sixteen

Auxiliaries were killed and the 6th Division Record alleged that some had been axed to death after surrendering. Tom Barry, who led the ambush, stated that the Auxiliaries offered their surrender, but this proved to be a trick when they opened up on Volunteers who stood up to take the surrender. Two of the men were killed and it appears that after this the Volunteers gave no quarter. The incident became a pretext for the British government to declare martial law.

During this period, Moylan remains a shadowy figure. We know he was organising, training and moving from one billet to another with his men. In north Cork his battalion was providing logistical support to the brigade column as and when required; usually in the form of intelligence gathering, transportation, signalling, storage, road blocking and scouting. In the late autumn the brigade column was disbanded and each battalion was required to set up its own smaller column. They had less firepower but they were easier to billet and would prove to be more elusive, flexible and difficult to fight.

Training camps took place at Toureen, where Moylan was in charge and Tom Roche was the training officer. The course lasted ten days and included instruction on the use of arms, signals, first aid, scouting and the selection of ambush positions. Dan Flynn recalled: 'We were put through a course of cross-country night marches, during which many hard words were used towards the officers who selected the routes to be followed'.[18]

Additionally Moylan set up an engineering section to oversee the making of landmines, bombs and the repair of guns. Engineers were recruited; a workshop was found; a lighting system, an engine and a dynamo were stolen; equipment was bought; and scrap iron was collected.

In the midst of all this activity, Moylan passed his young cousin Liam Moylan into the care of Paddy McCarthy. There was a plan to go into Millstreet for a shoot-out with local Black and Tans who had committed a number of street robberies and thrown a bomb into the house of a Volunteer. Moylan was always keen to give the less experienced Volunteers the chance 'to be shot over' and, with some misgivings, agreed to allow Liam to take part. Liam returned that night spattered with the blood of Paddy McCarthy, who had died in the shoot-out. Moylan felt a strong sense of personal loss at the death of a man who had been a tower of strength; a man remembered by Ernie O'Malley for his unfailing good humour, resourcefulness and tendency to break into song.[19]

In the aftermath of this unsuccessful raid Lynch ordered the column to return to Millstreet each night that week. They did, but the military refused to leave the barracks. On the final night Dick Willis and Jack Bolster set up their Hotchkiss in a draper's shop opposite and fired into the barracks' gate and windows – without response. While this was happening, Moylan had a coffin made in Kiskeam and took it to Millstreet for McCarthy's burial. Despite the curfew, the coffin was carried at midnight along the byroads towards Kilcorney and as the miles slipped by the cortège became immense.

There were, of course, many painful funerals on both sides. In Gort, Captain Cornwallis and Lieutenant McCreery of the Lancers and District Inspector Blake and his wife were killed in an ambush.[20] No ballads were written about this ambush nor were there any reprisals by the Lancers.

But the spiral of violence continued. In December the Auxiliaries burned part of the city centre in Cork and martial law was proclaimed first in Limerick, Cork, Kerry and Tipperary and then extended to Kilkenny, Wexford, Waterford and Clare. This development permitted the imposition of the death penalty on anyone found to be wearing a Volunteer uniform, carrying arms or aiding and abetting rebels.

7

Meelin

We did it alright, never mind how much the well-intentioned Hamar Greenwood would excuse us ... in all the tales of fiction I have read I have never experienced such orgies of murder, arson and looting as I have witnessed during the past sixteen days with the RIC Auxiliaries. It baffles description. And we are supposed to be officers and gentlemen.

An Auxiliary writing home to his mother[1]

At Westminster the policy of bluster and denial continued into 1921, when a new government policy took effect: official reprisals. The 6th Division Record of the Rebellion states with quiet satisfaction that two houses in Midleton, County Cork, had been burned in response to the killing of three RIC men. The record suggests that this, the first official reprisal, was regarded as an appropriate and measured response to attacks on British forces.

The flaws in this policy were fundamental and apparently obvious to all but those commanding the British forces and those implementing the policy at Westminster. The illegality of burning the homes of civilians and the immorality of burning homes and putting very poor people, young and old, with no other resources out on the streets in winter needs no elaboration. The archives of the 6th Division contain a cluster of pathetic and anguished letters written by the victims of this policy: a sad echo of other imperial campaigns in India and against the Boers, where British policy had employed similar tactics to subdue rebellion. An Auxiliary writing home recorded that 'many who had witnessed similar scenes in France and Flanders [said] nothing was comparable to the punishment meted out in Cork'.[2] The 6th Division Record shows that 192 homes were burned in one six-month period as part of this policy.[3]

Unofficial reprisals had been taking place for some months and it was hard for the citizenry of Cork to distinguish between official reprisals and those which were not. Certainly, no householder or shop owner would have taken comfort from the fact that the burning of their property was an official act. Naturally, the policy of reprisals generated counter-reprisals against those who were known to support the British government.

This was Cork in January 1921. At the same time, Moylan was about to engage British forces at Meelin. It was a time of 'incessant rain, intensifying sometimes into sleet and snow. I don't remember ever wearing a dry garment during the month ... on a few occasions, sleeping in the shelter of a fence, I awoke covered in snow.'[4] It was the first engagement for the new battalion column. The men who turned out at the Ballydrocane ambush formed the core of the unit – men such as Dan Guiney, Jim Riordan, Jimmy Cashman and Dan Flynn – but most of the column was untested. Moylan recalled that 'we had sufficient men now trained as far as it was possible to train them without bringing them under fire'.[5]

The difficulty, as always in this remote rural area, was in finding a target. A stage of the war had been reached in which all army units lived in barracks and the RIC patrols did not venture out except as part of a large force. It was known, however, that army units at Newmarket exercised their men along the Meelin road. Early on the morning of 4 January, the ambush party lay behind a fence about a mile south of Meelin:

We had half a dozen rifles, the rest of the men were armed with shotguns, it was therefore necessary that the fight should be at close quarters. Scouts were stationed in positions where an early view of the approach of the British could be obtained. There was nothing to do but wait and we waited well into the afternoon without result. We then got word of their approach, not from the south as expected but from the west, not a marching patrol but a strong raiding party in lorries … The position we occupied was exposed, without any real cover by way of retreat and quite unsuitable to this new problem. I decided that if we had time to get to the turn of the road … at Meenkeragh that we'd reach a position that would be reasonably satisfactory. On our way we got a further message that they were coming too swiftly towards us to enable us to reach the desired position. We had perforce to turn off the road when we had passed through the village and take the cover that immediately offered itself.[6]

The ambushers hurriedly took up position on a slope about 300 yards above the road and took what cover could be found. Moylan continues:

Scarcely had we done this when the lorries arrived. Our position was, from the point of view of success, rather hopeless. Nevertheless we opened fire with the rifles and succeeded in stopping the lorries. The British dismounted quickly and there began a duel that lasted till dusk and then the arrival of British reinforcements … there was nothing to do but retire.[7]

A slightly different account is given by Tim Cronin in his witness statement:

… the column under Seán Moylan attacked a party of British troops travelling in two lorries on the Meelin–Newmarket (commonly known as 'The Line') road. One lorry got through to Newmarket, while the party in the second lorry came under heavy fire, to which they replied. The fight went on for almost an hour, after which the IRA party was forced to withdraw due to the arrival of enemy reinforcements.[8]

A communiqué issued by General Macready's headquarters in Dublin the following day stated:

> Two military lorries each containing five soldiers and one policeman were ambushed on Tuesday afternoon near Newmarket, County Cork, martial law area. Machine-gun fire and rifle fire was opened on them by a large party of civilians and after an exchange of fire lasting a considerable time the attackers made off leaving a quantity of ammunition behind them.[9]

It appears from the army report that the reinforcements made their way to the rebel position at the crest of a hill where 'they found blood and other evidence that the attacking party had suffered injuries'.[10]

The 6th Division Record provides a little more detail on the ambush: 'An unsuccessful attempt was made by a large band of rebels to ambush a party of the Kerry Brigade [British Army] under the brigade intelligence officer at Meelin on 4 January and several casualties were inflicted on them.'[11] There are differences in the accounts given by opposing sides in every war, particularly on casualty figures. Moylan recalls that they neither sustained or inflicted any casualties and none of the Volunteers who made witness statements mentioned casualties.

The Meelin ambush was inconclusive but it had wider implications. Moylan had been fortunate to avoid disaster. He was engaged in a steep learning curve and had discovered early that there was some truth in the old military axiom: no plan survives contact with the enemy. He also judged that the late change of plan had unsettled the inexperienced ambush party. They had continued to fight but the chain of command had disintegrated in the heat of the struggle and he resolved to use a smaller and more carefully selected group in the future.

In keeping with events elsewhere, Moylan noted that the following day 'a punitive party of British military arrived in Meelin, looted and burned half a dozen houses, rounded up all the men they could find and in general behaved in a bullying and brutal manner'.[12] Florrie O'Donoghue reported that an unarmed youth, Morgan Sweeney, was killed.[13] A communiqué from British Army headquarters the day after the ambush records that the governor of the martial law area ordered the destruction of four houses in Meelin.[14] This was the second official reprisal in Ireland. Maud Gonne MacBride and the indefatigable campaigner for the oppressed, Charlotte Despard (sister of Lord Lieutenant Sir John French), made the journey from Dublin to witness the destruction inflicted on the inhabitants. A pathetic photograph of the burned-out ruins of Tim Murphy's house was carried in the *Cork Examiner* on 22 January.

Moylan's rebel party was elsewhere when the reprisals took place. They were thawing out gelignite that had been in cold storage. The effect of the chemicals was to render the party ill for some days. Moylan's experience echoed events in East Clare where Michael Brennan and a party of Volunteers were also laid up for days after experimenting with gelignite.[15] Explosives had become necessary because the RIC barracks were so heavily fortified. Some brigades had acquired gelignite but often lacked the expertise to use it. January saw no less than three assaults on RIC barracks in west Cork, all led by Tom Barry, each of which was repulsed after an explosive charge laid by the wall failed to detonate.

8

MEENEGORMAN

... there were hardly any cases of convoys accompanied by a 'mascot' being attacked.

6th Division Record of the Rebellion[1]

One of the tactical difficulties identified by Moylan in laying an ambush was the need to stop all the lorries in an army convoy to prevent the military spreading out along the road and outflanking the ambush party. Occasionally the terrain or other obstacles could be deployed to meet this difficulty. An example of this occurred on 14 January about two miles west of Newmarket, near Meenegorman. A Humber car had been involved in an accident and lay deserted for some days. Moylan takes up the story: 'I felt sure that when the British came upon the car they would halt to examine it and arranged my ambush accordingly.'[2] The ambush party, which was more than usually well armed with twenty rifles:

> ... arrived at the ambush position at about 4 a.m. It had been raining heavily. The rain had now ceased but it was bitter cold. I crept under a hedge and went to sleep for a few hours. When I woke there was a slight drift of snow. It was not yet daylight and the boys had begun to gather ... a messenger cycling furiously from Newmarket brought the news that four lorries of soldiers had arrived in the town. They were at

the military barracks as he left. This was the number we had expected and prepared for so there was no need to make any alteration in the arranged position … Then another breathless cyclist arrived with a hurriedly written note from Con Moylan. The British had a number of hostages in their lorries and were then engaged in gathering a number of others … I was in a quandary. I had made every effort and taken all care to make a success of this fight. Now, if I fought it meant certain death for a number of non-combatants … I still hoped against hope that an opportunity would present itself for an attack which would at the same time embody a sporting chance for the hostages. I explained the position to my comrades and ordered that except on my whistle there was to be no attack. I got back to my own position beside the fence outside which the car lay.

We soon heard the sound of approaching lorries, immediately they were in sight. They were crowded with men in civilian dress and these seemed to outnumber the soldiers they carried. My anticipation was sound. When the British sighted the car they slowed, their rifles were pointed outward. Two lorries moved past it, one pulled up in line with it. The last lorry twenty yards to the rear of this. Had there been no hostages there would have been slaughter. Each lorry was in perfect position for our purpose. An officer and some men dismounted to examine the car. The others remained in the lorries with the hostages, all of whom were handcuffed. Where I lay half a dozen British Tommies were five yards away, no member of the group more than fifty yards from an IRA rifle. Yet I could not blow my whistle. I could not condemn those unarmed, handcuffed men to the death that would be surely theirs if the fight started. The British remounted their lorries and drove away, never suspecting how close they had been to death. We waited all day in the hope that on their return the position might have altered. But their return through the ambush site was a repeat performance. They again halted, some dismounted and again examined the car while the majority stood guard over their prisoners. Had these prisoners been young, I might have taken a chance, but some of them were old and most were middle-aged, breadwinners with dependant families, I couldn't do it. And so again we marched away disgruntled. We had worked hard for success but success evaded us.[3]

The practice of carrying hostages had been foreshadowed the previous month in Cork city when Brigadier General Higginson announced that captured Volunteers would be carried on lorries as protection, although it should be pointed out that the Newmarket hostages were civilians.[4] It appears from the 6th Division Record that the carrying of civilian hostages had become official policy: 'Another measure introduced was the carrying of "hostages" on all road convoys. How far such action prevented ambushes it is difficult to say – as a matter of fact, there were hardly any cases of convoys accompanied by a "mascot" being attacked.'[5]

What happened outside Newmarket that day was not an isolated instance. Towards the end of the month, in Dublin, British Army vehicles on patrol started to carry IRA prisoners to deter attack. It seems this practice ceased swiftly in Dublin, but it carried on elsewhere. It was particularly prevalent in west Cork, where captive Volunteer Tim Connolly was carried battered and bruised on the back of a lorry. Jeremiah Fehily recalled being carried as a hostage 'first on a lorry and then astride the engine of a Ford car'.[6]

In any event it must have been a small consolation for Moylan to learn that other elements of the No. 2 Brigade were having more success elsewhere. The same night as the Meenegorman ambush, the No. 3 battalion laid an ambush at Shinanagh by digging a trench in the road. A British Army car, coming upon the ditch unexpectedly, tried to jump the trench, failed and slid back into it while some of the ambush party were still digging. The driver put the lights out and there was an exchange of fire before the British party was able to slip away. A small quantity of guns and ammunition was captured along with dispatches from the British intelligence officer in Limerick to the intelligence officer in Buttevant.

For the men under Moylan's command, however, one stalemate followed another. Nevertheless it may be gleaned from Moylan's account that he was developing a tactical appreciation of the war that must be fought and that the Volunteers under his command, although still ill equipped, were coalescing into a disciplined unit.

9

TUREENGARRIFFE

As January 1921 drew to a close, Moylan's men were still grappling with the problem of attacking fortified barracks:

> It was no longer possible to attack a police barracks by the methods that were successful in 1920. Now the garrisons were strongly reinforced by the Black and Tans, there were sandbag emplacements, steel shutters, barbed wire and machine guns, while we sadly lacked explosives. In the centres where the police still remained, military posts were set up, garrisoned by from sixty to one hundred men. While we were able to keep both military and police closely confined within a narrow circle, we had no equipment with which to drive them from the positions they occupied. I began to consider the possibility of using an old seventeenth-century cannon. We got one of these from Killarney. I think it came from Ross Castle. We cleaned it up, built a frame for it and one night Dan Vaughan, Tom McNamara and I went into Newmarket railway station and collected two wheels from a railway truck which we attached to the frame. We tried it early one morning. We set it up one hundred yards from a disused limekiln, loaded it with a quantity of black powder and a ten-pound sash weight, set off the charge with a short piece of fuse. It worked perfectly. We hit the face of the kiln dead centre and burst a hole through it. We were elated. When the British travelled through our district they were sheltered behind a screen of hostages. Now … we could attack them in their own barracks.[1]

While preparations were made for an artillery attack, Moylan's men continued to lay daily ambushes on the roads without encountering the enemy. In view of the unrelenting bad weather, he decided to send most of the men home for a break. At that point an event occurred that put experiments with the cannon on hold. Moylan describes walking the roads with Dan Vaughan when:

Suddenly Vaughan pointed to the road surface. There in a patch of mud was a wet tyre track, that of a heavy, wide type … We were sure the track was left by a British military car. We decided that the British had gone to Kingwilliamstown to post their latest proclamation and we both cursed the decision that had dispersed our group. We … proceeded to Kiskeam to make inquiries about the matter. The rain came down in sheets. Kiskeam was a deserted village. Con Murphy had no knowledge of the passing of any cars, nor could we elicit any information anywhere … on our way we met a man loading rushes into a cart. As a last hope we questioned him. Yes he had seen the cars, two of them, loaded with Black and Tans, they had a cannon. He described the cannon. I diagnosed a Lewis gun. We proceeded to Kingwilliamstown and made inquiries. A few people had seen the cars passing; they had gone through the village toward Castleisland. It was natural for us to think that they had gone to Tralee, which was the British headquarters in Kerry, and we considered that owing to the lateness of the hour they were unlikely to return.

I decided … to ambush the cars on their return, if they did return, at Tureengarriffe, two miles west of the village. I sent a note to the commandant of the Kanturk battalion, explaining to him what I intended to do and suggesting that, as there was a possibility that the return route would be by Killarney and Rathmore, he should lay an ambush at Clonbanin. I sent another message to the Kerry Brigade O/C …

That night was a scene of tremendous activity. Men came and went, guns and ammunition were examined, the attacking party selected.

We got to bed for a few hours in the early morning and at 5 a.m. were again astir. We marched off an hour later and having reached the selected position began to dig a trench across the road. It was a vile day, fog so thick that one could see only a few yards, and so wet that it seemed to penetrate to the bone.[2]

The ambush site itself was in Thade Daly's Glen, where a narrow road winds back and forth around the contours of the hills. On one side of the road there is an escarpment, about twenty feet high, with a good deal of foliage. On the other side of the road, the land falls away. Jim Riordan, one of the men who dug a trench around the bend of the road, recalled the intense cold and 'hailstones hopping off the road'.[3] Moylan continues:

All day long we waited and well into the night but there was no sign of our quarry. A number of men were left on guard, the majority of us snatched a few hours sleep. At six the following morning the whole party was in position again. The fog had disappeared, it was a clear dry day. At noon I decided to let half the men go so that they might try to get a cup of tea in the nearest houses but before I issued the order the sun shone out and I focused the glasses on the road at Scartag schoolhouse which was a bright yellow colour and easily identifiable. Just as my glasses rested on the patch of road two cars swung in. I shouted to the others and told them what I'd seen. I had determined at this time that nothing was going to stop the attack.[4]

Tim Cronin recalled the position of the ambush party:

North of the road and on high ground overlooking the same was a party of seven shotgun men under Dan Vaughan. This party was under cover of a sod fence about twenty yards from the road. They were extended over a distance of about thirty yards. I was with this party.

South of the road was a party of about eight riflemen in position behind some rocks and stones. They were extended over a distance of about forty yards.

Bill Moylan and Seán Healy with the Hotchkiss gun were also

south of the road but some thirty to forty yards farther east. The column O/C Seán Moylan was with this party, which from its position could enfilade the road to the west.[5]

The net result, in Moylan's words, was 'our position approximated to a semi-circle with the road cutting it in half'.[6] The Hotchkiss gun was one of those captured at Mallow Barracks. It had a disconcerting tendency to jam. The ambush party had only about ten rifles so others were armed with shotguns. As always, ammunition was in short supply.

Moylan continues:

From the viewpoint of observation we had perfect cover, from that of protection, none. The fight had to be fought to a finish. There was, too, no retreat for the Tans. If they came into the position their retreat was cut off by the men of the local companies armed with shotguns.[7]

Jimmy Cashman, a lieutenant with Kiskeam company, was crouched in an exposed position behind rocks and stones on the south side of the road. He described what then took place:

The convoy, consisting of two cars, was allowed to drive into our position, where it was greeted by a burst of machine-gun fire and a call to surrender. The driver of the leading car accelerated out of the straight stretch round the bend at the eastern end where he was held up by the trench. The second car halted and the occupants of both cars dashed for cover behind the roadside fences. As the enemy did not surrender at the opening burst all sections of the IRA party opened fire.[8]

Dan Guiney, the O/C of the Kiskeam company, was up on the high ground above the road. He later recalled that the first burst of machine-gun fire was directed above the heads of the RIC men, which appears to have given them a chance to find cover, and that 'the fighting continued for about twenty-five minutes during which time the enemy had been called upon to surrender on a number of occasions'.[9] Then Moylan signalled for a ceasefire by a blast of his whistle. He called for the men below to surrender and this time they threw down their weapons. The ambush party went down and found Divisional Commissioner Holmes badly wounded. There were seven other RIC men with him. One, Constable Moyles, was dead and the rest were wounded, two seriously. Moyles was twenty-one years of age and had been in the RIC less than a year.

Kiskeam versus The Empire reports that one RIC man dangled his rosary beads in front of Moylan and pleaded, 'I am a Catholic like yourself, don't shoot me.' Unimpressed, Moylan turned to another prisoner and asked:

'What are you?'
'I'm a bloody Black and Tan, and you can shoot me if you want to.'
Moylan's response was to extend his hand saying: 'Shake, you are a man anyway'. So they clasped hands and found some fellowship.[10]

Moylan says little more about the ambush save that he suffered a minor wound to the leg. Arms seized from the captured party included rifles, automatic shotguns, grenades, revolvers and ammunition. The prisoners were searched and paperwork was seized. One of the rebels found a large sum of money on Holmes and was staring, mesmerised by the wad of notes, when 'Moylan came up behind him and reduced him to reality by stuffing them back into the Divisional Commissioner's pocket'.[11]

Holmes was very seriously wounded. His right leg was broken, he had sustained bullet wounds in his left leg, left shoulder and above the eye, and he had other lesser injuries. A cigarette was lit for him and a coat laid over him. In the distance a scout signalled the approach of another car, which generated a flurry of activity. Fears that this car contained more police quickly evaporated when it came into view and the driver was identified as a school inspector. Tim Cronin later recounted that 'first aid was rendered to the wounded and they were loaded onto the car of a national school inspector who happened to come [our] way. He was instructed to take the wounded to Castleisland for medical attention.'[12]

The two cars were inspected. The first, an Austin, was damaged and the rebel party set it on fire. They loaded the captured weapons into the other, a Crossley, which was still in good running order and drove off. Steps were taken to disguise the tyre tracks and at a fork in the road the car went one way while the other road was blocked with trees to lead the army on a false trail.

Holmes was delivered to hospital by the school inspector as requested. A special train was laid on to bring two surgeons from Cork to attend to him. He was then brought back to the Central Military Hospital at Victoria Barracks, where he died the next day. His father and grandfather had served in the RIC. He had served in France, where he had been wounded twice and gassed. He had only recently taken over his position after the shooting of Divisional Commissioner Smyth. Holmes was buried with full military honours at Glasnevin in Dublin.

Some months later when Moylan was on trial for his life, evidence was given by the prosecution to the court-martial that at the Tureengarriffe ambush Moylan had warded off an attempt to shoot the captured police officers. 'Shoot them and I will shoot you' were the words attributed to him.[13] One of the RIC men later related that Moylan had indeed threatened to shoot some of his own men who were searching the captured and throwing their possessions into a ditch.[14] Moylan's account makes no mention of this incident. Nor is it mentioned in the accounts given by other Volunteers. Did it happen? There are a number of pointers. On the one hand, successful ambushes of the army almost always ended with the disarming of prisoners and their release. These ambushes were usually marked by invitations to surrender. It does appear that this practice was motivated by a reluctance to take life. Of course, for soldiers crouched under a lorry under fire, the knowledge that if they surrendered they would be back in barracks within hours must have been a strong inducement to do so. On the other hand, Moylan never denied that the words were spoken by him and prosecutors do not usually make statements in court that are favourable to an accused unless they are true.

By early 1921 there were many cases where British forces had killed or mistreated prisoners or civilians and martial law was in force in Cork with the consequence that any rebel captured with arms faced execution. This situation must have been the subject of intense debate amongst Volunteers living rough or crowded into cold cottages with little else to talk about. The debate would have had an extra piquancy that January after the capture and court-martialling of Cornelius (Con) Murphy of the Millstreet battalion, who was then awaiting execution at Victoria Barracks in Cork.[15]

Typed rough notes kept by the intelligence officer of the Gloucestershire Regiment, which are more or less contemporaneous, record the Tureengarriffe ambush and, with a little surprise, note that the wounded were not killed after capture. Immediately after this entry there is recorded in direct speech a remark made by one of the attackers: 'We are not the murder gang' an oblique reference to the description of the IRA penned by British Prime Minister David Lloyd George.[16] This sounds like Moylan's voice (in personal correspondence written during the War of Independence he was apt to write ironically of himself and his men as 'the Murder Gang'), but whether his words were addressed to the prisoners or to his men remains unclear.

In any event, there is no doubt that the ambush caused considerable dismay at British Army headquarters. It was described in the 6th Division Record of the Rebellion as the 'biggest encounter which had so far occurred ... between the army and the rebels'.[17] And a high-ranking civil servant at Dublin Castle wrote in his diary for 28 January: 'This afternoon a party of six police with Major Holmes, DC Cork, were ambushed at Castleisland near Tralee by about sixty men. One constable killed. All the rest wounded and disabled. Holmes wounded dangerously. Both cars and all arms captured. A bad business.'[18] A press communiqué issued by General Macready the next day also suggested that the attacking party numbered sixty or more and was heavily armed with machine guns.[19] Volunteer sources, however, suggest the rebel party was far smaller.

This misapprehension about the size of the rebel party may explain the unusually strong reprisal raid that was launched the next day. Thirty lorries of troops arrived at Ballydesmond. Officers demanded to know the identities of those responsible for the Tureengarriffe ambush, but no information was forthcoming. A house and grocery shop belonging to Tim Vaughan were burned along with William McAuliffe's home and drapery store.[20]

The planning and execution of the Tureengarriffe ambush cannot be faulted on any account. Events elsewhere that day show that the difference between success and failure could be slim. At Godfrey's Cross near Dripsey, elements of the Cork No. 1 Brigade were lying in ambush for a column of Auxiliaries, when they themselves were ambushed by the Manchester Regiment. Ten Volunteers were captured, six of whom were badly wounded. Immediately after this encounter a report written by the officer commanding the Volunteer unit was captured. It gives the flavour of the ambush:

> In the retreat, three of our men were wounded, but were able to come along with us, and, as far as I can ascertain there are seven others missing … we lost about three rifles and some shotguns, also some bombs. Some of these articles were hidden by the men, so we may recover them. The military attacked from the front, rear and left flanks, and also scoured the roads all around, so it is evident they got information.[21]

January 1921 ended with a further spate of killings. The 6th Division Record notes: 'On 31 January, a particularly brutal outrage was committed. Mrs King, wife of the County Inspector at Mallow was shot while walking with her husband at Mallow Station. The CI was also wounded.'[22] There had been a determined effort to kill the county inspector, which had been badly botched. The inspector and his wife were severely wounded and 'a few hours later Mrs King after suffering much agony died'.[23] Reprisals were swift. The railway union had been a staunch supporter of Sinn Féin for some time and had been refusing to carry troops on the trains. For this reason, and as far as can be discerned for no other, the Auxiliaries sought out a number of local railway staff, who were invited to run and then were shot in the back as they tried to escape. Three railwaymen, Devitt, Mullane and Bennett, were killed.[24]

10

FEBRUARY 1921

Con Murphy of Cork No. 2 Brigade was arrested on 4 January 1921. He was charged with possessing a revolver and seven rounds of ammunition.[1] His execution at Victoria Barracks on 1 February was the first to be carried out following the declaration of martial law in Cork and the neighbouring counties. A few days later, eight of the ten men captured in the Dripsey ambush were brought before a court-martial at Victoria Barracks. Five were found guilty. Sentence was put back while the military debated their fate.

Despite this the ambushes continued. On 1 February the Drimoleague company ambushed four RIC men, killing Constable O'Connor and wounding Constable Griffin. In Tulligbeg a few days later a four-man RIC cycle patrol was ambushed; Constables Edward Carter and William Taylor were killed and another constable was wounded.

On 4 February Patrick Crowley of the Kilbrittain company was killed by Auxiliaries as he tried to shoot his way to freedom. A few days later at Skibbereen, Cork No. 3 Brigade launched an attack on the barracks. They captured two unarmed privates from the King's (Liverpool) Regiment, who were held for some hours and then released. It appears their release was a response to the chivalrous manner in which their commanding officer, Colonel Hudson, had conducted operations. On 11 February there was an attack by the flying column of Cork No. 3 Brigade on the Drimoleague RIC Barracks. On the same day the Millstreet flying column of Cork No. 2 Brigade attacked a train carrying troops near Rathcoole. According to Con Meaney, one British soldier was killed and the others surrendered and were released after they handed over their rifles and ammunition.[2]

Men under Moylan's command were lying in ambush for a military convoy near Newmarket when the convoy diverted unexpectedly around the ambush site and then split into two. One section of the convoy passed through the village of Knocknagree. Moylan describes the events as they were relayed to him that night:

A hurling match was in progress between a number of small boys. These little lads had no anticipation of danger and stood in groups about the small playing pitch to watch the approaching lorries. Two bursts of machine-gun fire directed towards them was the first indication they had of any danger. Some of the boys rushed southwards, others lay on the fields and beside the fences. The British soldiers advanced, pouring volley after volley on the fleeing boys and on the playing pitch. When the firing ceased the boys were rounded up ... Michael J. Kelleher, aged seventeen, had been shot through the head; Michael Herlihy, aged thirteen, was shot through the thigh and Donal Herlihy, his brother, was shot through the lung.[3]

The army did not deny that the boys had been shot but asserted that they had been caught in the crossfire: 'A military patrol saw a party of armed civilians in a field near Knocknagree. Fire was opened and replied to resulting in the deaths of one youth and the wounding of two others.'[4] Local people rejected this official account. There is no evidence that any of these youths had a connection with the Volunteers and Moylan's account suggests there was no Volunteer activity in the area that day. Indeed all Volunteer engagements have been scrupulously recorded by historians in recent years and there is no mention of an engagement at Knocknagree. Also, there is no record of any incident at Knocknagree in the 6th Division Record of the Rebellion, which logged every significant ambush.

Such incidents were becoming increasingly common. Hansard is full of detailed reports coming from all parts of Ireland in which the killing of women and children are related in compelling and painful detail. Writing over thirty years later Moylan's anger had abated little. The moral authority of the British government was seeping away and British rule in Ireland disintegrating.

Another notable incident in February 1921, casts some light on the conflicting tensions in the senior ranks of the military. A number of Auxiliaries had burned and looted a pub in Robinstown. General Crozier, commander of the Auxiliaries, tried and dismissed twenty-one members of N Company. Five more Auxiliaries were arrested pending a court-martial. All of the Auxiliaries were reinstated by General Tudor, Chief of Police. On 22 February, Hansard reported on the bare facts of what had taken place and noted that Crozier's resignation had been tendered almost immediately. Crozier later alleged that the British government had succumbed to threats by the Auxiliaries to reveal the true extent of what was taking place in Ireland.[5]

The weather remained bitterly cold and back in north Cork Moylan and his men spent much of February lying in wait for convoys that never materialised or trying to engineer an attack on the barracks in Newmarket. Dan Flynn described his life at this critical time: 'I was engaged nearly full time on the destruction of enemy lines of communication, digging trenches, demolishing bridges and blocking roads'. His story is typical of many others.[6]

Seán Kennedy recalled a miserable February evening returning through the fields after inspecting a possible ambush position:

We came to a stream, swollen after recent heavy rains. We did not know how deep it was, so Seán Moylan told me to ask the people in a nearby house. They said it would be up to our hips, but they offered me a donkey and cart to get across. I accepted ... Seán wanted to wade across, and it was only after some persuasion that he consented to get into the cart. Everything went fine until we got to the middle of the stream, then the donkey fell and Seán was pitched out head foremost. The other two laughed but I didn't as I knew what was coming ... Seán did not mind about himself it was his gun and ammunition getting wet that annoyed him so much ... but he never kept up his anger very long and soon it was forgotten.[7]

Moylan and his men moved from one billet to another. Years later he recalled the generosity of local people who would put him and his men up: 'It was now that the magnificent spirit of the people manifested itself. Capture of a wanted man in any house meant imprisonment or worse for every male member of the household. It meant the destruction of home and property ... Yet in every household were the wanted men made welcome.'[8] This experience of local generosity was echoed by Paddy O'Brien: 'I travelled through the greater part of north Cork from August 1920 until the Truce on 11 July 1921. Only once during that time was I refused shelter for a night.'[9]

Nora Moylan's grocery shop in Newmarket did little trade during the War of Independence. Many local people were afraid of being targeted by the military if they shopped there, but there were some loyal customers such as the O'Flynn family. The shop was closely watched by the military and Moylan's visits were rare:

... one night I called home to see my mother. She and my sisters had been subject to a good deal of annoyance from the military. The doors had periodically been kicked in and the house ransacked. All my books had disappeared as a result. She and I talked together in the shop. I asked her if she had had any recent raids and she confessed that for several weeks things had been quiet except for the day after the Tureengarriffe ambush when raiding Auxiliaries had taken over the town. Just then I heard footsteps on the road outside. Since curfew was being rigorously imposed I knew whose they were. I suggested she should go upstairs and ascertain if all was clear as I intended departing. My real reason was that I didn't want her to be present when the fight I believed to be imminent started. I moved to the back of the shop and looked through the glass door leading to the room behind. There were two soldiers in the room. One, an officer, whose head was within a foot of my revolver, was talking to my sister. The other, a sergeant, was near the outer door engaged in animated laughing conversation with a Miss Baby O'Mahony who was that night staying in the house. I stood still as a statue until, after a few minutes, they both left.[10]

Moylan's reference to his books may be revealing. It is one of only two occasions in his lengthy witness statement when he talks of personal possessions. The other was when he received some money and used it to buy guns. The books, it seems, were all that he owned. Even the suit he wore had been donated by his friend Con Flynn. His witness statement, written in the late 1940s, is heavily laced with classical allusions and references to Charles Dickens, Victor Hugo, Robbie Burns and William Shakespeare. It is likely that this learning did not come late in life.

Moylan had now been on the run for almost three years. He had given up his trade as a carpenter, his workshop and the family business for a life of hardship and danger. His sacrifice was no greater than many of his generation: men and women driven by a vision of a fairer and more just society. It involved, in their view, the end of British rule in Ireland. It was a life of isolation, which he summed up in this way: 'Generous friends gave me food and shelter. I needed nothing more. I didn't smoke. I drank only when wearied muscle had to be flogged to meet unexpected demands or as a remedy for complaints caught from soaking rain and chilling winds. An occasional pound and an odd parcel of underclothing came from home.'[11]

The arduous life meant that ill health was never far away and many senior Volunteers were hospitalised or confined to bed for weeks on end. As well as Moylan, George Power, Liam Deasy and Paddy O'Brien, to name but a few, were laid low by the effects of poor diet, privation, cold, exposure and a lack of clean, dry clothes.

The consequences of being taken off guard could prove fatal. For example, a flying column had stayed some weeks at a farmhouse near

Clonmult but failed to post guards on the day they were due to move out. The 6th Division Record of the Rebellion shows that this large party of rebels was surprised at the farmhouse. A siege of some hours followed until the brigade intelligence officer, showing considerable bravery, climbed onto the roof and set fire to the building. Hand grenades were then thrown into the gaping hole. What happened next remains a huge controversy. The 6th Division Record states:

> Six or seven rebels came out with their hands up, and the Crown forces went forward to take them prisoners; on this, fire was opened again by the rebels in the house. The Crown forces returned the fire immediately, and as the men who were surrendering came into the line of fire, several casualties were inflicted on them. The Crown forces then rushed the house and captured it, and found eight rebels – four wounded and four unwounded. These were taken prisoner.[12]

After a few days a very different picture began to emerge from the survivors: an account of surrendering rebels shot down with their hands up. The dying were robbed and finished off with enthusiasm. But for one officer's intervention, all would have been killed. One of the survivors, Paddy O'Higgins, wrote the following account in the closing years of his life: 'We were told to come out with our hands up. We did so. We were lined up alongside an outhouse with our hands up. The Tans came along and shot every man.'[13]

One soldier and two police officers were injured. Twelve rebels were shot dead and eight were captured of whom four were wounded.

Moylan had other matters to deal with following the Tureengarriffe ambush. First, the ambush party had seized papers from General Holmes which needed to be analysed. Moylan describes the outcome:

> ... as a result of the shooting of Inspector Sullivan, a number of Kerry men were prisoners in Cork Barracks. General Holmes' chief mission ... was to collect the evidence which would condemn these men. He

got it but it never reached the official files … Those who gave the information were unfortunately unable to repeat their story. They met a fate intended for the prisoners.[14]

It is likely that the execution of informants was carried out by the local Kerry Brigade and one suspects that Moylan was glad to be relieved of that duty. He had a marked disinclination to kill informants or unarmed soldiers.

Second, the seized car, which is described in one contemporary account as a touring car capable of cruising at speeds of up to forty miles per hour, needed to be dealt with. Its hiding place was becoming something of a tourist attraction and people travelled for many miles to have a look. Moylan issued instructions to three young Volunteers, who he remembers as the musketeers, to move it. He recalls cycling many miles to Andy Horan's to deal with the car:

I asked him if he knew anything about the car.

'I do, of course,' he said, 'the boys are after carrying it off with them to the wedding.'

'To the wedding?' I asked.

'At the cathedral at Killarney,' he said.

I swore to high Heaven. Here was a car, the description of which was in every barracks, a car in size, power and colour standing out from the ruck of cars like a sore thumb.

'Do you mean to tell me,' I said, 'that they drove the car to a wedding at the cathedral?'

'They did,' he said, 'and what's more, they took the bride and bridesmaid with them. The car that was to take them broke down on the road and the boys, sooner than disappoint the girl, drove her to town.'[15]

Moylan observes in his witness statement 'there is a special providence watching over fools and children'.[16] He avoided contact with the men until his anger abated. Several days later they were called upon to deploy in ambush. The senior musketeer reported to Moylan with disgruntled self-righteousness: 'I snapped at him, I don't need a report, you're to get out a machine gun and go with Commandant O'Leary and I'll be at no damn loss if I never see you again.'[17] The truth about the car was more prosaic. It had been taken to the wedding but not to the cathedral. One of the Volunteers recalled:

> It was one of those old type weddings, there was the hauling home of the bride on the third day, the straw boys and every old time thing you can think of ... Moylan was mad. I know I kept out of his way on my return. He would be mad one day and the next day he would have forgotten all as there was something new to worry about.[18]

A summary of the events that took place on one day at the end of February 1921 gives some insight into the prevailing conditions. Five of the men captured in the Dripsey ambush were executed: Volunteers Tim McCarthy, Thomas O'Brien, John Lyons, Daniel O'Callaghan and Patrick O'Mahoney. Mary Lindsay, who had given information to the authorities about the Dripsey ambush, and her butler had been taken hostage to ensure the safety of the captured Volunteers; both their lives were now at great risk. One other prisoner, John Allen from Tipperary, was also executed. Also in that month, five soldiers were shot dead in Cork city and eleven others were wounded.[19] Such was the reality of life for Moylan and many others like him in early 1921.

11

CLONBANIN

Dublin, March 6 – Brig. Gen. H. R. Cumming, DSO was killed in an ambush in west Cork yesterday afternoon. He was in control of a Kerry brigade and was returning heavily escorted from Killarney to his headquarters at Buttevant.

New York Times, 7 March 1921

Any analysis of recent history runs the risk of reopening old passions and grievances and may perhaps be seen as trivialising what took place. Three generations on, the ambushes and killings are still argued over with a disconcerting passion. There are disputes about atrocities and about acts that deserved acknowledgement and some expression of regret. There are also, even now, allegations that one or other side misrepresented casualty figures.

There are many versions of what took place at Clonbanin. Some will even argue over the date, although that, at least, can be fixed with a degree of certainty. Moylan recalls that while lying in wait on the morning of the Clonbanin ambush, they flagged down a car carrying two American journalists and a photographer. The Americans gave their word they would not pass on information about the rebel party and were allowed to proceed. The *New York Times* carried the story of the ambush on 7 March and placed the date as 5 March.

The Clonbanin ambush was the result of intelligence showing that on the third day of each month two pay lorries of Auxiliaries travelled from Killarney to Rathmore. A joint operation was set up involving units from Cork and Kerry. Moylan set the scene in his witness statement:

> We arrived in Kerry … and on 1 March got into position at the Bower, which is about midway between Killarney and Rathmore. Its name is deceptive; it is a cold, bare and windswept glen. The country here is, particularly in winter, rather desolate, with none of the scenic beauty for which the south and west of the county is famous. When we arrived the Kerrymen were in possession and while arms were few there were men in plenty. All the local companies had turned up, some with shotguns, most of them completely unarmed. We lay in position all day without result. Still another day passed and still nothing happened. On the morning of the third day we discovered the reason why the British had not come our way. General Strickland … was on an inspection tour in Kerry. We read the details of his tour when somebody arrived with a newspaper. He had rounded up the people of Tralee and given them a minatory talk, informing them, amongst other things, that there were armed men with Cork accents hanging round the borders of the county and threatening dire consequences for Kerry if anyone gave aid or comfort to any of these people. He seemed to be fairly well informed of our movements.[1]

Major General E. P. Strickland was the commander-in-chief of the 6th Division. The previous autumn the IRA had attempted to kidnap him in Cork and later launched a determined effort to kill him. As the days passed at the Bower, the prospect of any ambush receded and it seemed probable that the military would know of their position. A new ambush position was reconnoitred about half a mile west of Clonbanin crossroads. The terrain was favourable and the road curved only gently and was lined on each side with banks and heavy foliage, which allowed fire from both sides of the road without endangering attackers on the other bank. The only disadvantage was that the location was just six miles from the heavily garrisoned town of Kanturk.

Arrangements were made to billet the men and provide horses for transport in the morning. The column moved off into the night. What had started as a plan to ambush any convoy that passed seems to have evolved into a determined plan to kill Major General Strickland. We know this because Moylan's report of the action, which was later captured by the army, reads: 'Intelligence arrived from Killarney that Major General Strickland would probably travel from there towards Cork on Friday. This news strengthened our desire to remain on until Friday.'[2]

Con Meaney, commandant of Cork No. 7 Millstreet battalion, recalled receiving a request from Moylan in the early hours of 5 March to reinforce him as soon as possible. Meaney later recounted: 'The message arrived at about 5.30 to 6.30 a.m. Horses and traps were immediately procured, and still under cover of darkness, the column, consisting of about twenty men, was drawn to within three miles of Clonbanin.'[3] The reinforcements marched from there to find the men from Newmarket, Charleville and Kerry lying or crouching behind bushes and fences on the banks overlooking the road. At the eastern end, the Hotchkiss machine gun was positioned so that it could fire down along the road.

Moylan's decision to move the ambush site proved to be astute. The 6th Division Record of the Rebellion shows that the army had sound and detailed information about the location of the proposed ambush. The convoy travelling from Killarney to Buttevant that afternoon carried General Hanway R. Cumming, not the hoped-for Major General Strickland. The Royal Fusiliers escorting General Cumming debused and reconnoitred the area on foot. The East Lancashire Regiment, walking the ground on the approaches from Rathmore, carried out a similar search and found the abandoned ambush site, before escorting Cumming onwards. The 6th Division Record suggests that they may have let their guard down a little at this point.[4]

It is worth stepping back for a moment to consider the audacity of the plan. None of the IRA party had experience as professional soldiers. Moylan had been a carpenter, most of the others were farmers or labourers. It is fair to describe them as men with a conservative outlook in which family life, Catholicism and a strong work ethic were the defining elements. It was a momentous step for such men to set upon a course of action that involved the taking of human life. To engage in an armed conflict with the largest empire in the world was an ambitious enterprise and to attack a heavily armed convoy carrying the commander-in-chief of all armed forces in the southern Ireland region illustrated their breathtaking determination.

Moylan describes the scene:

> It was a beautiful calm morning, we had an unusually strong force, riflemen from Charleville, Newmarket and Millstreet, as well as the riflemen from Kerry who had come with us. We also had one of the Hotchkiss guns captured at Mallow and half a dozen road mines. Commandant P. O'Brien had put the troops in position while I arranged for the laying of the mines. When I had finished he took me round to each section. In our tour we had the leader of each section with us so that each man should have a clear idea of the plan of attack. We made it quite clear that General Strickland and his party were the objects of our attack and we intended to ignore every other opportunity for attack offered, no matter how tempting the offer proved to be.[5]

At this point Moylan recalls that a messenger arrived. Liam Lynch had been waiting for some days for Moylan and O'Brien to arrive for a brigade meeting and was now, it was reported, 'in a towering rage'.[6] Moylan and O'Brien decided to press on with the ambush:

> At ten o'clock we got word from the signallers that the British were coming. I had a good view of the road leading from the west and turned my glasses on it. The road was empty. I sent a messenger swiftly to the nearest signaller. Yes, the British were coming from the east. On they came, three wire-covered lorries, one man playing

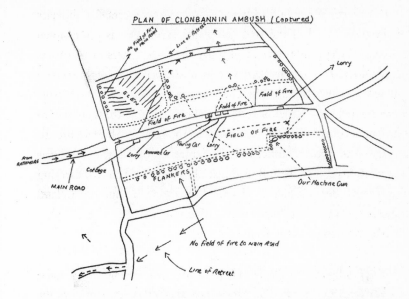

A plan of the Clonbanin ambush taken from the Strickland Papers, Appendix 11 of the 6th Division Record of the Rebellion. Courtesy of Imperial War Museum

an accordion, the others singing … the lorries travelled away to the west, went over the crest of the hill, disappeared. Until then there was silence. But now a murmur of excited speech broke out in every group. Men were questioning the wisdom of the order given. What if we got no second chance? I confess that I, too, began to have doubts … if our prediction was wrong any shred of reputation we had was lost.[7]

There is a divergence of evidence here. Paddy O'Brien later stated that this convoy got through because the mine operated by Moylan failed to detonate and O'Brien's trigger misfired.[8] As the convoy passed from view, one other Volunteer noted that Moylan shed a tear of rage.[9] It may not be necessary to resolve this conflict. If Moylan chose not to fire then it was a tough decision and he must have been racked by doubts. The brigade O/C and most of the senior officers had been waiting for Moylan and O'Brien for some days. The entire brigade was tied up. Losing the confidence of Liam Lynch was one thing, but Moylan also risked losing the confidence of his men. Some hours passed without movement. Moylan picks up the story:

At 2.15 p.m. an excited signaller came with the news. This time they were coming from the west. The signallers on the hill behind us had seen them. They were not yet in view from the position in which I stood. I focused the glasses on the hill crest. In a few moments the first lorry appeared, then two other vehicles, next came an armoured car, behind that again three more lorries. They were spaced at such intervals as to cover a half mile of the road. We had expected this and had spaced our section and the road mines accordingly.[10]

An officer of the East Lancashire Regiment later described the attack: 'At a point approximately 400 yards west of Clonbanin crossroads, fire was opened on the convoy from both sides of the road, which at this point takes a curve north-east and is flanked by high banks, which are covered by furze bushes and intersected with banks and hedges.'[11]

Watching from above, Moylan followed the progress of the armoured car:

The mine in the centre of the ambush position was destined for it. As it passed over the mine I pressed the switch on the battery. I got a shock that almost knocked me over. It had short circuited. But all the others were watching too and at once a burst of rifle fire rang out. The leading lorry was ditched. And now we had a slice of luck; Liam Moylan with his Hotchkiss gun had concentrated on the armoured car and one lucky shot got through the slit in front, wounding the driver. The armoured car, too, was ditched. The British dived for cover.[12]

Other Volunteers recall the armoured car hitting the back of the touring car before getting bogged down in the road. A tall officer jumped from the tourer and, in response to a call for surrender, shouted, 'Surrender hell. Give them the lead.'[13] The officer sustained a head wound and fell dead. A press release issued later by British GHQ suggests this must have been Cumming.

Moylan takes up his account: 'Apart from the advantage of surprise which we had, they were now in as good a position as we were, and then began the long duel that ended only at dusk ... In numbers we were about equal, but in armament we had no answer ... to the heavy maxim that roared continuously from the armoured car.'[14]

Jimmy Cashman recalled Moylan appearing beside him at the height of the fighting. He took three Volunteers and crossed to the south side of the road in an attempt to drive in the flank of the enemy, but they were beaten back by fire from the armoured car which dominated the fight.[15] Flanking attacks by the British were also driven off. The Hotchkiss jammed and could not be unblocked, further limiting the Volunteers' ammunition. The British unit was buoyed up by continuous fire from the armoured car and at least one Lewis gun.

One of the untold stories of the ambush concerns a Miss Leader, the daughter of a local Church of Ireland clergyman who lived nearby. She heard the shooting from her home and ran out to the road, at considerable personal risk, to tend to the wounded soldiers. Her courage has never been recognised.[16]

Moylan recalls:

The fight started about 2.30 p.m. It seemed to me that it had been in progress less than an hour when I looked at my watch. It was 5.30 p.m. My worry then was British reinforcements. Kanturk and Newmarket, where there were strong garrisons, were but a few miles distant ... It was not until darkness had fallen that the reinforcements arrived, and when they came, they came in strength ... As darkness fell we moved away.[17]

Moylan's report describes the encounter developing 'into a series of skirmishes over a wide area. We retreated in good order after inflicting heavy casualties and without suffering any on our side.'[18] The attackers melted away into the dusk: the Millstreet and Kerry troops to the west;

those from Charleville and Newmarket retired north to Kiskeam. Breaking off was not easy for some of the rebels when the army units attempted to outflank them. Moylan recalls slowing his departure to wait for stragglers and being fired upon by a large party of British troops. Moylan's party pressed on and disappeared into the night.

Initial reports to the outside world were sketchy. A communiqué issued by General Macready that evening stated: 'A party of about thirty-five military were ambushed at 2 p.m. this afternoon between Killarney and Buttevant and two officers and two other ranks were killed. The fighting was still in progress at 6 p.m.'[19] Moylan learned the same night that Major General Strickland had not been aboard the convoy, but Cumming had been killed and it was believed that the military had sustained many casualties.

Because of the heavy firing from the armoured car there was no opportunity for the rebels to gather weapons dropped at the scene. Some days later a small silver revolver, believed to have belonged to Cumming, was found by a local woman and given to Denis Galvin, one of the attacking party.

The 6th Division Record shows that Colonel Commandant Cumming, CMG, DSO, was killed, as was Lieutenant Maligny. Another officer and seven men were wounded. It described the ambush as:

One of the worst reverses suffered by the army and, making all allowance for the elaborate and undoubtedly skilful preparations made by the rebels, there is no doubt that the two facts which were more or less responsible for the disaster were (1) finding the original ambush position, of which information had been received, evacuated, precautions were somewhat relaxed; (2) owing to the armoured car, in its efforts to avoid a collision, getting ditched, it never properly came into action.[20]

The bodies of Cumming and Maligny were removed to Buttevant Barracks and the next day to Dublin. The following morning the bodies of the dead officers were placed on gun carriages, each covered with a Union Jack, and taken from King George V Military Hospital at Arbour Hill along the quays to an awaiting ship at the North Wall. They were followed by senior officers acting as pallbearers. Behind, walked General Macready and a number of staff officers at the head of hundreds of troops stretching out into the distance. Traffic was blockaded by Auxiliaries armed with rifles and fixed bayonets. Those civilians who failed to uncover their heads had their hats knocked to the ground.[21]

The ambush at Clonbanin and Cumming's death made international news. It also had a deep impact on the British Army's Dublin GHQ and on the parliament at Westminster. Cumming was remembered with affection by his own regiment and his obituary read: 'Fearless and just, he died as he lived.'[22] He had enjoyed a distinguished career, had been mentioned in dispatches at Ladysmith and had served with distinction in France where he was awarded the Distinguished Service Order (DSO) and the Legion of Honour. He left behind a widow.

At the time of his death Cumming had been undertaking a court of inquiry into the death of Mrs King and the Mallow railwaymen. The inquiry exonerated the British forces from the murder of the railwaymen and Macready later wrote that Cumming had gained 'the esteem and respect of all parties concerned'.[23] In fact, courts of inquiry, which had replaced inquests, did not command public confidence because they were seen to cover up unlawful killings and had become known, disparagingly, as courts of acquittal. Florrie O'Donoghue, with typical understatement, condemned the Mallow inquiry as an exercise in 'mendacity'.[24] It is doubtful whether any person on the republican side had a favourable view of Cumming. Many Volunteers recalled that the convoy at Clonbanin carried a civilian hostage, Maurice Slattery, who escaped in the confusion of the ambush. The Volunteers had strong views about the propriety of carrying hostages.

Most of the casualties of the Clonbanin ambush were members

of the East Lancashire Regiment. Moylan would next encounter this regiment after his capture in May, when it appears they remembered him well.

In the immediate aftermath of the ambush, Moylan laid low all night and the following day before collecting the unexploded mines from Clonbanin and making his way on foot to the brigade meeting at Nadd. On his arrival he found Lynch reading the newspaper reports of the Clonbanin ambush, his temper of previous days forgotten.

After the meeting he describes walking on towards Lisgriffin where he had an appointment with a local company to destroy the bridge on the road from Buttevant to Kanturk. The destruction of bridges and trenching of roads had become a primary tactic in disrupting enemy troop movements. The demolition was completed in the hours of darkness with picks, wedges and bars. The working party learned as they dismantled the bridge that the Kanturk battalion had ambushed an RIC patrol at Father Murphy's Bridge in Banteer and disarmed a number of Black and Tans and RIC men. The dismantling of the bridge finished at about 2 a.m. Moylan's work rate was still quite prodigious but it was taking its toll. As he put it: 'I was not physically robust, for months I had no more than a few hours sleep nightly. During the few recent weeks even these short hours had been cut in half.'[25]

The job at the bridge finished, Moylan set out to cycle from Lisgriffin to Dromagh, fifteen miles away. There he was due to meet the Derrygallon company to carry out the destruction of another bridge. On his journey he was forced to take cover from a convoy of troops. He learned later that the convoy was part of a round-up in the Nadd area. The army had acquired an important informant: a former British soldier named Dan Shields, who had gone over to the rebels and had been captured. Moylan knew Shields and describes him as 'an uncouth individual, a blackguard given to drink … I got a distinct shock when I heard he had been recruited into the Kanturk battalion'.[26] It appears from records held by the Gloucestershire Regiment that Shields told the army he had been conscripted into the Volunteers and held more or less prisoner. Shields was able to pinpoint the No. 2 Brigade headquarters at Nadd about a thousand feet up on the slopes of the Boggeragh Mountains.

The 6th Division Record relates the operation:

The inclemency of the weather, and the rough nature of the ground, rendered the operation a most difficult one to accomplish. The troops were on the 'jumping off line' at six a.m. and at eight a.m. had advanced over the portion of the mountain covering the rebels' headquarters and preventing escape. Shortly after daybreak a small party of rebels were encountered by some of the troops. These were immediately attacked, three being killed and two wounded; one of the wounded men escaped, and the other was killed by the troops forming the cordon on the north. A quantity of munitions was captured and their stronghold destroyed.[27]

The Volunteers killed were David Herlihy, Edward Waters and Timothy Kiely. They had been surprised at Herlihy's farm. According to local Volunteers, the situation that unfolded was grim: 'They brought the lads out in front of the house in their bare feet and told them to run for it. The military had a firing party in readiness.'[28] Morgan and Moloney ran and were wounded but were able to get away. The others were shot dead. Another Volunteer, Twomey, who was not on duty that day, was also shot dead in unknown circumstances. The brigade staff escaped after fighting a running retreat.

Elsewhere there were more ambushes. In mid-March an ambush at Castletownroche resulted in the death of Constable Elton. And in west Cork, Tom Barry led a major engagement at Crossbarry, inflicting and sustaining significant casualties.

On 22 March, the RIC in Cork captured an unnamed Volunteer in possession of a revolver. According to the 6th Division Record, the man was threatened with a drumhead court-martial and execution. He then gave information that led the army to a barn at Clogheen where an exchange of fire resulted in six IRA men from Cork No. 1

Brigade being killed. The army sustained no casualties. The Volunteers were William Deasy, Michael O'Sullivan, Daniel Crowley, Daniel Murphy, Jeremiah Mullane and Thomas Dennehy. The informant was paid £150 and put aboard a destroyer bound for England.[29]

On the last day of March, Tom Barry led an attack on Rosscarbery RIC Barracks. The wall of the barracks was partially blown in and there followed a desperate battle in which Sergeant Shea and Constable Bowles were killed. The rest of the defenders retreated room by room under the onslaught until eventually, with the barracks in flames and all eight defenders wounded, they threw their weapons into the blaze and surrendered.

Closer to home Moylan had been working on the destruction of Clonfert Bridge. It appears he hoped the demolition of the bridge might draw out a military convoy. He had laid an ambush party, but the convoy did not materialise and the Volunteers departed. The following day Moylan, Charlie O'Reilly and Mick Sullivan of Knockacluggin returned to the bridge where they ran into an ambush laid by the military. O'Reilly was wounded and died the next day. Moylan recalls that 'his funeral was the occasion of a great demonstration of force and intimidation on the part of the British'.[30]

On 21 March, the IRA had killed two hostages in Cork: Mary Lindsay, who had given information about the Dripsey ambush, and her butler, James Clarke, although it is not clear what he did to deserve this fate. There is evidence of ongoing debates in the IRA about the propriety of taking hostages. Moylan's witness statement appears to be an accurate and reliable account of the period, however, he is unaccountably silent on important issues such as this.

12

THE GUN AND PROMOTION

By April 1921 there was something of a stalemate in north Cork. The ambush war meant that the RIC was increasingly confined to barracks and the army only ventured out in large convoys, taking care to vary their routes. Unaware that communications from British military headquarters in Cork were being successfully intercepted by an attentive telephonist at the Mallow exchange, the army issued instructions to surround a Cork column that was 'resting' in the east Kerry area. The telephonist, Annie Barrett, sent out word that 'arrangements were being made for troops from Limerick, Killarney, Buttevant and Fermoy to surround the area' and a round-up was successfully foiled. There was a subsequent telephone call from Mallow to Cork headquarters stating that the 'birds had flown' and assuming that 'Moylan must have tapped the lines'.[1] While the rebels had reliable intelligence on planned raids, information on the movement of patrols that might be ambushed was much harder to come by. Moylan recalls that 'a dozen times plans were made, ambushes arranged. Men endured an endless weary wait in all weathers without success.'[2]

One of those plans involved the destruction of the bridge at Barley Hill just north of Newmarket. The plan was to tempt the British garrison out to a site near the bridge where they could be ambushed. Moylan suffered a recurrence of the illness that had laid him low in 1919. He recalls being:

... put to bed, where I lay helplessly. I had scarcely enough strength to speak yet I forced myself to discuss the proposed ambush with Mick Sullivan ... as he left with the others to take up their positions my last instruction to him was to send for me at once when he had word of the arrival of the British and under no circumstances to leave his position until after dark.[3]

The Volunteers deployed and waited all day before retiring. It transpired that a military unit visited the bridge within a few minutes of the Volunteers leaving. It was another chance missed.

Elsewhere in Cork there was little overt activity. There was a skirmish at Kildorrery in which Constables Boynes and Woodward were shot dead while out walking and another action in which Tadhg O'Sullivan from Cork No. 1 Brigade was killed. In Cork city Constable John McDonald was attacked by two men while he was out walking with a girl: one jumped on McDonald's back holding his arms and the other produced a hand gun. The constable tried to fend off the weapon but was shot in the head. While he lay on the ground four more shots were fired at him but missed. The attackers ran off and McDonald died of his wound some days later. This was the brutal reality of war in Cork.

Meanwhile Moylan was striving for a way to break the deadlock in his north Cork area by launching a direct attack on the police barracks. The cannon seized from Ross Castle had been refurbished and tested in late January, but had then been put to one side owing to other pressing issues. Moylan arranged another test towards the end of April 1921:

The gun was housed in a barn. We trundled it out and got it into position. The powder was tamped in place and a newspaper was rammed home. The bore was rough and jagged, eaten by the years of rust, this must have caused the accident. As I placed the iron projectile in the mouth of the gun there was an explosion. The piece of iron was torn from my hand. I was blinded with smoke. My hands were numb and as I looked down I found my left hand covered with blood and gobbets of flesh hanging from it. That, for me, completed the day's experiment. The hand was tied up somehow.[4]

Jim Riordan drove him to Dr Riordan in Boherbue. Moylan continues:

He stripped off the bandage, took one look at the hand and produced a bottle of whiskey. He gave me a stiff drink by way of anaesthetic and then proceeded to operate. He was at the time practically retired from practice but the job he did was as perfect as any of the most eminent surgeon. He could not replace the missing tissue but otherwise the work was perfect. A glass of whiskey, however, does not produce a sufficient condition of insensibility to pain and when the operation was over I was weak and exhausted. But though the result of such an accident would in peacetime conditions have meant a month in hospital to me, now however, invalidism had to be ignored. I was due for a meeting on the morrow with the brigade O/C near Millstreet. The 1st Southern Division was to be formed.[5]

The meeting that gave rise to the 1st Southern Command took place at Kippagh near Millstreet on 26 April 1921 and involved some of the most senior IRA men in south-west Ireland. This meeting would result in Moylan's appointment as O/C of Cork No. 2 Brigade.

A final experiment in the search for heavy weaponry took place shortly after the Kippagh meeting, but can sensibly be recounted here. Within days of the explosion of the first cannon, a second was located and brought from Kerry to a remote farm outside Ballydesmond. The movement of the gun was not easy:

It was a lump of metal ten feet long, fifteen inches in diameter, tapering to nine. It smashed the cars onto which it was loaded, lamed the horses that drew it, crushed fingers and toes. It slipped off a cart, rolling madly downhill, in erratic circles, transforming in their effort to avoid it, a column of marching men into a mad riot of dancing dervishes; smashed through a gate, came to rest so deep in a slimy ditch that nothing of it appeared but the little lump of metal round the touch hole which stared up from the slime like an eye, glaring in gleeful malice at those who had retreated madly from its onslaught and were now engaged in recovering it from its slimy bed.[6]

Liam Lynch and Moylan withdrew to allow more technically minded men to fire the gun:

> They heard a deafening bang. Moments later they heard something falling on the field beside them while another weighty object went westward towards the Blackwater and Kerry. There was silence again. A bright torchlight announced the approach of Liam Lynch. Seeing the brigade O/C, Lynch remarked: 'I wonder Seán did we hit it?' To which Moylan replied: 'Damn you Liam did we hit Scartaglen.'[7]

The purpose of the Kippagh meeting was to get local commanders to agree to a reorganisation of the IRA. At local level the structure worked well: each parish was the basis for a company of Volunteers. A battalion was formed by a group of companies from the same area, and up to eight battalions comprised a brigade. In the spring of 1921 there were three Cork brigades. It was at brigade level that the difficulties and inflexibilities arose. A convention had developed that one brigade did not intrude into the operational area of another. Such intrusions were thought to reflect badly on the local brigade's fighting reputation and to risk jeopardising its planned operations. Opportunities for brigades to co-operate in raids were being missed. Moylan recalls the meeting:

> There now were gathered IRA leaders from Cork, Kerry, Waterford and West Limerick Brigades. Some were old friends and associates of long standing, others were strangers, known only to me by reputation. Seán Hegarty, O/C Cork No. 1 Brigade, I hadn't seen for several years. He was now bearded, with homespun trousers and blue coat, the whole ensemble roofed in a bowler hat. He looked like an old-time music hall artist; a stranger seeing him would not be surprised if

he broke into song. He was, however, no comedian but a serious man of keen intellect. If he had a sense of humour, it was of that sardonic and devastating type peculiar to Cork. I had heard so much of Tom Barry and of his high reputation as a leader of troops in action that I was anxious to see him. Here he was; like Ernie O'Malley, he looked like a soldier and didn't care a damn who knew it. He was slight and erect, his smart coat, riding breeches and gaiters giving an impression of uniform. Later as he sat across the table from me I watched him. His face was that of an intelligent, earnest, determined and intolerant man, one whose mind was closed to all issues other than that with which he was concerned. I don't think that his appearance belied his character. A few weeks before he had had at Crossbarry a great success against the British. Other Cork men were Florrie O'Donoghue, Adjutant Cork No. 1 Brigade, shrewd, brainy; Liam Deasy, Cork No. 3; West Waterford was represented by Pax Whelan; West Limerick by Garrett McAuliffe, newly appointed brigade O/C on the death of Seán Finn; from Kerry came Humphrey Murphy. Liam Lynch was accompanied by George Power, his six foot frame dwarfed by Power's appalling inches. Ernie O'Malley represented GHQ and was to preside at the meeting.[8]

The meeting was difficult. A communication from GHQ was read out, which appears from Moylan's witness statement to have had an unreal notion of tactics based on an outdated British Army training manual and a copy of General Vorbeck's account of resistance to British rule in East Africa. GHQ's attempt to impose a tactical straitjacket on the local commanders was met with a hail of derision. They plainly took the view that those at GHQ had too much time on their hands and too little military experience. The local commanders had their own views about fighting a guerrilla war and the meeting gave rise to a useful exchange of views. Moylan 'was very much impressed by the contributions of the men from Cork No. 3 Brigade, it indicated experience and thought'.[9] One of those men was Tom Barry, whose anger with GHQ was shared by the other commanders. He recalls Moylan jumping to his feet and exclaiming: 'We started this war with hurleys, but, by Heavens, its seems to me, we will all finish it off with fountain pens.'[10] Once the dust settled, the principle of divisionalisation was accepted and Lynch was appointed O/C of the 1st Southern Division.

According to Florrie O'Donoghue, the other main issue was the torture and shooting of IRA prisoners, which had become endemic in Cork.[11] There were five IRA men awaiting execution at Victoria Barracks. Barry urged that a letter be sent to Major General Strickland threatening reprisals and 14 May was set as a 'shoot-up day' if the executions were carried out.

Many years later both Moylan and Barry wrote critically of GHQ at this fractious meeting. Barry in particular regarded the new divisional structure as a waste of time and declared that 'not a gun, a round of ammunition, a shilling or a plan of action came out of it'.[12]

After the meeting dispersed Moylan was called on by Lynch, who 'was delighted with his new post ... he had an amiable boyish touch of vanity which did not detract from his earnestness and determination. "You'll take over the brigade," he said.'[13]

13

CORK NO. 2 BRIGADE O/C

Moylan's reaction to the news that he was to command Cork No. 2 Brigade is instructive:

> I was not prepared for this. A brigade O/C has to concentrate on staff work and cannot personally concern himself with the clash of arms. It seemed to me that the life of a staff officer would be intolerably dull for one of my experiences. It seemed to me that George Power of

- - - - - - - - - **Cork No. 2 Brigade boundary area (not to scale).**
Battalions at Millstreet, Kanturk, Newmarket, Mallow and Charleville formed Cork No. 4 Brigade in July 1921 on division of the original Cork No. 2 Brigade. See Florence O'Donoghue, *No Other Law* (Irish Press Ltd, Dublin 1954) p.346. Seán Moylan took operational command of Cork No. 4 Brigade on his release from Spike Island prison in August 1921.

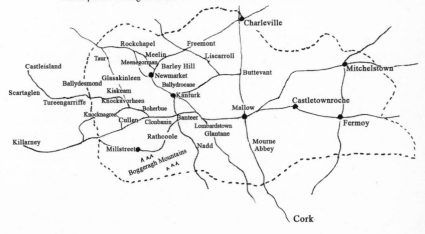

Fermoy should be appointed. He was deputy brigade commandant. He had done his work well and was the obvious choice.[1]

Writing many years later Power recalled that he had been offered the post but declined because Moylan was 'a more obvious choice'.[2] There were good reasons for appointing Moylan, who had developed a reputation for sound judgment and forceful leadership, and who had trained and sustained a battalion of Volunteers until they were an effective fighting force. He had made impressive use of intelligence in his handling of the ambushes at Ballydrocane, Tureengarriffe and Clonbanin. The Meelin and Meenegorman ambushes showed a leader with a cool head. The Clonbanin ambush is also memorable for similar reasons: the ambush site was relocated when it seemed likely that the military had intelligence about their whereabouts, the convoy was successfully ambushed and there was an organised withdrawal that owed a good deal to discipline and careful planning.

The casualty rates may be another significant indicator of ability. Cork No. 2 Brigade suffered many casualties in the war, often as the result of shoot-outs in isolated farmhouses or executions following capture. In the ambushes led by Moylan there were no fatalities on the republican side. He was cautious with the lives of his men and laid ambushes on ground of his choosing and only when he was satisfied that his men had sufficient arms and training for the task. Instinctively he and Tom Barry shared the view that one of the functions of a column was simply to survive and avoid disaster as the mere presence of an armed column was a threat to the government and tied up army resources.

Like the capture of General Lucas the previous year, the ambushes at Tureengarriffe and Clonbanin had attracted international press attention. They were also widely reported in the *Cork Examiner* and other local papers, making Moylan a household name in north Cork.

He also owed his appointment to a more prosaic and obvious reason. Thus far, he had been fortunate enough and able enough to evade capture or death. Many Volunteers had perished in the

Spanish flu epidemic of 1918; many, such as Paddy Clancy and Charlie O'Reilly, had been killed in action; and others, such as Con Murphy, had been executed by firing squad at Victoria Barracks in Cork.

Moylan's objections were overruled and he took on his post and determined to reorganise the brigade. The operational area of Cork No. 2 extended north of Midleton from Ballynoe to the Kerry border west of Millstreet and Newmarket. The northern border was the Limerick county boundary and in the south it was the Boggeragh Mountains. There were eight battalions: Fermoy, Castletownroche, Mitchelstown, Charleville, Mallow, Kanturk, Newmarket and Millstreet, and approximately 5,000 Volunteers.[3] Only a fraction of these Volunteers would be actively engaged at any one time, but it was plainly a heavy responsibility.

One new initiative was the development of an engineering section. Moylan had noted the need for a facility to repair guns and make mines. An engine and dynamo were stolen and a workshop was developed under the supervision of his cousin Con Moylan.

Seán Nunan was appointed Newmarket battalion commander and Jim Riordan became quartermaster. Battalion headquarters had been at Riordan's farm at Knockavorheen and brigade headquarters would also be based there. An increasing burden of responsibility fell on Nunan and Riordan.

There were other matters to attend to. The debacle at Nadd in March had almost resulted in the loss of the entire brigade staff. Moylan viewed this as a failure of intelligence that could not be overlooked and one of his first steps was to replace the battalion O/C at Kanturk who had permitted the informant Shields to be recruited into the ranks and who had failed to act decisively when suspicions were raised.

Two British Army deserters, thought to be spies, were captured about this time and gave details of a man who was passing information to the army in Kerry. The man was identified on description and following questioning at Moylan's headquarters was found to be guilty.[4] Moylan had him sent to the Kerry Brigade to be dealt with by those whom he had given information against. Moylan then ordered the two deserters to be sent to work on remote farms.

There were other difficulties in the offing. Éamon de Valera wanted to spend a month with an active service unit in the field and the Cork No. 2 Brigade had been chosen. In his witness statement Moylan was polite about this development but the responsibility for caring for de Valera cannot have been a welcome idea. It was planned for and arrangements were put in place, but the visit was cancelled at forty-eight hours notice when de Valera became involved in responding to overtures for peace.[5]

Moylan's involvement in Sinn Féin carried with it added duties, such as running the Republican Courts and collecting taxes. While he was so engaged some of his men took part in what became known as the Bog Road ambush. Again, the strategy turned on luring the RIC out of barracks. Elements of the Kerry Brigade and the Newmarket column joined forces to lay an ambush on a remote section of the Bog Road near Rathmore. The IRA left the body of an informer on the road and awaited developments. There was an anxious discussion about whether they had enough ammunition, but the decision was taken to go ahead. The large RIC patrol that came out to investigate the body was ambushed and suffered heavy losses: Constables Thomas McCormack, Walter Brown, William Clapp, Robert Dyne, Alfred Hillier, James Phelan, Samuel Watkins and Headley Woodcock lost their lives.[6] Some of the constables were badly wounded and were brought back to barracks but died within a few days. A single constable cycled to safety and raised the alarm. A number of farmhouses and the Rathmore creamery were burned in reprisal.

A minor incident about the same time, which would have significant consequences, is described in *Kiskeam versus The Empire*:

A man called Danny Sweeney came to Kiskeam searching for Moylan whose whereabouts were a closely guarded secret. He told Jim Riordan that the local Sinn Féin committee wanted Moylan to stand in the forthcoming election. Sweeney was allowed to see Moylan who was lying up in bed. Moylan declined to sign. Sweeney would not take no for an answer and there then followed a furious row between Big Jim Riordan and Moylan. Which ended with Moylan acquiescing: 'You'll have to get a candle and bring light.'[7]

Riordan and Sweeney bore witness and Sweeney departed for Dublin with the nomination papers. It was a step that probably later saved Moylan's life.

14

THE ARRIVAL OF THE
GLOUCESTERSHIRE REGIMENT

At the end of April 1921, four IRA men were executed at Victoria Barracks in Cork: Maurice Moore and Paddy O'Sullivan, who had been captured at Clonmult some weeks previously, and Patrick Ronayne and Thomas Mulcahy, who were captured during the failed Mourne Abbey ambush in which four Volunteers were killed. The IRA had been holding a hostage for some weeks to guarantee the safety of the prisoners, Major Compton Smith of the Welch Fusiliers, who wrote home to his wife: 'I am now prisoner, but being very well treated. I have no doubt I shall get out of this scrape just as I have got out of others. There is nothing to worry about.'[1] He was shot dead shortly afterwards. In further attacks in Cork, Constables Smith and Webb were killed while fishing and Constable Arthur Harrison was kidnapped and shot dead near Coachford railway station.

Another significant event towards the end of April 1921 was the deployment of the 1st Battalion of the Gloucestershire Regiment to Kanturk. Under the command of Lieutenant Colonel F. C. Nisbet, the battalion comprised eighteen officers and 572 other ranks, mostly based in Kanturk, with smaller units in Newmarket and Banteer. The advance party was headed by the battalion's intelligence officer, Lieutenant R. M. Grazebrook, who was provided with temporary transport in the form of the late Brigadier General Cumming's purple tourer. He was disconcerted to find the car was 'riddled with bullets'.[2]

The main force was billeted in the Old Union Workhouse on Coolacusane Hill overlooking Kanturk. Grazebrook recorded that he arrived:

> ... armed with the authority to take over the building and to eject within a certain number of days all the inmates and the attendants. To one who doesn't know Ireland, and the squalor and filth of the cottages and of that country, it would be impossible to describe the condition of the building and the inhabitants. There were about a hundred or so male and female inmates of all descriptions, some absolutely bed-ridden, others stone deaf, many real imbeciles and continually creating ghastly noises. Besides this there was one block full of orphans and one set apart for fever cases.[3]

The workhouse was run by Pat O'Keefe under the stewardship of the Board of Guardians. It appears that O'Keefe was reluctant to co-operate. According to Grazebrook: 'O'Keefe said it was impossible for the poor dear patients to leave ... he was told to get on with it', but it seems that the shock of the move was too much for some of the residents and 'a certain number died of fright'.[4]

The workhouse appears to have been chosen because the building was sufficiently large and enjoyed a useful strategic position just outside Kanturk, at the heart of the rebel activity. It was also easily defended: a two-storey building with a yard surrounded by a fourteen-foot wall. There was a single gated entrance through which a lorry could pass and a narrow gate to a recreation field. The old hospital block was used to billet the men, the boardroom was used by the sergeants and the officers' mess was located in the fever hospital annex, which fronted onto the courtyard. There was a single detention room. Some of the inmates continued to live in the top storey for a few weeks until they were re-housed elsewhere. The men complained of fleas dropping down from above and soon became adept at trapping them with a piece of soft soap.

Grazebrook described the workhouse as filthy and squalid, and the task of cleaning the building involved many buckets of Jeyes Fluid. One of the officers found a tub and enjoyed his first bath for some weeks until his satisfaction was dented by the information that the tub was used to wash the dead before burial. The soldiers' first night was disturbed by movement on the other side of the wall and the duty sergeant threw a Mills bomb over the wall just to be on the safe side.[5]

Captain A. H. Richards recalled: 'The locals were quite affable and we did drink with them knowing full well that they were at least IRA sympathisers. They were nearly always able to tell us where we had been on our latest operation and what we had been doing whether it was by day or by night.'[6]

The operational role assigned to the Gloucestershire Regiment (known as the Glosters) was to restore order, arrest known rebels, seize arms and provide escorts for lorry convoys. The capture of Moylan was high on their agenda. Moylan recalls their deployment:

> Our difficulties had been augmented by the fact that a Battalion of the Gloucester [sic] Regiment had come to Kanturk ... I lay one sunny afternoon on a hillside watching a column of troops pass by on their way to Kerry. The column consisted of twenty-five lorries and two armoured cars. They proceeded slowly, stopping to search roadside farmhouses and to make excursions into the fields to search the farmhouses at some distance from the roads. They held up and questioned everyone they met and after several hours passed out of my sight. They were proceeding at a rate of not greater than one mile an hour.[7]

Most of the bridges and culverts around Kanturk and Newmarket had been destroyed and many roads were bisected by trenches. The trench diggers were careful to allow space for the ass carts carrying milk to the creameries to pass around the edge of the trench. The Glosters responded by carrying metal girders on Crossley tenders, which could be laid over road trenches to enable their lorries to continue. They also took to seizing farm carts, or sometimes just their wheels, as a means of persuading the local farmers to repair the roads. Occasionally local people were rounded up and forced to fill in the trenches; however, Volunteers such as Dan Flynn were on hand to dig fresh trenches once they had finished. The Glosters also combated the transport difficulties by using bicycles, though most of their 500 bikes had seen service in France and were regarded as boneshakers. The emphasis was on swift movement and, according to one soldier, the standard order was 'Bondook [rifle] bandolier bike and away'.[8] The IRA responded by covering the road with broken glass and tin tacks.

The IRA used a complex system of fires to signal troop movements and local people also signalled the movement of troops at night by blowing 'conchies', which were usually fashioned from an old whiskey bottle that had been filled with an inch of water and then held over a fire until the bottom dropped off. The horns were loud and created a disquieting sound at night.

The Glosters strictly enforced the curfew and people found outside at night were either 'invited' to walk all night with the patrol or locked up in the barracks. A number were brought before the summary court. Moylan recalls going into Newmarket on the night of 14 May – the day designated at the Kippagh meeting for a 'shoot up' – with a body of twenty men: 'there was no movement of British troops, RIC or Tans. All these stuck closely to their barracks. The only activity open to us was the sniping of these posts and this did not seem wise to me as it would only lead to indiscriminate fire from the posts and would possibly involve the death or wounding of a number of civilians.'[9]

There was something of an impasse. While the IRA faced the difficulties presented by the numerical superiority of the Glosters, the Glosters were unable to move by day or by night without being observed. It quickly became apparent to the officers of the regiment that the workhouse master informed on their movements. This was particularly easy for him to do, because the workhouse had only a single exit to the road. In response Grazebrook billeted men in tents in the recreation field, thereby allowing units to leave unobserved at night.

At first the Glosters had very little local intelligence and were heavily reliant on a number of local RIC sergeants of considerable experience and determination. Soon informants were cultivated and paid where necessary, and the Glosters developed an extremely accurate picture of the local company and battalion structure and quickly came to know the identity of most of the active Volunteers, including those who had taken part in the Tureengarriffe and Clonbanin ambushes. They were still using the turncoat Shields, who by then had a British Army uniform and a new name. Shields assisted at interrogations and was occasionally called to give evidence at courts-martial.

Local Volunteers were aware that the Glosters were slowly building up their intelligence. They had seen members of the regiment in civilian clothes drawing up maps, aided by spotter planes and high-powered binoculars.[10]

According to Grazebrook, 'raids, searches and round-ups were taking place almost continually, morning, noon and night'.[11] A favoured tactic involved surrounding the church on Sunday mornings and pulling out suspects from the congregation. Some arrests were more productive than others: one junior Volunteer was so taken up with the drama of the conflict that he allowed himself to be captured with a photograph of himself in uniform and another photo showing his friends parading in uniform. In this way the Glosters built up a picture of their opponents. Many arrests were made and documents were seized, which sometimes led to further raids. Where there was evidence, the case went to court-martial. Other less serious cases were dealt with by the battalion summary court-martial. Where there was suspicion, then internment followed at Spike Island.

The rebels were also actively looking for intelligence. Surveillance on the military was a Volunteer pastime and they were adept at identifying informants. Telephonists such as Annie Barrett continued to support them by passing information and occasionally simply obstructing efforts by the military to use the telephone system. The rebels also cut telephone wires and raided the mail, surprising

Grazebrook when they returned registered mail and packets containing pension books.[12]

It is clear from Lieutenant Grazebrook's intelligence notes that Moylan was a prime target from an early stage. His name had been widely reported in the press after the Tureengarriffe and Clonbanin ambushes and his mother's shop in Newmarket was often raided, more in hope than expectation one suspects. Grazebrook accumulated specific information about Moylan: that he had been a building contractor in Newmarket (this was nearly right), that he was dying of consumption (he was certainly very ill by then), that he was about to be married (again, there may have been a shred of truth in this) and that he was often seen in a black trap on Saturday evenings on the Tullylease to Kiskeam road.

We know from Moylan's witness statement that he had set up brigade headquarters at Knockavorheen close to Kiskeam and that he returned each weekend after a tour of the brigade area. There may have been other reasons to visit Kiskeam on a Saturday night. Moylan was friendly with Katie Murphy, who was the principal of the girl's school in Newmarket, and her sister Mollie in Kiskeam and would later write to both women from Spike Island. Perhaps we can infer from Grazebrook's intelligence that Moylan's weekends had a social dimension. In the life of a revolutionary the opportunities for banter, card playing or even a dance had to be snatched.

But Moylan was also quite unwell. He later wrote: 'Ill health had reduced me to a shadow, and now I had a note from the Divisional O/C saying that GHQ had made provision for my admission to a Dublin hospital and urging me to make arrangements to go there.'[13] He declined to take up the offer. This incident illustrates how his debilitating illness had developed from a personal matter for him to solve in 1919 to an operational matter for the organisation in 1921.

There were other challenges to be faced. The enduring good weather, the firmness of the ground underfoot and the long daylight hours that summer allowed the British forces to deploy a new tactic – the round-up – involving thousands of troops sweeping vast areas of the country. A series of round-ups in May and June focused on Kerry and Cork. The Volunteers in north Cork had been expecting a big raid and preparations were in hand. Most of the roads had been trenched and there were plans to light warning fires when the army was known to be on the move.

The raid on the Millstreet battalion took place on 5 May.[14] Moylan was awoken in the early hours and went down to the yard: 'Fire blazed on the hilltops, not only to the east, but north, south and west also.'[15] Volunteers began to assemble; many armed, some not. The raid was much bigger than they had anticipated. Although the roads were trenched, the dry summer of 1921 meant that army lorries might easily pass over fields where previously they would have become embedded in mud. There was every prospect that the rebels might be surrounded. Moylan's approach to the crisis was typically cerebral:

I spread a map on the table and lighted a candle … One may have a most perfect knowledge of terrain but the lines of the map bring swiftly to mind matters of important detail that the memory is too apt to overlook … There was an opening to the north towards a mountainy district, where if the odds proved too great, it would be hard to find us. Here we had driven in several police barracks. The only forces that could successfully intercept us were a brigade of British military garrisoned thirty miles to the west.[16]

Moylan left his dispatch rider behind, a young man called Taaffe who had proved reliable and enterprising in the past. The rest of the Volunteers set off: 'The ASU fell in, with them was every Volunteer known to be wanted or likely to be wanted by the British; the others were to scatter and disappear.'[17] The Volunteers marched off into the night and took cover at daybreak:

We lay until the forenoon in a deep glen with the heather high above us and with hidden outposts placed at strategic points. Children passed to school on the road above us. Farm carts rattled on their way to the creamery. It was as yet too early for news. The creamery carts began to return. It was noticeable that the drivers were the older men. The younger men had gone to ground.[18]

When news of the round-up was brought to Moylan, he learned that 'The roads were black with soldiers and police. They were searching everywhere, firing on everyone who failed to halt when called upon. Three men had already been shot, one an old man working in the fields.'[19] Food was also sent up from nearby villages: 'homemade bread in huge buttered slices, jars of tea, bowls, mugs and cups as drinking materials. Brought by women and young girls driving donkey carts; leaving their jars and baskets at a gap in the roadside fence and departing.'[20]

A long hot day lying in the grass followed. A spotter plane wheeled above them, no smoking or movement was allowed. As nightfall came, local Volunteers arrived and brought the men down to the farms and villages where dinner was provided and further news of the round-up filtered through. Moylan recalls that the British forces had conscripted local people to fill trenches and move barricades and:

Armoured cars cruised to and fro. Road intersections were held, all civilian movement brought to a stop. Soldiers in extended order moved across fields, beat the fences and searched farm buildings closely ... In the afternoon they arrived to my headquarters of the day before. Here the search was more thorough than elsewhere, the questioning more intense.

According to Moylan, the encircled area was about 100 square miles and the troops engaged numbered 6,000.[21]

When the troops packed up that night they departed with five truckloads of prisoners, one of whom was Moylan's dispatch rider, Taaffe, who had been detailed to bring Moylan news of enemy activities. He exceeded his brief, leading the Glosters on a wild goose chase and implicating dozens of men who had no connection with the IRA, including his father. Taaffe appears to have thought it was all a great joke. The records kept by the Gloucestershire Regiment conclude: 'As far as we were concerned the operation was almost a blank. We rounded up ninety-one men but there was a surprising lack of young men – all we got were practically all over forty.'[22] The spotter plane was also ineffective and the only message dropped in the course of the round–up said: 'No enemy visible, is it time to go home?'[23]

One man was interned. There is no mention of any arms being seized from the civilian casualties or during searches. It does appear probable that the casualties were civilians fleeing in panic. There were also round-ups in Donoghmore, the Boggeragh Mountains, Clare, Glenville and the Dingle Peninsula. However, the 6th Division Record of the Rebellion shows that 'In none of these cases were any very good results achieved ... most of the worst characters slipped away.'[24]

On 11 May, three Volunteers from the Liscarroll company were resting up at a farmhouse in Aughrim when the British Army arrived in force. John O'Regan the battalion quartermaster was badly wounded and taken prisoner. Dan O'Brien stopped to help his comrade and was captured. His brother Paddy O'Brien, the battalion O/C, carried out a running gun battle during which he outran his pursuers, wounding an officer before getting away.[25]

The reorganisation of the Cork No. 2 Brigade continued against this backdrop.

15

CAPTURE

The Glosters' battalion intelligence officer, Lieutenant R. M. Graze-brook, recalled Moylan as an ephemeral, elusive character, who could not be pinned down, but 'one always found him leading the most violent outrages and ambushes … without doubt he was a most clever and able man'.[1] But the net was closing in. Not everyone in north Cork was on the side of the rebels and, as in any guerrilla war, the spectre of the informant was always close at hand. Snippets of information allowed Grazebrook to piece Moylan's movements together with some accuracy.

The 6th Division Record of the Rebellion shows:

In the middle of May, the Gloucester [*sic*] Regiment carried out a round-up in N. W. Cork with a view to catching John Moylan, a well-known rebel commandant … it was believed that rebel forces were billeted about the townland of Knockavorheen, one mile south-east of Kiskeam. The locality of a dugout where four men lived had been roughly given, and lastly John Moylan had passed through Meelin supposedly for Kiskeam and Rockchapel. The object of the operation was to carry out a round-up of the Knockavorheen area, and during a weekend when there would be more chance of finding Moylan.[2]

The planners of this operation faced certain difficulties. They could not use motor transport because of the extensive road trenching and although the Glosters tended to move silently on bicycles, the rebels always had advance notice through their warning systems. The closely observed single exit from their Kanturk base meant they had to billet men in the field beside the workhouse who could then slip away unnoticed and march through the night before taking cover in a copse during the daylight hours. The Glosters also had to cut telephone wires at Newmarket to isolate Moylan from news of troop movements. Eventually they hoped to throw a ring of soldiers around three sides of the farms under suspicion, while another section of soldiers would come up on bikes to close the cordon.

The plan involved the deployment of four officers and fifty-eight troops supported by four RIC sergeants. The raiding party was billeted in tents beside the workhouse for several nights. On Sunday 15 May, the unit left their tents at 1 a.m., making their way on foot through undulating land and over many ditches. It took them three hours to cover seven miles. Arriving at the copse at 4 a.m. they found that the trees had been cut down and so took cover in a barn overlooking the village of Boherbue to avoid imminent discovery. From the barn the Glosters watched the villagers come and go to Mass. At one point they were disturbed by a farmhand who had come to milk his cows. They could not hold the man prisoner because he would be missed and their plan would be discovered. Therefore, according to Grazebrook, the unfortunate farmhand was threatened by the RIC men and when told that if he informed 'he and his family would suffer the direst consequences, he went off a very frightened man'.[3]

When night fell the raiding party moved off in the direction of the Mahoney and Riordan farms. As they approached and circled round to the north, a party of eight men was dropped every 400 yards. At this point a conchie sounded and their cover was blown. In the distance a party of fifty Glosters was moving up to cover the fourth side of the cordon. A search of Mahoney's farm yielded no arms and no information. Two of the men of the house were seized and taken on with the raiding party towards Riordan's farm.

What followed is logged in the regimental records as the Battle of

Riordan's Farm. It seems a rather grand title for a skirmish in which no one on either side was killed or even wounded. As the raiding party closed in on Riordan's farm they were raked by heavy rifle fire. It now appears certain that the fire was coming from the Glosters approaching on bikes to close the cordon, because Moylan's account makes it plain that his men were thoroughly surprised and unable to offer organised resistance. According to the Gloucestershire records, a figure was then seen walking towards the party of soldiers. An order was given to halt. The figure halted and raised his hands then bolted and was fired upon. Other shadowy figures moved off swiftly. As dawn broke the sound of conchies grew and figures were seen doubling away in the distance. Grazebrook wrote: 'Temple and his party were searching gorse bushes and cover. I heard a shout and one of the men brought in a prisoner, armed with a loaded revolver and two Mills bombs. This turned out to be Seán Moylan … Later we rounded up fourteen of the active service gang.'[4]

The raid had been well planned and executed, but every military operation needs luck and the Glosters had their share. Seán Finn of the West Limerick Brigade had been killed a few months previously and Moylan had set out late that night to meet the new West Limerick Brigade O/C. He had walked some miles before a messenger caught up with him and told him that members of the Kerry Brigade were at Knockavorheen to see him. He walked back to meet them and by the time their business had been concluded he decided to stay over at Riordan's farm. The Glosters might have had even more good fortune as Florrie O'Donoghue and Liam Lynch were also heading to Knockavorheen, but their horse tired and they were forced to find shelter near Taur.[5]

Moylan recalls the raid:

I was awakened about 3 a.m. and told that the British had passed through Boherbue, about four miles away, and that there was every likelihood of a raid. I got out of bed, went into the yard where half a dozen others were collected. They expressed the opinion that the

British were much closer and suggested we should move off to the west at once … In view of the fact that the active service unit had left the district, the usual care in relation to sentries and signals had not been taken and it was quite possible we might have been taken unawares. We went out on the roadway and at the yard gate we met a Volunteer who informed us that he believed we were surrounded. Fifty yards away in the passage leading to the next house, he had heard the rattle of rifle butts which led him to believe that the British had arrived. I ordered those who were with me to get inside the fence on the north side of the road and decided to investigate. If the British were here the sooner we knew it the better and the only way of finding out was for one man to walk into the trap, if a trap it was … I walked down the passage about twenty yards. And then heard a shout 'halt, hands up'. I halted and put up my hands and was then instructed to come forward I advanced one step, turned swiftly, ran a few steps and dropped to the ground. A volley rang out over my head. I jumped to my feet and got round the corner of a fence before the second volley came. The volley was sufficient signal to my comrades to get away swiftly, which they did, and luckily they got out of the ring before it was finally closed … the air seemed to be alive with bullets … Escape was hopeless. I crawled back again into cover and got on top of a fence between furze bushes. As the day broke brightly I could see everywhere around me khaki-clad figures of the British soldiers … I lay down and fell asleep … Possibly an hour later I was dragged from the fence … into the yard.[6]

The owner of the farm, Johnny Riordan, was questioned sitting in his bed. Moylan was brought in and the old man was asked to identify him. According to *Kiskeam versus The Empire*, Riordan feigned deafness and met every question with 'Hah?' Eventually the soldiers relented, 'You can lie down now, old man.' As Riordan sank back into his bed the officer leaned forward and said, 'How well you heard that!'[7]

Moylan's interrogation took place a little after dawn in Riordan's farmyard. The prisoners were under heavy guard. Each of the captured men was brought to a table and questioned in turn. According to the

Gloucestershire Regimental Record, Moylan gave the name O'Connell but was immediately identified by the RIC men.[8] He said little else: he did not deny possessing the revolver and the Mills bombs; he did not say where he had been staying the night or who his associates were; in short, he implicated no one. His possessions amounted to no more than a whistle, revolver, compass and binoculars, all of which had been captured from the British Army. Moylan's account states:

> An officer sat at a table in the yard. Beside him stood an RIC man. This man recognised me and gave to the British officer a history of my activities. The British officer questioned me and while he was questioning me I was busy reading the names which lay before him on the table. He seemed to have the name of every member of the active service unit, and also had the names of some of the prominent undercover men, at which I was surprised.[9]

The officer at the table must have been Lieutenant Grazebrook, who had planned and led the raid. He noted that 'very little could be got out of Moylan, he looked decidedly ill and frightened … he obviously expected to be court-martialled and shot right away.'[10] Grazebrook appears to be a shrewd observer. We know that Moylan was very ill and was under instructions to admit himself to hospital, and he certainly had every reason to be frightened as IRA prisoners were either shot after arrest (sometimes they would be invited to run from the guns, which became known as 'a sporting chance') or brought into barracks to face a court-martial or drumhead court-martial. The first execution by drumhead court-martial had taken place only two weeks previously when Patrick Casey had been shot hours after capture.[11] It should be said that the five soldiers who captured Moylan and gave evidence at his court-martial did not suggest he showed any fear or the slightest trepidation.

The search of Riordan's farm led to the arrest of fourteen men. It was the opinion of the Glosters that they were all part of an IRA active service unit. Moylan disagreed: he recalled that the unit had left the area before the raid and that only a few of the arrestees were Volunteers and low-ranking ones at that; the rest were farmers and labourers swept up in the raid. It appears that after an investigation the only charges brought were against Moylan and Johnny Riordan (in respect of the arms found on his land). Dan Flynn was captured in the raid and moved to Kanturk, but there was no evidence against him and he was interned at Spike Island.

There were other valuable finds made that night and Grazebrook records that 'a search of the area revealed a box cunningly concealed in a hole in the bank contained the Hotchkiss gun which had been captured from the 17th Lancers at Mallow … another revolver, ammunition, telephone apparatus.'[12] This was a valuable find, particularly the machine gun that had been used to devastating effect at Tureengarriffe and Clonbanin. Also found close by were Moylan's new Corona typewriter, a dispatch case, a batch of letters to the commanding officer of the Southern Command and a list of secret IRA codes. The typewriter was later put to use by the Glosters. The rest of the finds were enough to have Moylan shot. They also seized a cheque for £115 which was thought to be pay for IRA men. Some days later the Glosters took the cheque to the bank and compelled the bank manager to lodge it 'to the Battalion Summary Court A/C'.[13]

Moylan recalls that he and the other thirteen arrested men were marched several miles until they came to a road trench where lorries were waiting. He was handcuffed, taken to Kanturk and placed in a cell:

Small as my wrists were, the handcuffs were still smaller. And as I lay all day in my cell I suffered a good deal of pain from my swollen arms. In the evening as the guard was changed, the Orderly officer visited me. He was a small man wearing the ribbons of the MC and Bar. He and I had a conversation for fifteen minutes then he ordered one of the soldiers who was with him to get me a new pair of handcuffs. These were much more comfortable … I expressed my surprise at his kindness, to which he stated 'I am British.' The term British did not to my mind connote any form of chivalry or fair play and at that time I could not realise that it could mean those things to anybody. However, there are some British who do play the game.[14]

The next morning, Moylan – O/C of Cork No. 2 Brigade and Sinn Féin candidate for the Second Dáil – was brought before the Glosters' commanding officer, Lieutenant Colonel F. C. Nisbet, a tough professional soldier who had been decorated for bravery in France. Grazebrook, who witnessed this interview, wrote: 'Moylan … had pulled himself together and in a passage of words with the C/O he came out rather the best. There was no doubt he was a very quick-witted and clever customer.'[15] Writing over thirty years later Moylan recorded what passed between them:

The Colonel told me he wanted to get some information about the reasons for the trouble in Ireland. I asked him what good the supply of such information would do me. He replied that it would do me no good, that I was going to be shot anyway. He said he was really anxious to know something of the reason for Ireland's rebellious attitude. I said, of course, if he proposed to discuss the matter on that basis, I was quite willing. He put a number of questions to me to which I replied …

Finally he said, 'I am not anxious to remain here in Ireland. I want to go back home.'

I said, 'I am most anxious that you should do so and possibly the whole reason for our attitude is to ensure that every English soldier and official in Ireland should go back to England and cease interfering with matters in this country.'

'Your chief difficulty,' he stated, 'in this country is that you are living in the past. You take no cognisance of modern conditions. You think that the world has not progressed since the days of Wolfe Tone and Emmet and still think in the terms in which those men thought …'

'By the way,' I said, 'as I was coming into the office, I saw outside a gong with the word "Egypt" on top and the date "1798" in the centre. What does that signify?'

Lt Col Francis Courtney Nisbet. Courtesy of the Soldiers of Gloucestershire Museum

'Oh,' he said, 'that commemorates a great battle which this regiment fought in 1798. Surrounded there, our men fought back to back till the finish. You will notice,' he said, 'that there is a badge both in front and back of the caps worn by the men of this regiment. We are not known as the Gloucesters [*sic*] but as the "Fore and Afts".'

'I understand,' I said. 'I assume,' I continued, 'that regimental tradition is a great force.'

'Undoubtedly,' he said.

'And British regiments,' I said, 'must remember 1798 and Irishmen must forget it.'

'I am afraid,' he said, 'we have not shot you soon enough.'[16]

The Gloucestershire Regiment had fought a battle in Egypt – the Battle of Alexandria – in which, as their number thinned to a few dozen, the order had been famously given, 'Rear rank about face', which gave rise to the 'Fore and Aft' nickname. Although the date of the battle was 1801 not 1798, the substance of Moylan's recollection appears correct.

Grazebrook and Moylan never met again. Grazebrook's record was made more or less contemporaneously, whereas Moylan wrote his account over thirty years later. Both versions record the detail of events in a very similar way. Two inferences can be drawn: first, Moylan and Grazebrook were reliable historians; and second, Moylan's account of other episodes in the War of Independence is equally reliable.

After the meeting, Moylan was:

> ... handed over to a party of soldiers from Buttevant. My handcuffs were removed and a new set supplied. The sadist who locked these on took care to dig away a portion of the flesh on my wrist as he snapped on the handcuffs. I was then tied hand and foot with a rope, thrown into a lorry. A huge convoy of lorries waited outside the barracks to convey me to Buttevant.[17]

Grazebrook recalls, with what one suspects was a degree of under-statement: 'I fear Seán Moylan TD did not receive too gentle handling in the hands of the East Lancs who acted as the escort.'[18] The capture of Moylan was something of a coup for the British Army. The news was passed to Major General Strickland's headquarters and then to GHQ in Dublin. General Macready's weekly report to the cabinet at Westminster contains a short reference to the incident: 'In the country there have been only minor actions, but a very prominent rebel, Moylan, was captured together with twelve of his followers at Kiskeam.'[19]

Moylan's imprisonment was a severe blow for the rebels. Worse still, the IRA codes had also been seized. The cyclist party in the Knockavorheen round-up had also captured two more Volunteers: Maurice Clancy, Captain of the Derrygallon company, and Pat Cronin. There was yet another blow for the brigade that day when Volunteer Dan O'Brien was executed by firing squad at Victoria Barracks in Cork. It seemed that Moylan would soon follow in his footsteps.

16

A Writ of Habeas Corpus

'On arriving at Buttevant I was thrown out of the lorry onto the barrack yard and lay there for an hour watching a cricket match that was in progress ... the general in charge of the troops, whose predecessor I had killed four months before ... came along and ordered the rope which bound me should be removed.'[1] Moylan was then marched to the provost marshal's office and booked in. He recalls being 'ragged, unshaven, bloody'.[2] Life was about to get worse. 'I was immediately put into a small cell and a few moments later had a visit from two corporals who gave me a sound drubbing. These were men of the East Lancashire Regiment.'[3] It is difficult to resist the inference that this beating was in revenge for the Clonbanin ambush. It was well known that Moylan had run this engagement and he must have known that the East Lancashire Regiment suffered significant casualties. Moylan makes no mention of anything being said by the soldiers.

The conflict in Ireland was described by British Prime Minister David Lloyd George as a small war. It was, and Moylan was about to meet another man he had shot at before: the brigade intelligence officer who had led the army convoy ambushed at Meelin some months previously:

I was left in the cell all day and was not further attacked. At night the brigade intelligence officer paid me a visit, talked to me and questioned me for several hours. I don't think he succeeded in getting any information from me as a result of our conversation but he was so assured of my immediate death he must have felt it quite safe for him to let me have all the knowledge he had gathered about my brigade and much of this information was to prove very valuable in the months to come. I feel it right to state that he used no violence, intimidation or threat.[4]

Moylan was fortunate to have been captured by the Glosters. They were a tough but scrupulous outfit and their tour of duty was not marked by ill treatment or shooting of prisoners. Elsewhere, in west Cork in particular, the torture of prisoners was widespread and is well documented.

The following day Moylan was taken to Victoria Barracks in Cork city. He recalls that 'the place was quite silent. There was a chill air of certain death.'[5] Con Murphy had been executed at Victoria Barracks in February and Dan O'Brien of the Millstreet battalion had been executed the week before. O'Brien's court-martial lasted only a few minutes. When he was asked for his plea he told the court: 'I was a soldier of the Irish Republican Army when I was captured and I expect the treatment of a captured soldier. I would not shoot a soldier if I captured him myself and you can do as you like to me.'[6] He was sentenced to death and shot within a few days.

Not all the captors were hostile. Moylan recalls an older Scottish sergeant who took him out of the custody of the East Lancashire Regiment. There was a book detainees had to sign and Moylan noted the signature of Dan O'Brien immediately above his own:

The Sergeant asked me if I knew him. I said he was my comrade. I had seen Dan O'Brien in action and I knew his character … The Sergeant casually said, 'Well you will follow him in the morning.' I was in no doubt about it. However, he said, 'Soldiers, like everyone else, must die. Maybe you would like to have a bath before I lock you up.'[7]

A bath was provided. After this Moylan was put in a cell and the chaplain came to hear his confession. He went to bed and somewhat surprisingly fell asleep. As he explained in his witness statement:

> When a man who had lived as I had lived, had been inspired with the ideals such as had inspired me, had faced disillusion every day over a prolonged period, it is easy to die. There was never heroism in my action. My attitude was quite matter of fact. My time had come and there was no more to be said.[8]

Moylan did not, it seems, express a desire to see or to write to anyone, not even his mother. He was unmarried and childless. He owned no property of any kind and had no stake in society as it was then structured, but he had an aspiration, an ideal to which he had given himself. Death in these circumstances might be easier to bear but it must have been hard to face knowing that the struggle he had been part of was still in the balance.

According to Lieutenant Grazebrook's record, the court-martial witnesses from the battalion came up to Cork to give evidence the next day but matters did not proceed, probably due to a backlog of cases. Moylan paraded with the rest of the prisoners the following day, and the next. He appears to have found the delay difficult to deal with. On the third day he asked to see a solicitor. 'The Sergeant Major replied: "You don't need a solicitor; you are going to be shot." I said I was fully aware of the fact but said that I was fully entitled to see a solicitor so as to dispose of my private property.'[9] The property consisted of the suit he was wearing, which itself had been given to him by a friend. To this request, the military acceded and he was given permission to see Barry Sullivan of Mallow.

Sullivan had been an active supporter of Sinn Féin for some years and was acting for the families of the Mallow railwaymen killed by the Black and Tans in January. He was at Victoria Barracks to defend the Mourne Abbey men: Owen Harold, Denis Barter, John Murphy, Daniel McCarthy and Timothy Breen, who were charged with the murder of Sergeant Gibbs in the raid on Mallow Barracks. Their court-martial had been delayed twice – first, because the summary of evidence had been lost; and second, because while the Lancers were out on a raid a grenade had been thrown into a lorry injuring many of the witnesses – but proceedings were finally under way. Moylan writes:

> My desire to meet Barry Sullivan was not rooted in any hope to save my own life but I wanted a reliable man to whom I could pass the information I had got from the intelligence officer at Buttevant and whom I could inform of the whereabouts of certain documents and arms and ammunition.[10]

Sullivan, like all competent solicitors, kept a careful but selective note: '24 May 1921. On court adjourning at 5 p.m. I was informed by an officer of the Legal Department of 6th Division headquarters, that Brigadier Comdt Seán Moylan TD who had just been arrested wished to see me as he had been charged with possession of arms and levying war against the Crown.'[11] The following exchange captures the moment: 'I stated to the officer that I could not visit the prisoner immediately as I expected to be working most of the night with the court-martial.'[12] The officer's reply is recorded in direct speech: 'Moylan will be tried on Thursday morning and as no defence is possible and his record is well known the divisional confirmation will immediately follow and he will be shot on Friday morning.'[13]

Sullivan wrote: 'I crossed to the detention barracks and asked for the prisoner … In an interview I told him what the officer said to me … that he was to be sentenced to death on Thursday and executed on Friday. He refused under any circumstances to be defended.'[14] Moylan recalls him asking: '"What about your own case?" I said I have no case, they intend to shoot me and it is a waste of time to do anything about it. It is certain that I am to be shot and I may as well go down with colours flying rather than in any way recognise the legal authority of the British.'[15]

*Albert E. Wood, KC, and his
wife Edythe in the 1930s.
Courtesy of Chris Wood*

Sullivan was not about to leave it there and he persuaded Moylan
to see Albert Wood, KC, who was defending the others being court-
martialled at the barracks. Sullivan then returned to his hotel 'where
Albert Wood, KC, was waiting. I told him of my interview with
Moylan and we decided that everything possible should be done to
avert the imminent execution.'[16] Wood had defended a number of
courts-martial without fee. He and Sullivan drafted an affidavit in
support of an application for a writ of habeas corpus. The writ of
habeas corpus is a command issued by the High Court to anyone
holding a prisoner to show legal cause for imprisonment. It is one
of the oldest and most effective common law powers to prevent
oppressive and unlawful conduct by the state. Sullivan's notes read: '25
May 8 a.m. Dispatched affidavit on train leaving Cork this hour.'[17]

The prospect of saving Moylan's life must have seemed remote.
Military action was intensifying everywhere. In Dublin that day the
custom house was burned; six IRA men were killed in the action

and over eighty were captured. In London the British cabinet had reconstituted the Irish Situation Committee. The committee decided that if the newly elected southern parliament failed to function then martial law should be extended throughout the twenty-six counties. It also decided that a further sixteen battalions should leave for Ireland immediately. Back at Victoria Barracks Sullivan wrote: '25 May, 8.30 a.m. Accompanied by Albert Wood ... visited Moylan in detention barracks ... He persisted in his determination to ignore the court.'[18]

Moylan later described the meeting:

> I was called again to the office ... There were three men ... one was Barry Sullivan, the other a tall, good-looking man, whom I knew immediately. His name was Bourke. He was a barrister and a son of the recorder who lived at Banteer. A year before I had got him out of bed to get the keys of his car which I needed for the removal of the mails at Banteer. He did not know me. I made no reference to our previous meeting. The third man present was, to my unsophisticated seeming, a typical Englishman, beautifully dressed and groomed, with an accent which seemed to me then to be the quintessence of Oxford. This was Albert Wood.[19]

Their discussion lasted over an hour. Moylan recalls that he did not think he had any case to fight. Wood referred to the case of Wolfe Tone in which the power of the military in times of war had been challenged by the civil courts. Ultimately Tone's untimely death meant that the issue remained undecided. The legal argument had been revived in 1921 when martial law had been declared, although it had not saved John Allen who had been executed at Victoria Barracks some weeks previously. In Allen's case the court decided that where the country was in a state of war, the civil courts had no power to intervene. Moylan wrote:

> Wood insisted that negotiations were going on and that a truce was imminent. He said it was very important for many reasons that my case should be defended. It might mean eventually saving the lives of

other men … Finally I said that if I am ordered by IRA Headquarters to defend my case, I shall obey orders, but, I said I must absolutely be permitted to refuse to recognise the British court. Wood said immediately, 'If we meet your conditions will you guarantee to say nothing in court other than the fact that you will refuse to recognise the court?' I agreed and we parted on that note.[20]

The practice of refusing to recognise the court had died out just a few months previously when martial law was proclaimed and it had been announced that any rebel captured in arms would face the death penalty; it had become too high risk. As to the strategy of getting a writ of habeas corpus: this was a forlorn hope. The case of John Allen had more or less exhausted the legal remedies. Having made up his mind to face execution it must have been difficult for Moylan to embark on a positive course of action. It is likely that he did not wish to raise his hopes unduly or to make a futile plea for clemency.

Three days later at the High Court in Dublin an application for a writ of habeas corpus was made in the matter of *Moylan J. R. v Major General E. P. Strickland*. The basis of the writ was that Ireland was not in a state of war, the civil courts were still sitting, therefore the civil courts prevailed and did not permit trial by a court-martial. Justice Powell was sceptical and counsel A. Meredith, KC, remarked, 'It is highly unpleasant for us all, we hear the revolver shots'.[21] Somewhat reluctantly the judge issued a conditional writ of habeas corpus, pending full argument from both sides. By leave of the court the order was 'telegraphed' to Major General E. P. Strickland in Cork where Sullivan and Wood were still fully engaged in the Mourne Abbey case.[22] Sullivan's notes read: 'The court-martial of the Mourne Abbey men is concluded. Timothy Breen is acquitted. The decision in the case of Harold, Murphy, McCarthy and Barter would be announced in due course. This means conviction.' Sullivan's notes continue: '29 May – In conference all day dealing with the Mourne Abbey appeal and the Moylan case listed to be heard tomorrow.'[23]

17

The Court-Martial

Moylan was brought before a court-martial on 30 May 1921. He had been given a suit by a local tailor. It was not the first or the last time that someone was moved by his obvious penury to buy him clothes. Moylan describes the walk to the court:

> As I walked across the yard to the room where the court was held I had no fears and no regrets but I was young and it seemed to me that the sky was never so blue or the trees never so beautifully green … it seemed to me a pity to depart so young from all this earthly beauty … The court was composed of three officers. I assume that it was in order to emphasise the fact that it was a Court of Justice that there was a loaded revolver in front of the Chairman of the Bench. The gallery was crowded with a number of curious onlookers – all British officers – and soldiers stood round the chair where I sat with drawn revolvers. The lawyers arrived and the charge was read out to me.[1]

The court-martial was short, probably less than two hours. It is rare to have a full transcript of a trial such as this and it is worth setting out. There are two observations before turning to the record. First, it was not usual for the names of witnesses to be reported and these remain deleted. Second, since Moylan chose not to recognise the court or participate in any way, there was no cross-examination of the evidence presented and therefore no record of the extent to which Moylan disagreed. The record of the court-martial shows:

John Moylan, of Kiskeam, County Cork, was charged with (1) committing an offence in that he, near Knocknagree, Co. Cork, on or about 16 May 1921, did levy war on His Majesty the King, by joining with other persons unknown in an armed attack on a detachment of His Majesty's forces; (2) was improperly in possession of arms, ammunition and explosives, namely one revolver, thirteen rounds of revolver ammunition and three Mills pattern bombs.

Mr A. E. Wood, KC, and Mr J. F. Bourke, BL, appeared for the accused.

Counsel for the accused stated that they had no objection to his being tried by the members of the tribunal individually, but took exception to their jurisdiction.

The court having been duly sworn, the accused was arraigned on both charges. Counsel for the accused pleaded in bar and quoted proceedings in the High Court of Justice in Ireland (Chancery Division), in the case of John R. Moylan (plaintiff) and Major General E. P. Strickland and the Attorney General for Ireland. Counsel pointed out that the Court of Chancery was the court which formerly issued writs of habeas corpus, for the protection of His Majesty's subjects.

President – Does the accused admit that he is a subject of His Majesty?

Counsel – I make no admissions.

Counsel handed in a formal objection marked 'A' signed by the President and attached to the proceedings.

The court decided to proceed with the trial.

Both counsel announced that they had decided to withdraw from the trial, and accordingly did so.[2]

One suspects the writ was simply a delaying tactic. It was never expected to succeed, but it was designed to cause a rift between the civil courts and the military and thereby generate a crisis. In due course, in the case of *Egan v Macready and others*, this tactic succeeded. But on this day it had no effect on the determination of the military court to try Moylan.

Moylan's solicitor Barry Sullivan records his next step: '30 May – telegram to House of Commons: Military Court is sitting this day at Victoria Barracks to try John R. Moylan, MP for Southern Ireland … Counsel produced an order of a chancery judge dated 28 May ordering the writ of habeas corpus directed to the military governor … The charge is levying war – Penalty – death.'[3] This appeal to the backbenchers at Westminster seems another forlorn hope. There was little sympathy to be had and this last week of May brought news of further killings in Cork. In an action at Midleton the officer commanding fourth battalion, Cork No. 1 Brigade, Diarmaid Hurley, was killed. At Castletownroche an attack on the RIC barracks resulted in the death of a Black and Tan. At Youghal a culvert bomb killed seven bandsmen of the Hampshire Regiment. Many more were wounded.

Back at Victoria Barracks the court-martial continued. The record shows: 'The accused declined to recognise the court and a plea of not guilty was entered in respect of all the charges. The accused declined the assistance of an officer in his defence.'[4] Evidence was then given and the accused declined to cross-examine each witness. The first witness stated:

On 16 May 1921 I was on duty with a party of military near Knocknagree and Kiskeam, Co. Cork, before daylight. I was a sentry and at about 05.30 hours, we started to close in on an area we had surrounded. I was posted in a small field with Private ——, about 06.45 hours. At about 07.00 hours I noticed about 100 yards on my right that there was a movement amongst the bushes of a hedge. I went towards the place with ——. I was armed with a revolver and —— had a rifle. I then saw a man lying on his back who appeared to be asleep. I told —— to cover him with the rifle, and I told the accused to get up. As he did not get up I kicked his foot. Before accused got up I took hold of the revolver [produced] and a detonated bomb similar to that produced, which the accused held in his right hand. The revolver was loaded in six chambers with the ammunition [produced]. I marched accused back. Accused said to me 'You are a lucky fellow to find me, but you are unlucky to me today.' I was present when —— searched accused, and I saw him find seven rounds of revolver ammunition [produced] in the right-hand breeches' pocket of the accused. The revolver [produced] is a six inch 445 Webley and the ammunition is of the same calibre. The bomb is of Mills pattern and detonated.

The statement of the second witness was similar in detail. The record of the third witness' evidence states:

I was with a cycling patrol of my regiment ... We advanced across country. Accused was brought to me by the first witness. I proceeded to search accused and in his right-hand breeches' pocket I found the seven rounds of .45 ammunition. Accused made no statement. In the presence of the accused the first witness showed me the revolver and a Mills bomb. The first witness said he had found the accused lying in some gorse with a revolver and bomb in his hand. Accused still said nothing.

The fourth witness stated:

Parties were dropped at various points. My party consisted of about twenty. We were proceeding on foot up a track ... when a lot of horns were sounded all around us.

We came to a farm, and I skirted it and came to the lane on the other side of it. I went up the lane with a member of the RIC and two men. There were high hedges on each side, and a mud wall at the turning beyond us. My party were fired on by one shot from this mud wall, and the bullet went between me and the RIC man. We replied to the fire, and retired to a bank. Three more men appeared on the bank and rushed up as if to line it. I could not see if they had arms, as the light was still bad. They were twenty yards from me. About two minutes after, I heard a human whistle, which I took to be a signal from the top of the lane. Then I heard —— challenge someone, and then I heard a rifle shot in the lane. I was only three yards from ——, and it was he who fired this shot. Dawn was about 04.30 hours, and we then moved forward. In a farm 150 to 200 yards in advance we found a pair of puttees and two revolver holsters. Then I went about 400 yards from the place I was fired at previously, and there found some of my men around a dugout, which contained a box about four feet high and about two feet sunk into a bank. I saw men pulling out of this a Hotchkiss gun, and some ammunition and some literature. I saw the accused later under escort at a farm 150 yards from where we were shot at.

In response to questions by the court the witness said: 'The horn sounded about three miles around. From the noise I judged there were about 100 men ahead of the troops. Later in the day I saw four or five armed men moving away. I also saw two men blowing horns on a hill. We took twelve prisoners that day.'

The fifth witness stated:

Just before 04.00 hours I heard a shot up a lane near a house I was searching. I went up the lane towards where I heard the shot … I got into the lane and a few minutes later I heard a signal whistle from the top end of the lane and it was repeated, then someone walked down the lane towards me, and then I said, 'Halt. Hands up!' I could see that he was wearing an overcoat and a light cap. The man answered, 'All right I have got them up.' Then I could see he had his hands above his head. I covered the man with my rifle and told him to come on. Immediately, he dropped his hands and bolted up the lane. I fired at him with a rifle. At about 04.30 hours we started to search the country and houses. At the top of the lane I saw the bank and then I proceeded to a farm on the right. A greatcoat, Sam Browne belt and a holster were brought to me. The greatcoat was the one the accused is now wearing. Accused was brought into the lane by the first and second witnesses, and they handed him over to an officer, together with the revolver and the bomb produced. The officer asked accused if the revolver and bomb belonged to him and the accused replied, 'Yes.' This reply was quite voluntary ... Accused asked me if he could proceed down the lane to find a pair of glasses he had lost. I went down the lane to the spot where I had fired. I had noticed that the accused had on a light cap and spoke like the man I had heard when I fired. So I asked him if anyone had shot at him during the morning. He said, 'Yes' and that it was down the lane. I said it was I who had fired at him, and he said, 'It was a pretty near one.' He went down the lane with me and said, 'Where was it that you fired at me?' I showed him and he said, 'I did not think it was so far down as that.' I noticed that accused was searching up one end of the lane. He found nothing there. I saw accused at Buttevant with his glasses, and he told me one of my regiment had found the glasses and given them to him. I asked accused if the greatcoat and Sam Browne belt belonged to him, and he admitted it. Accused put the greatcoat over his shoulders, and said something about me finding more of his equipment if I was lucky. I then told the second witness to take me to the place where the accused was found. On arriving at the bank about 150 to 200 yards from the lane I noticed that the grass and bushes were flattened out, as if someone had been lying there, and I saw witness number two pick up a Mills bomb similar to that produced from the top of the bank amongst some gorse bushes and grass. When I first saw accused under arrest, he was wringing the sleeves of his coat, which was very wet. There was a heavy dew that night. Accused had on a light cap. I thought accused seemed glad to be caught. He was white and cold. Accused said he had been in the district about three weeks, and had not been there overnight but had evidently arrived at about the same time as us. I asked how many men were with him, and he replied, 'Only two or three but the whole countryside is on the run.' All statements made by the accused to me or in my presence were quite voluntary. I escorted accused from Buttevant to Cork, and his attitude was friendly towards me and the other soldiers. Accused talked freely to me.

The record shows:

> The accused was informed in open court of the finding of not guilty
> on the first charge.
>
> The president announced that in view of the communications
> received, which were favourable to the accused, the court wished to
> give the prosecutor ample opportunity of enquiring into the character
> of the accused before sentence was passed. And the court adjourned
> accordingly until 3 June 1921 until sentence was passed.[5]

The acquittal on the charge of levying war on the Crown must follow
from the fact that the charge was expressly tied to the night of his
capture. The evidence suggested that there were many others who
might have fired on the military and the absence of firm evidence
that Moylan had fired upon soldiers on that night was decisive. The
reference to 'communications received' must refer to the fact that
Moylan's capture was well publicised and his record was well known to
the military, in particular his treatment of General Lucas and others,
and his conduct in other actions. Representation had been made. But
Moylan's life still hung in the balance and events were taking place at
Westminster that might yet have had a bearing on his fate.

Hansard records that at Westminster on 1 June Sir Hamar
Greenwood, Chief Secretary for Ireland, was questioned about the
court-martial:

> Captain W. Benn asked the Chief Secretary whether a Chancery
> Judge at Dublin on 26 May ordered the issue of a Writ of Habeas
> Corpus to the Military Governor of Cork to produce on 6 June the
> body of John R. Moylan, at present in custody in Cork; meanwhile
> will he restrain action by the military in respect of Mr Moylan's
> person, and further, whether he is aware that Moylan's execution
> may take place on 4 June and will he see that the Writ is obeyed
> ...
>
> Sir H. Greenwood: John R. Moylan came before a court-martial
> yesterday at Cork on two charges, one of levying war against the

King, and the second of having in his possession improperly one revolver, thirty rounds of revolver ammunition, and two Mills pattern bombs. The trial commenced yesterday ... the court now stands adjourned until tomorrow.

Captain Benn: Will the Right Hon. Gentleman say whether the Writ of Habeas Corpus which has been issued will be obeyed by the Military Court or does it not run?

Sir H. Greenwood: That is one of those very difficult legal questions which I cannot answer off hand ...[6]

Over the preceding three years Captain Wedgwood Benn and a number of other backbenchers had held the British government to account over events in Ireland. The government, the military and other parts of the British establishment regarded Benn as a traitor who was taking the part of assassins and criminals. The exchanges in Westminster were widely reported in Ireland and we see Grazebrook, the Glosters' intelligence officer, furiously note 'that swine Wedgwood Benn'.[7]

Hansard records further exchanges at Westminster on 2 June:

Captain W. Benn asked the Chief Secretary whether he has given orders that the Writ of Habeas Corpus issued by the Dublin court in the case of John R. Moylan shall be obeyed by the Cork Military Court.

Sir H. Greenwood: I am informed that the court before which Moylan is being tried has not yet pronounced sentence. If it is ultimately decided that there is power to issue this Writ, it will of course be obeyed.[8]

This was the nub of the matter: did civilian law or military law prevail? Who decided? It was not just Moylan's life that was at stake; there were a number of men from Cork who had sought a Writ and others who were awaiting court-martial. Greenwood continued to dodge and Benn continued to press for answers:

Captain Benn: Cannot the Right Hon. Gentleman say, the Writ having been issued by a competent court, whether it will be obeyed or not?

Sir H. Greenwood: As a matter of fact the Writ has not been issued, I may inform the hon. and gallant member that a conditional order for the Writ has been issued, but not the Writ.

Captain Benn: If the conditional order is made good and the Writ is issued, will the Military Court obey it?[9]

This question produced no answer.

A contemporary press report shows that Moylan's court-martial reconvened on 5 June when the prosecutor set out the findings regarding the character of the accused:

This case was heard earlier in the week and after finding [conviction], an application was made by the prosecutor for an adjournment which the court granted. At that time certain information concerning the accused had reached the prosecutor. This information the prosecutor wished to investigate and consider. This has now been done and I consider it my duty to lay the information before the court for consideration before passing sentence.

Shortly, the information is as follows. I understand and believe that the accused was in charge of a party of rebels who ambushed a party of police near Kingwilliamstown on 28 January, when Divisional Commissioner Holmes was mortally wounded. Certain of the rebels wanted to shoot some members of the RIC who were lying on the road, but their lives were saved by Moylan, who said to his own men, 'If you shoot them, I will shoot you.' On another occasion two army deserters were caught by Moylan's gang, who were about to shoot them, when Moylan intervened and sent them on their way, saying, 'You have me to thank, or else you would be shot. I don't believe in shooting in cold blood.'

The president said the Military Court had tried some 5,000 cases within the last twelve months, and this was, he thought, one of the first cases in which chivalry had been displayed by the IRA. The court would give full consideration to the statement of the prosecutor.[10]

Sentence was not pronounced and it is unclear whether Moylan was present at this hearing. The president's remark about the lack of chivalry was something of a back-handed compliment: in praising Moylan, the military made a passing swipe at the IRA. The assertion of a lack of chivalry cannot be sustained: the number of cases in which successful ambushes on the military resulted in soldiers and RIC men being disarmed and sent on their way are too numerous to mention and are well documented in the 6th Division Record of the Rebellion. There are also a number of recorded instances of the ambushers providing medical treatment for the wounded. Other ambushes were plainly far less palatable. Moylan later wrote: 'This talk of chivalrous treatment of prisoners was meaningless. No British prisoner falling into the hands of the IRA anywhere was ill treated. Irishmen with arms in their hands captured by the British were always executed. The British soldiers so captured had always been freed.'[11] This statement is also inaccurate: it does not deal with ambushes of RIC men, some of whom were off duty or unarmed, or the taking and shooting of hostages in response to the shooting of rebel prisoners.[12] Nor does it correspond with the treatment of Moylan which, setting aside the conduct of the East Lancashire Regiment and the later decision of the civil courts that the declaration of martial law was contrary to civil law, was fair.

The next event took place on 6 June when the Chancery Division of the High Court heard counsel for Moylan in support of an order to make the Writ of Habeas Corpus absolute. After argument the conditional order was continued pending the decision of the House of Lords in a similar case – *R v Clifford and Sullivan*.[13]

On 9 June, and in defiance of the Writ of Habeas Corpus, the court-martial sat again on the Moylan case, anxious it seems to bring matters to a conclusion before the civil court took further action. Fifteen years penal servitude was ordered.[14] Moylan was not sentenced to death. Had he been convicted of the charge of levying war then it is highly likely that execution would have followed. He was still at risk on the second charge but may have been spared because of his election to the Dáil and the ongoing covert discussions about a truce. The reason may also lie in a desire by the military not to force a confrontation with the civil courts.

Other men were still under sentence of death. There was the case of the Mourne Abbey men sentenced to death for the murder of Sergeant Gibbs during a raid in Mallow; however, Barry Sullivan got a stay of execution and the sentence of death for these men was never confirmed. Others were not so fortunate, such as Thomas Keane, who was executed in Limerick on 7 June.

Moylan's court-martial had wider implications. There is always a danger in applying contemporary standards to the events of 1921. However, even by the standards of that time, the defects in the system were profound and demonstrate the ease with which the rule of law may be abrogated in times of crisis. Later that summer the High Court, in the case of *Egan v Macready and others*, found that the Military Courts in Cork and the rest of the martial law area were illegal.[15] John Egan had been arrested near Quin, County Clare in possession of ammunition. He had been tried and convicted by a Military Court in Limerick. Another man, Higgins, had been court-martialled and sentenced to death for levying war. Both men, like others before them, had sought a Writ of Habeas Corpus with little prospect of success. As with most landmark judgments, this one turned on a fine piece of law. The Master of the Rolls decided that parliament had laid down a process to deal with the rebellion, and that process included court-martial procedures as defined by statute and regulations. It was not open to the military to supplement this procedure by declaring martial law and imposing their own brand of law. This dramatic judgment created the crisis that lawyers for rebel prisoners had long since tried to engineer. The Writ of Habeas Corpus was granted for Egan and for Higgins. The military declined to produce the prisoners and there followed a sharp exchange in court. Counsel for the Crown, Sergeant Hannah, KC, told the court:

... an appeal lies, and notice of an appeal having been served, and the

Crown did not propose to produce the prisoners or release them
pending the appeal.

Judge: I will not listen to any such answer to the Writ. The Writ must
be answered in the ordinary way. Has the Writ been obeyed?

Lynch, KC [for the prisoners]: No, my Lord.

Judge: Then I will order a Writ of Attachment to issue against the
three parties for whom Sergeant Hannah appears. It is a quite
deliberate contempt of court.[16]

The Master of the Rolls then issued Writs for the arrest of General
Macready, Major General Strickland and Brigadier General Cameron,
while the generals made ready to arrest the judge. The next day the
government at Westminster gave way and ordered the release of the
prisoners and the constitutional crisis was averted.

The consequences of what had transpired were grave. There were
fourteen executions in the martial law area. The first was Con Murphy
in February. Then there was John Allen and the men convicted
of involvement in the Dripsey ambush: Tim McCarthy, Thomas
O'Brien, Daniel O'Callaghan, John Lyons and Patrick O'Mahoney.
They were followed by two Volunteers who escaped the massacre at
Clonmult: Maurice Moore and Paddy O'Sullivan, and two others
found guilty of involvement in the Mourne Abbey ambush: Patrick
Ronayne and Thomas Mulcahy. Patrick Casey was executed on 2
May, Dan O'Brien on 16 May and Thomas Keane on 7 June. At the
time of the Truce there were approximately sixteen men awaiting
execution and 133 serving sentences of penal servitude. The courts-
martial also show a revealing pattern. All the men executed in the
martial law area were from Cork with the exceptions of John Allen
and Thomas Keane. Of the twelve Corkmen, none were from west
Cork. According to Tom Barry, this was because prisoners were not
being taken in that area.[17]

There were other basic flaws in the Military Courts sitting in
Cork. The British Army was acting as both prosecutor and judge,
and was regarded by most of the population as partisan. And there

were miscarriages of justice. For example, it is now known that one of the men sentenced to death for the murder of Sergeant Gibbs in the Mallow raid, David Buckley, was not involved in the raid or the Volunteers in any way.[18]

The legal experience of officers sitting on courts-martial and Military Courts was limited. In the case of Joseph Murphy of Thomas Street, Cork, who was charged with taking part in an ambush in which Private Squibs of the 2nd Battalion of the Hampshire Regiment was killed, the tribunal refused to allow questions to be put to soldiers giving evidence that would show that they had given contradictory evidence in another court hearing. Murphy was sentenced to death, but this was eventually commuted to twenty-five years penal servitude because of the distress caused by the repeated deferral of his execution while the lawyers argued.[19] The High Court recognised the unfairness of what had taken place but declined to interfere for legal reasons. Errors of this magnitude were not unusual.

Other hearings were hurried. The court-martial of Dan O'Brien took just a few minutes and he was executed before his family was made aware that he was being court-martialled. Then there was John Allen from Tipperary, who was charged with possessing ammunition, a revolver and a book called *Night Fighting*. He was tried and convicted under martial law and executed for an offence that did not carry the death sentence in civil law.[20] Clifford and Sullivan were similarly at risk of execution for offences that did not carry the death penalty in civil law.

Another flaw was the drumhead court-martial system, where suspects could be executed without any proper safeguards. Indeed, the purpose of a drumhead court-martial was primarily to ensure that the trial and execution went ahead without the suspect having any opportunity to be represented or to get the protection of the courts.

The executions generated an increasingly bloody spiral of violence. One of the consequences was the IRA reprisal shootings of Mary Lindsay, James Clarke and Major Compton Smith. After the execution of Dan O'Brien, the Charleville Battalion determined to take no more prisoners and four soldiers were killed as a result.[21]

Outside the martial law area men were tried by courts-martial convened under the Restoration of Order in Ireland Act. Between November 1920 and July 1921 ten men were executed under these courts-martial. The first was Kevin Barry and the last were Jim Foley and Paddy Maher. These courts-martial were carried out according to law, but they were fraught with the same potential for injustice.

18

Spike Island

About ten o'clock the land-fog rose, and far to the northward I could recognise the coast about Youghal, the opening of the Blackwater, and beyond these, faint and blue, the summits of Knockmeldown [sic]. We had kept a wide berth from the land all night, but were now making straight for Cork harbour. Soon it opened; within half-an-hour more we came to anchor opposite Cove, and within five hundred yards of Spike Island – a rueful looking place, where I could discern, crowning the hill, the long walls of the prison, and a battery commanding the harbour.

Jail Journal – John Mitchel[1]

The battery commanding the harbour was Moylan's first view of Spike Island. He remembered reading *Jail Journal* as a young boy in Kilmallock, never imagining that one day he too would be imprisoned on the island. Moylan had spent some weeks at Cork Detention Barracks where, he later recalled, discipline was tight and the building was spotlessly clean. The guards were on edge and sometimes fired needlessly at each other; one was killed, a number had narrow escapes. He would visit the prison again in 1922 when Free State soldiers were being held at the barracks. In his witness statement he recalled that the conditions the Free State men encountered were far worse than those he had endured in 1921. The skills of running a prison, he observed, were not obvious but they were important. Plainly the British Army had extensive experience.

One night at 3 a.m. Moylan and the other long-term prisoners were taken from their cells to the ground floor. The place was crowded with officers, who had their revolvers drawn, and soldiers, many of whom had their bayonets fixed. The prisoners were handcuffed, put on lorries and driven through silent streets to the quayside where they boarded a boat. No information about their destination was given and Moylan speculated that he would have to serve his sentence at Dartmoor or elsewhere in England. But when the prisoners emerged from the hold they could see Cobh in the distance; this was Spike Island. They were marched from the pier to Fort Westmoreland, an oppressive six-bastioned fort complex.

Moylan found a very different regime on Spike Island. Prisoners did not take orders from the warders but from their own commandant. The accommodation consisted of a series of huts, each housing fifteen to twenty long-term prisoners. There was an exercise yard but no other facilities. A large number of internees were held separately, some in the old fort. John L. O'Sullivan from Cork remembers being held in one of the fort's cells and drawing some comfort from reading the names of the Fenian prisoners of the previous century that were carved into the limestone walls.[2] New internees were arriving constantly and O'Sullivan recalled many of them bore the marks of ill treatment, although their spirit was remarkable. Security was tight, however, since in April three prisoners had escaped and one of the internees had been shot dead.[3]

Medical treatment was a problem. The hand injury Moylan sustained in the experiment with the Ross Castle cannon continued to trouble him, but the prison doctor's attitude was contemptuous. Seán Hales was also refused proper treatment for an eye complaint. Another prisoner, Con Conroy, pointed Hales out and told the doctor:

'That man is an MP.'
'My God, is he?'
'And so is the man who came to see you a few days ago with the wounded hand.'

Seán Moylan with a Fáinne in his lapel, *c.* 1916.

Seán Moylan's parents, Richard and Nora Moylan, *c.* 1890.

Mamie Moylan
(Seán's sister),
Newmarket,
c. 1916.

The Moylan women, August 1921. *Left to right*: (rear) Annri and Nora
with Seán and Pats O'Regan; (front) Gret and Mamie.

Lieutenant R. M. Grazebrook, Intelligence Officer, Gloucestershire Regiment, stationed at Kanturk 1921–22. *Courtesy of the Soldiers of Gloucestershire Military Museum*

Brigadier General Henry Tyndall Lucas. *Courtesy of the Rifles (Berkshire and Wiltshire) Museum*

Seán Moylan captured by the Gloucestershire Regiment at Riordan's
farm, Knockavorheen, 16 May 1921.
Courtesy of the Soldiers of Gloucestershire Military Museum

North Cork Volunteers posing in Seán Keating's studio, 1921.

Print of '1921, An IRA Column' by Seán Keating, RHA.
Left to right (front): Michael D. O'Sullivan (Meelin), John Jones
(Ballydesmond), Roger Kiely (Cullen) and Dan Browne (Meelin).
Left to right (rear): Jim Riordan (Knockavorheen), Denny O'Mullane
(Freemount), James Cashman (Kiskeam) and Seán Moylan, O/C Cork
No. 2 Brigade.

Double wedding of Mollie and Nellie Murphy, Cork, October 1921.

Left to right (front): Johnny Murphy, NT; Mollie Murphy; Kathleen Doyle; Nellie Murphy; Lilly McAuliffe; Seán Moylan (in uniform).

Left to right (rear): Katie Murphy, NT (Gaelic League, Newmarket); Bob Kenny; Jim Daly; Fr Tim Murphy; John McAuliffe; Larry Singleton; Con Murphy; Lena Singleton.

Courtesy of Katty Sheahan, Newmarket

Seán Moylan and Gearóid O'Sullivan en route to Dublin for the Treaty debate.

Retreat from Kilmallock, August 1922. Moylan is standing front left.

Seán MacEoin, Richard Mulcahy, Seán Moylan and Eoin O'Duffy, 1922.

Dan Breen lights up, Civil War, 1922.

Seán Moylan and Seán MacEoin, 4 May 1922.

Seán and Nora's wedding day, 2 December 1922.

The Moylan shop, with workshop to the rear.

Seán Moylan and his mother, Nora Raleigh Moylan, holding Moylan's
first child, Peig, December 1924.

Seán Moylan presided at the inaugural meeting of the Kiskeam branch of Fianna Fáil in 1935. Messrs Maurice Murphy, MCC, Michael Cronin and Daniel Guiney were appointed Honorary Treasurer, Vice-Chairman and Honorary Secretary respectively. (Moylan seated front row.)

Seán Moylan, June 1937. The referendum vote for the Irish Constitution was held on 1 July 1937.

Seán Keating and Seán Moylan at the World's Fair, 1939. *Courtesy Dr Éimear O'Connor, Trinity Art Research Centre, Dublin*

Detail of the mural by Seán Keating, RHA, created for the World's Fair, New York, 1939.

Receiving the seal of office as Minister for Agriculture from President Seán T. O'Kelly, 16 May 1957. Also in the photograph are Frank Aiken and Éamon de Valera.
Copyright: Irish Press Plc

'You mean that ragged chap?'[4]

The ragged chap was sent for. Moylan scathingly reminded the doctor of his duty to Hippocrates and declined further treatment. It appears that the experiences of Moylan and Hales were not isolated. Johnny Collins (brother of Michael), who was also at Spike Island, lost the permanent use of his right hand due to lack of proper treatment.[5] The prison doctor later appears to have been replaced by a better doctor quite suddenly and without explanation. The timing of Moylan's row with the doctor could not have been worse, as soon afterwards he suffered a collapse and was dispatched to the prison hospital for some weeks. Conroy was in charge of the hospital unit and nursed him to recovery.

News of events in the martial law area was scarce. Letters were allowed in but were heavily censored. Occasionally a newspaper would be smuggled in from the internees in the adjoining camp and more rarely a new prisoner would arrive with news from the outside. Details filtered in from north Cork of a successful ambush on the Auxiliaries near Millstreet and also at Abbeyfeale. There was also news of large sweeping operations in north Cork and Kerry, which IRA columns evaded but not without great difficulty. One of Moylan's last acts before being captured related to two British Army deserters, who were suspected of being spies. Moylan had sent them to Kerry to work on farms. It appears that during one of the big sweeps some Volunteers decided that they knew too much about Volunteer activities and the two men were executed. There is little doubt that Moylan, like many Volunteers, would have profoundly disagreed with the execution.

Despite the minor hardships and shortcomings of medical treatment, the prisoners' conditions on Spike Island were tolerable. We know from personal correspondence that Moylan was in Hut 17 and that he sent and received mail; some of those letters survive. He also received food from home and was able to smuggle out personal correspondence. News trickled into Spike about the Truce dances and celebrations in north Cork. In his own letters he speculated that

Kiskeam would once again echo to the resonant reveille of Tim Kiely's battered cornet, which he expected had come down off the shelf to play an enthusiastic rendition of the 'Soldier's Song'. There were a few rueful words of regret that he would miss hauling home the turf from Knocknaboul that scorching hot summer. But there was also a note of optimism: the thought of 'a bottle of stout at Pateen's' and a message that if anyone heard of his release to 'keep the kettle full'.[6]

Conditions in the prison were hard but adequate. There were showers on Saturdays and a march to Mass on Sundays. The long-term prisoners, who had been convicted of offences contrary to martial law or the Restoration of Order in Ireland Act, were allowed to hear Mass with the internees, who were there on suspicion of involvement in rebel activity. It was a chance for the internees to pass food and tobacco to the long-termers, who had few privileges and whose concerns mainly seemed to relate to food, cigarettes and the bullying behaviour of one of the sergeants of the Welch Fusiliers.

Once Moylan was back on his feet, he and Conroy got to work. The food was improved by the simple expedient of a letter to the brigade, which passed on their concerns to the food contractors. The oppressive sergeant of the Welch Fusiliers was dealt with in a similar fashion. It was learned that his wife and mother-in-law lived in Cobh; there followed a short discussion in which Moylan outlined the consequences if the sergeant did not mend his ways. The matter was resolved. Moylan did not smoke but appears to have enjoyed bribing orderlies to bring in cigarettes on a large scale for the benefit of the long-term prisoners.

At home the constant raids on Nora Moylan's shop in Newmarket had stopped, although in a curious entry in the Glosters' diary Lieutenant Grazebrook records that Moylan's mother and other women of the family had gone on a picnic near Newmarket and that 'someone' had put laxatives in their drinks with devastating effects. It appears that Grazebrook knew what was done, how it was done, who attended the picnic and what the results were. How he knew this is not recorded.[7]

The Truce came quite suddenly. In north Cork Volunteers who had been on the run for months, or even years, emerged from hiding. Few thought the Truce would hold and the Glosters took the chance to get a look at the men they had been hunting. Denis Galvin appears to have excited a lot of interest: he had been an active and able Volunteer, but as an athletic man of six feet and four inches he had escaped capture on several occasions. He was seen in the marketplace at Kanturk and his appearance was carefully noted by the Glosters, who had one eye on the resumption of hostilities.

There was little to do for the prisoners at Spike Island, except await developments. Éamon de Valera was negotiating with David Lloyd George. One of the issues was the release of republican members of the Dáil. There was no difficulty in relation to Seán Hales, Seán Moylan and others, but there was an impasse in relation to Seán MacEoin, who had been convicted of murder. A diary entry at Dublin Castle dated 7 August 1921 notes:

> There is an influential section of Sinn Féin not so much in Dublin as in the country, who want to fight and are prepared to make McKeown [*sic*] the test. Dáil Éireann is to meet. 'Where,' they say, 'is the logic of withholding from the meeting one member and that a Cabinet Minister? True he has been convicted of murder but you are prepared to release others who according to you are equally guilty of murder, Moylan for instance.'[8]

De Valera held firm and Lloyd George gave way.

Moylan wrote to his mother from Spike Island on 7 August 1921, just before his release to take part in the Anglo-Irish Treaty debates:

> Dear Mother,
> I reckon I've nothing to report. I got Mamie's letter and parcel OK. I also got K. T. Murphy's letter and hope she got mine in reply. Will you get me some stuff when you get this. Butter, some cake and bacon (cooked). Had a note from Dublin notifying me of meeting of An Dáil. I have me doubts about its meaning anything else. Did Joe come

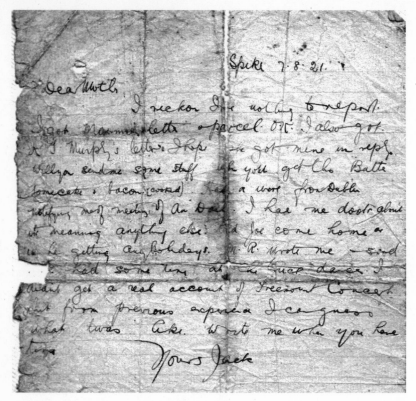

Letter from Moylan to his mother from Spike Island, dated 7 August 1921.

home or is he getting any holidays? M. R. wrote me and she said she had some time at the Truce dances. I didn't get a real account of Freemont concert but from previous experience I can guess what 'twas like. Write me when you have time.

Yours Jack[9]

According to contemporary press accounts, Moylan left Spike Island on 8 August, dressed pretty much in rags. He was taken to Mrs Martin's house in Cork where he met other senior Volunteers: Seán Hegarty, Michael Leahy and Dominic Sullivan. Hegarty bought him a suit and he was then driven to divisional headquarters.

This is a good moment to address an inaccurate observation made by the historian Michael Hopkinson: 'Moylan had notoriously frosty relations with his brigade leadership and regarded Lynch, whom he could not bring himself to name in his witness statement, as a mere "pen pusher".[10] Unfortunately a number of historians have taken this canard up as an established fact. What Moylan wrote in his statement was that when he got to divisional headquarters, 'Liam Lynch waited to drive me home. It seemed an age since we had met though scarcely two months had passed and we talked far into the night of hopes and plans for the future.'[11]

The remaining convicted prisoners on Spike Island were left pretty much to their own devices; the internees fared less well and by autumn the atmosphere was volatile – sanitation and overcrowding were the major issues and led to hunger strikes, riots and a prisoner breakout in November. The governor wrote despairingly, 'I am dealing with madmen.'[12]

19

THE TRUCE AND THE TREATY

The day after Moylan's release he was back at work. The Cork No. 2 Brigade had split in two while he was in prison: the eastern side was designated Cork No. 2, the western side was Cork No. 4 and under the command of Paddy O'Brien. O'Brien's brigade covered the Mallow, Kanturk, Charleville, Newmarket and Millstreet areas. O'Brien graciously stood down in favour of his old comrade and in fact became Moylan's deputy. The lion's share of the work fell on O'Brien as Moylan divided his time between his military and Dáil activities, spending part of each week in Dublin. The brigade staff included Seán Nunan, Michael Dennehy, Eugene McCarthy and Michael O'Connell, who were all experienced and able men.

The Second Dáil convened on 16 August at the Round Room in Dublin's Mansion House. Éamon de Valera, with an escort of hundreds of Volunteers, arrived to cheering crowds. Moylan does not share his feelings about these events. If he felt personal pride, he never admitted it. If he felt a moment of history when taking the oath, he did not share it. We do know that he did not believe that the British would permit independence or that the leaders of the republican cause would settle for anything less.

Similarly, the British Army's general staff did not believe that the conflict was over. The 6th Division Record of the Rebellion states that 'the whole time and energy of everyone during the period 11 July to 5 Dec was devoted to preparing for a possible resumption of hostilities'.

The focus of their preparations lay in intelligence: identifying guerrilla leaders and securing information about the structure of the IRA. Strenuous efforts were made to equip all units with wireless capabilities and to lay down aerodromes in every district.[1]

For Moylan and most senior Volunteers, the Truce was viewed as a breathing space, an opportunity to train, re-equip and organise. Foundries were developed and workshops were set up to produce munitions and to manufacture gunpowder. Residential training camps were also put in place. At a local level, there were many acts of indiscipline. Young men, sometimes on the fringes of the Volunteers, sometimes not even that, posed as hardened veterans and earned a bad reputation. New recruits, who became known derisively as 'trucileers', were also a mixed bag. Drunkenness was occasionally a problem and commandeering cars in the name of the IRA – sometimes with the words 'for Moylan of Newmarket' – was another. Commandeering transport had been necessary during the war, but with the Truce it was barefaced theft and Moylan strongly disapproved. Some of these incidents involved senior Volunteers who, because of the partly elective system of promotion, could not easily be replaced. Most of the committed Volunteers, however, were running or engaged in training camps and others had returned home to bring in the harvest. The 6th Division Record of the Rebellion reveals the British Army's perspective: 'As soon as all chance of immediate fighting was over, the scattered bands of desperados formed themselves into the companies and battalions to which they had always belonged on paper and started to train, practice musketry, hold reviews etc.'[2] These activities were reported up the line and General Sir Nevil Macready's memorandum to cabinet dated 27 September 1921 records 'flagrant breaches of the agreement specifically with regard to a notorious rebel, Moylan by name ... who was seen in Newmarket ... carrying a Thompson machine gun under his coat.'[3]

There were breaches of the Truce on both sides: soldiers were kidnapped but later released and arms were stolen; Dorothy Macardle records that some elements of the Crown forces continued to engage in acts of wanton violence.[4] In north Cork the protagonists appeared more relaxed. Captain Richards of the Glosters later wrote of his dealings with Moylan and, referring to Moylan's capture, he said: 'I am sure that Moylan fired a pistol at Reece at point blank range but missed.'[5] Richards recalled that a few weeks after Moylan was released 'he came to Kanturk and sought out Company Sergeant Major Reece for a friendly chat with him and others including myself'.[6]

Moylan also found time to court his future wife, Nora Murphy. She was the daughter of a formidable lady, Annie Mary Josephine Murphy, known to her neighbours and eleven children as 'The Mater', who, along with her husband Dan, owned the Shamrock House in Kiskeam. In an age when girls were not educated, 'The Mater' had educated all of her daughters. When the village apothecary was 'indisposed', as he often was, she took his place to dispense remedies, and occasionally her husband 'Dan the Shamrock' pulled teeth. Her daughter Nora Mary was a teacher in the north of England, who came home to visit her family during her holidays. By all accounts she was a self-possessed young woman of striking good looks. One evening her parents invited her to meet Moylan, who was at the house in some organisational capacity. She swept to the front of the crowded room but was not much impressed with the thin figure who sat cold and wet by the fire. He managed to engage her in some banter on the question of whether she might marry him. 'We will have to see,' she replied.

Moylan went to Dublin on 16 August and was invited to dinner at the Gresham Hotel by Hugh Harold, a businessman and brother of one of the men court-martialled for the Mallow Barracks raid. By chance he ran into Albert Wood. Days later, Wood commissioned the artist Seán Keating to paint a portrait of Moylan wearing the clothes in which he stood trial. This work was exhibited at the Royal Hibernian Academy in 1922 and is sometimes referred to as *The Trial*. Within weeks Keating would commence work on his iconic paintings of the north Cork flying column. While the painting was in progress, Moylan moved between his military duties in north Cork and his Dáil commitments in Dublin.

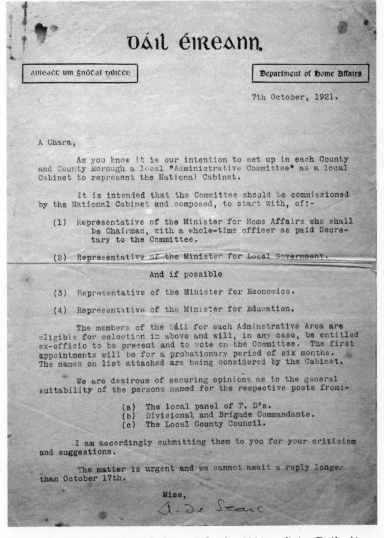

Dáil éireann,

aireacc um snócaí ohlcce

Department of Home Affairs

7th October, 1921.

A Chara,

As you know it is our intention to set up in each County and County Borough a local "Administrative Committee" as a local Cabinet to represent the National Cabinet.

It is intended that the Committee should be commissioned by the National Cabinet and composed, to start with, of:-

(1) Representative of the Minister for Home Affairs who shall be Chairman, with a whole-time officer as paid Secretary to the Committee.

(2) Representative of the Minister for Local Government.

And if possible

(3) Representative of the Minister for Economics.

(4) Representative of the Minister for Education.

The members of the Dáil for each Adminstrative Area are eligible for selection in above and will, in any case, be entitled ex-officio to be present and to vote on the Committee. The first appointments will be for a probationary period of six months. The names on list attached are being considered by the Cabinet.

We are desirous of securing opinions as to the general suitability of the persons named for the respective posts from:-

(a) The local panel of T. D's.
(b) Divisional and Brigade Commandants.
(c) The Local County Council.

I am accordingly submitting them to you for your criticism and suggestions.

The matter is urgent and we cannot await a reply longer than October 17th.

Mise,

A. de Stac

Letter from Austin Stack to Moylan on 7 October 1921, outlining Dáil cabinet proposals to set up a tier of local government in each county.

The Dáil cabinet was trying to set up a tier of local government to mirror the cabinet structure in Dublin. Moylan, no doubt like many other brigade commanders, was asked to become involved.[7] It is likely that he found this a distraction and felt that there were much more pressing problems to deal with. The following report was received from the intelligence officer of Cork No. 2 Brigade on 21 October:

> On a recent visit of Cope, Assistant Under Secretary, Dublin Castle, to Cork, the following outline plan was left with D. C. and General Strickland to work out details for immediate application in case hostilities are resumed: concentration camps for women and children and loyal members of male sex, to be established at various centres near coastal ports and railway centres such as Mallow. Loyal citizens to be given the opportunity to reside in England or in a camp. All males who elect to remain outside the camps in Ireland to be treated as hostile. Women and children to be removed compulsorily to camp, if necessary before the commencement of hostilities. Such operations expected to result in victory in a month.[8]

The knowledge of these plans must have been a heavy burden for men such as Moylan. Despite such intelligence, he remained unremittingly opposed to capitulating on the issue of the oath of allegiance and the Republic.

Meanwhile the politicians negotiated in London.[9] The Irish delegates were outmanoeuvred and worn down by their British opponents. They faced a strong team of able, professional politicians, including David Lloyd George, Winston Churchill, Austen Chamberlain and Lord Birkenhead. For them, negotiation and committee-room politics were meat and drink. The resulting Anglo-Irish Treaty, which would be debated in Dublin in December 1921, was very different to the terms most of the Deputies had expected or hoped to achieve.

The Treaty debates took place in the University College Dublin council chamber at Earlsfort Terrace. Each day the gallery was full to overflowing and it seems that no Deputy was denied the opportunity to speak on this critical issue. By 16 December, the British House of Commons and House of Lords had accepted the articles of the Treaty by a large majority. In Ireland the impetus slowly began to shift.

Moylan spoke on the issue on a number of occasions, but his most famous contribution was delivered on 22 December and took just a few minutes. A contemporary observer noted a 'smallish man, with glasses and long black hair' who spoke with powerful conviction.[10] Moylan was generous in his praise of the delegation that had gone to London and described the approach of the British government as 'throwing dust in the eyes of our too trustful representatives'. He labelled the proposal to abandon the northern counties as 'loathsome' and finished with this powerful appeal:

What I say is this: 'Hands off the Republic' and I am to be told this is a declaration of war on England? No English statesman will take it so. It is a definition of our rights, and Lloyd George, if he wants war will have to declare war. If he is giving us freedom he can do so without declaring war. All we ask of Lloyd George is to allow us to carry on. There is just one point more. It is this. As I said we have been fighting for the extermination of British interests in Ireland. We are told we have it. I don't believe we have it. If there is a war of extermination waged on us, that war will also exterminate British interest in Ireland; because if they want a war of extermination on us, I may not see it finished, but by God, no loyalist in North Cork will see its finish, and it is about time that somebody told Lloyd George that. The terms of reference must be interpreted in their broadest, and not in their narrowest, sense. For our Republic we are offered (1) An Oath of Allegiance; (2) A Governor General; (3) A new Pale; (4) An army entrenched on our flank; (5) Independence, internal independence; (6) The Treaty to preserve and consolidate British interests in our midst.[11]

Even before the Treaty vote, some members were beginning to fear the worst. Moylan recalled Liam Mellows telling him: 'Many more of us will die before an Irish Republic is recognised.'[12] Prophetic words, but even then no one seriously countenanced that there would be a civil war.

By mid-December hundreds of internees had been released from

Extract from Moylan's handwritten transcript of his speech on the Treaty debate, 21 December 1921.

prison in a general amnesty. The vote on the Treaty was adjourned to January and the newspapers reported many country Deputies returning to their homes. We can infer that Moylan took the train from Kingsbridge to Millstreet as he had in 1919 or hitched a lift going south. His journey home had a personal dimension. Nora Murphy was in Kiskeam for Christmas and correspondence between them over the preceding months had blossomed into something more serious. There was a sense of purpose in Moylan's journeys between Newmarket and Kiskeam, and Nora's parents, 'The Mater' and 'Dan the Shamrock', recognised that 'a match' was in the air.

In Newmarket, a cheerful if subdued bustle had returned to this country town. Just one year before 'an old man, John Murphy, took his Christmas candle to his bedroom where there were no curtains' and was shot through the throat by the military.[13] Twelve months later the atmosphere was lighter, less fearful and more hopeful. The Aldworths, who were the local gentry and landlords in Newmarket for over 300 years, moved to England in 1921. They had been considered relatively benign towards their tenants, especially in times of difficulty, and had supported local efforts throughout the nineteenth century. The family had donated a site and contributed towards the building costs of St Mary's Catholic church on the corner of Main Street and High Street, and in later years were the principal investors in the Newmarket railway. Within twelve months their residence at Newmarket Court would be occupied by Free State troops.[14] But no one thought of that possibility on Christmas Day 1921.

Elsewhere, in the Glen of Aherlow, the Lynch household celebrated the release of Paddy Lynch. His brother Seán was one of the Galbally men who successfully rescued Seán Hogan at Knocklong railway station in 1919. For two years the military pursued Paddy in the hope of getting information on his brother. Seán avoided capture but Paddy was finally picked up in June 1921 and interned at Tipperary Barracks, Spike Island, Bere and finally Maryborough. When he arrived home at Christmas his delighted brother gleefully remarked: 'Paddy, you never fired a shot yet you were in four different prisons, you must have done something terrible on the quiet.'[15] Similar homecomings, stories and banter were replicated all over Munster.

The adjournment on the vote proved to be a critical development. The churches favoured peace and made their views known. The press also favoured peace and supported the pro-Treaty faction. Many public bodies came out in favour of the Treaty. Amongst those supporting the Treaty, there was a wide divergence of reasons. Many were exhausted by war. There was also a fear, whipped up by statements of the British cabinet ministers Churchill and Birkenhead, about a new and quite terrible war. Some did not fear a war itself, but believed they could not win. Many felt what had been achieved was all that was needed. Others believed the Treaty was a stepping stone to a republic. In essence, although few were happy with it, the Treaty represented the least objectionable way forward.

As 1922 arrived, the fissures that ran through the country were mirrored in the IRA. In the course of the debates there were many passionate speeches but one carried in it the seeds of civil war. Seamus Robinson expressed the view that the IRA was entitled to hold a convention on the issue of the Treaty. Jim Riordan and Jimmy Cashman of Cork No. 4 Brigade listened intently from the gallery. Nora Murphy and her sister Mary were also in Dublin during those fateful days. Nora had just become engaged to Seán Moylan and there was excitement tinged with uncertainty on how the political landscape would develop. When the final vote on the Treaty was announced the scene was one of painful silence: 'nobody moved, nobody cheered, nobody even spoke'.[16] Seán Moylan, who was described by a contemporary as 'one of the most daring and gallant of our brigade commanders' broke down and wept.[17]

The Treaty was approved by a narrow margin of sixty-four to fifty-seven. De Valera resigned, Arthur Griffith was elected president and Robinson's observation gathered momentum. The direct result of the vote was that many senior IRA men pressed for a convention. Their logic was this: they had sworn an oath not just to Dáil Éireann but to the Republic. The effect of the Treaty vote was to revoke the

Republic and this placed them in an invidious position. Many officers pressed for the IRA to revert to a Volunteer organisation ruled by its executive. This was a most dangerous development, although it was not recognised as such at the time. As soon as the army developed a political agenda that brought it into conflict with the government, civil war became inevitable. This danger was heightened by two other factors: the decision of Ernie O'Malley and the 2nd Southern Division to refuse to recognise the authority of GHQ and the development of the Irish National Army at Beggars Bush in Dublin, where recruitment to the force was being carried out at a rapid pace. On 18 January, Richard Mulcahy, Minister for Defence, acceded to a request for an IRA convention; it would take place within two months.

The country was in a state of considerable turmoil. The general anxiety and uncertainty was mirrored in the Four Courts and, writing from the Law Library, Albert Wood remarked to Moylan that 'great rumours reach the courts each day of impending changes' and still 'the Liffey flows by unrippled'.[18] By the summer, every book in the library would be reduced to ashes.

As for Moylan, these precarious months were a tumult of military activities augmented by public speaking duties at major rallies in O'Connell Street and elsewhere.[19] The cabinet belatedly recognised that most IRA members were against the Treaty and reversed the decision to permit a convention. Indeed there was a growing risk the army would form its own policy. Oddly, the perception of this risk only seems to have dawned on the cabinet following Churchill's letter to Collins pointing out that the pro-Treaty Deputies were being drawn into an anti-Treaty argument rather than asserting themselves to implement the terms of the Treaty for the Irish nation. Despite the cabinet's order to cancel it, the army convention went ahead on 26 March against a background of a widening split between pro-Treaty and anti-Treaty forces. There were occasional clashes and a stand-off between the two sides in Limerick, where British barracks were being turned over to local republican forces and it was a matter of chance whether they were pro- or anti-Treaty. The Dáil, the Irish Republican

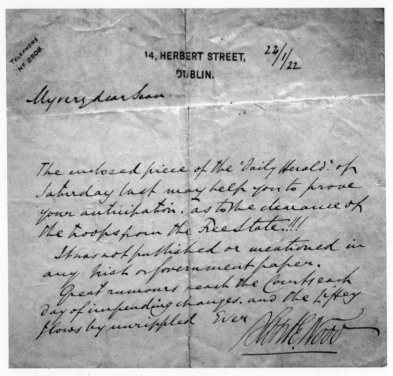

Letter dated 24/01/1922 from Albert Wood, KC, to Seán Moylan.

Brotherhood, the IRA, Cumann na mBan and other groups heaved with intrigue. The south hovered near civil war, while in Northern Ireland a pogrom against Catholics continued. Against this torrid background the convention re-affirmed the IRA's allegiance to the Republic and resolved that it would once again be ruled by an executive. A constitution would be framed for submission to another convention meeting on 9 April 1922. The new pro-tem sixteen-man executive issued a statement declaring that the Minister for Defence and the Chief-of-Staff no longer exercised any control over the IRA and called for recruiting to the embryonic National Army to be stopped.

The convention re-assembled on 9 April and agreed to adopt the new constitution giving control to an annually elected executive. The constitution was unequivocally republican in its outlook. Liam Lynch was appointed Chief-of-Staff and the sixteen-man executive included Lynch, Moylan, Liam Mellows, Rory O'Connor, Joe McKelvey, Florrie O'Donoghue, Seán O'Hegarty, Liam Deasy, Joe O'Connor, Seamus Robinson, Peadar O'Donnell, Frank Barrett, Tom Maguire, P. J. Ruttledge, Ernie O'Malley and Tom Hales.

Moylan and Lynch seemed joined at the hip on policy, although Moylan may have started to make his own overtures to the pro-Treaty faction. A meeting with Mulcahy in late April suggested a compromise might be found. Mulcahy noted in his typically convoluted style that Moylan was 'not worried about himself but about others being shot and he doing the shooting'.[20] Peadar O'Donnell later recalled coming upon Moylan in tears in the aftermath of a meeting with Mulcahy as the prospect of a civil war loomed.[21]

The British continued to supply armaments to the Provisional Government and gather intelligence on the Volunteers. As the weeks passed the split in the IRA grew and the army itself was becoming a potent political force. Moylan continued to dash back and forth between Dublin and Cork. He and Rory O'Connor were involved in a car crash at Carrick-on-Suir in late April during one such run.[22] Although they were avowedly anti-Treaty, the local pro-Treaty forces provided them with accommodation and fresh transport. This incident captures some of the chaos, muddle and also goodwill that still existed between the opposing factions at this time.

20

ON THE EDGE OF ANARCHY

In early spring 1922 the British Army began to withdraw to Dublin and the Curragh as the redeployment of troops to Europe and other parts of the Empire had finally commenced. In north Cork the Glosters vacated the Old Union Workhouse in Kanturk on 3 February. That night or the following day Pat O'Keefe, the workhouse master, died; as the battalion intelligence officer put it, 'he was pushed to his death' – although no details are supplied as to who pushed him or why.[1]

The Auxiliaries were leaving and members of the RIC were increasingly confined to barracks. Attacks continued on the RIC, mainly in the south-west. In this power vacuum the country stood on the edge of anarchy. Robberies of post offices and banks were frequent, some by anti-Treaty forces, others by those eager to line their own pockets. Clashes between anti- and pro-Treaty factions were common. On 26 April, three British intelligence officers and their driver were seized at Macroom and later shot.

At the end of April an incident occurred which later became known as the Dunmanway massacre. Thirteen Protestant civilians were killed by elements of the IRA. The spark was ignited when a group of IRA men tried to commandeer a car from the home of a loyalist in Ballygroman. The owner, Thomas Hornibrook, had taken the precaution of disabling his car by removing the magneto. This was to cost him his life. An IRA party led by Michael O'Neill tried to force entry into Hornibrook's house; eventually they slipped in through an unlocked window. O'Neill was shot dead by Hornibrook's son-in-law and this set in motion a spiral of killings that included two sixteen-year-old boys and a curate. The murders resulted in an exodus of Protestants from the west Cork area. No one was ever prosecuted for these events and it remains a black moment for nationalists.

Historian Peter Hart has used the killings to argue that an undercurrent of the War of Independence was sectarianism against Protestants, notably in Cork.[2] Moylan's famous Dáil speech against the Treaty was advanced as evidence of anti-Protestant sentiment. The extract from the speech reads: 'If there is a war of extermination waged on us, that war will also exterminate British interest in Ireland; because if they want a war of extermination on us, I may not see it finished, but by God, no loyalist in north Cork will see its finish'.[3] The context of this speech is worth setting out. As Winston Churchill had put it to the British cabinet some months previously: 'A hundred thousand new special troops and police must be raised, thousands of motor cars must be armoured ... the three provinces of Ireland must be closely laced with cordons of block houses and barbed wire; a systematic rummaging and questioning of every individual must be put in force.'[4] During the Truce General Macready sought and obtained consent for drumhead courts-martial throughout southern Ireland in the event that hostilities were resumed. The Treaty negotiations and debates were marked by threats from the British cabinet. At the House of Lords autumn recess debate, Lord Birkenhead (the Lord Chancellor) declared: 'Let no one blind himself to the conclusion that if this attempt at negotiation breaks down, we shall find ourselves committed to hostilities upon a scale never heretofore in my recollection of history, undertaken by the country against Ireland.'[5] In this context, Moylan's speech was a defiant rejoinder.

In terms of Hart's suggestion that Moylan may have harboured anti-Protestant attitudes, the following observations are relevant. First, the flaw in the argument advanced by Hart is to equate loyalist with Protestant; there was and still is a difference. Second, Moylan's directness of speech was legendary and if he had meant to espouse anti-Protestant rhetoric he would undoubtedly have said so in plain terms. Third, the truth is apparent from his actions after the massacre came to light. Local leaders – Moylan, Tom Barry and Liam Deasy – condemned the killings and ordered that armed guards be placed on the homes of known loyalists.[6] Isolated attempts to steal cattle belonging to local loyalists near Mallow and in west Cork, were also dealt with resolutely by Barry and Moylan.[7] And finally, on Moylan's death, as noted in the *Kerryman*, there were many tributes from Protestant churches and the Archbishop of the Church of Ireland, Dr Otto Simms, spoke from personal experience in paying tribute to his sensitivity to the interests of the Protestant minority.[8] It appears even Hart recognises the weakness of the allegation against Moylan in his footnote: 'In fairness, it should be noted that Moylan, despite his rhetoric, had nothing to do with the massacre and had the best record of any IRA brigade commander in treating the Protestant minority.'[9]

Meda Ryan's analysis shows that all but two of the men killed at Dunmanway were part of an organisation known as the 'Loyalist Action Group' and had connections to the Grand Orange Lodge and the anti-Sinn Féin League. All but two of these men also appeared in an abandoned Auxiliary log noting the names of 'helpful' citizens.[10] It is highly likely that their activities on this front led to their deaths. It is not attractive and does not make it right, but the argument that these men were killed simply because of their religion is hard to sustain. It may be that the killers acted with mixed motives, but, as they were never caught and tried, their position cannot be known with certainty. It is a controversial subject that has engaged some historians for many years.[11] What is instructive is that all the major nationalists, including Éamon de Valera, Seán T. O'Kelly and Arthur Griffith, spoke out against what had taken place. Finally, a convention of Church of Ireland leaders which sat at that time recorded that apart from the Dunmanway incident (which was then thought to be sectarian) 'hostility to Protestants by reason of their religion, has been almost, if not wholly, unknown in the twenty-six counties'.[12]

Meanwhile the developing fractures in the political consensus left the IRA sidelined with many members unpaid and without means. Moylan took his own steps to remedy the situation but his methods caused consternation in the Provisional Government. On 28 April he spoke in the Dáil in typically forthright terms and with some bitterness:

> During the war, the British enemy called me the leader of a murder gang. My hands are free from murder. The Minister for Defence, in his report yesterday called me the leader of a robber gang. I am as free from the crime of robbery as I am free from the crime of murder. ... We, unfortunate, plain soldiers, not being used to legal quibbles and legal methods of speaking, were easily gulled by the politicians here in the Dáil. Everywhere we were told that the Truce was a breathing space to give us a chance to organise to carry on the fight for the Republic. And we did organise. We took men away from their employments. We drilled them and trained and armed them and got them ready to fight. And they were ready to fight. These men have been out of employment, without a smoke, ill-shod, badly clad and – we are not all pussyfooters – in want of a drink too. That is the fault of the men who told us the Truce was a breathing space. We were guaranteed payment for those men, funds for the maintenance of those men. We did not get it. I have always seized every opportunity I could get to try and get comforts for my men – to clothe them, to put shoes on them, and to feed them. In February last, I issued an order in my area, seeing that no other action was taken by the Dáil, that the dog tax in the area should be paid to me. During the war, my word went in north Cork. In spite of any terms that would be applied to me today, my word goes there yet ... I put up a notice on Friday evening that I would come to the parish on Sunday to collect the dog tax. I did, and I collected £47, and the people willingly paid me ... That is the extent of my robbery. I am not ashamed of it ...[13]

In this speech Moylan's burning disappointment about the Treaty and profound anger against those whom he saw as betraying the cause can be sensed. His deep-seated concern for the men who served under him and the poverty and deprivation that marked their lives can also be discerned. In later years he would become a professional politician but the subjects on which he spoke and argued most vehemently remained social justice and the relief of poverty.

As to the accusation of robberies of post offices around Kanturk, the older people in the area today still remember the stories handed down by their parents: no one was shot, threatened or manhandled. Moylan arrived and the money was handed over for the use of the IRA. No one then or since, and certainly none of his political opponents, ever accused Moylan of profiteering.

THE SLIDE TO WAR

There will be no fucking civil war.
Seán Moylan in Michael Hopkinson's *Green Against Green*

Everyone shared Moylan's determination to avoid war. On 1 May 1922 a group of influential officers from each faction met to thrash out a compromise. Among their number was Dan Breen, Florrie O'Donoghue, Michael Collins, Humphrey Murphy, Richard Mulcahy, Seán Hales, Seán O'Hegarty, Gearóid O'Sullivan, Eoin O'Duffy and Seán Boylan. They signed a document calling for unity on the basis that the majority of people in Ireland accepted the Treaty and that there should be elections to provide a government which would have the confidence of the people. The context in which this document was drawn up should be stated briefly. In Northern Ireland the IRA continued to attack British forces as a wave of killings of the Catholic minority persisted unabated. Elsewhere, stand-offs between pro-Treaty army units and anti-Treaty forces were becoming common. People had been killed and wounded. Prisoners were being held by both sides.

The call for unity was submitted to the Dáil on 3 May. The author of the document, Seán O'Hegarty, was permitted to make an appeal for unity. However, not everyone found the proposal an acceptable compromise and Moylan spoke against it in the following terms:

I was a member of the Conference from which this statement has come. I was the only army officer there who did not sign it. Every thinking Republican views with horror the possibility of strife between comrades. To myself, personally, the idea of fighting the men who fought with me is particularly abhorrent and I was willing to explore every avenue to peace. It was for that purpose I went to the Conference. I went there and said to the other side that one of my great failings was that I found it difficult to believe evil of anybody and they all the time said they are as good republicans as we are. I am willing to meet any man who is a republican, because a republican can only work for the Republic. Rightly or wrongly, I took up the Truce as an opportunity of making preparation to carry on the fight for the Republic. I am not a politician. I am simply a soldier of the Republic. I will remain a soldier of the Republic and I will serve no other government but a republican government; but I am very anxious to accept, if possible, an assurance that the Treaty can be made a step to the Republic, that the Constitution, when drafted, will prove that this assurance is correct. I and the men I represent will anxiously await that. But in the light of the knowledge I have at present, and in the highest interests of the country as I conceive them, the men who are republicans, like myself, cannot agree, much as we want peace, with the document that has been presented here. We must stand by, or act to preserve the Republic.[1]

The Dáil appointed what became known as the Committee of Ten to try and find a solution to the impasse. The committee members were Seán Hales, Joe McGuinness, Seamus O'Dwyer, Seán MacEoin, Pádraic Ó Máille, Mrs Tom Clarke, Harry Boland, Seán Moylan, Liam Mellows and P. J. Ruttledge. A truce was agreed between the factions while the committee deliberated.

A Joint Army Committee was also formed in an effort to bring the IRA factions together. Moylan was appointed together with Lynch, Mellows, Rory O'Connor, Seamus Robinson, Michael Collins, Richard Mulcahy, Diarmuid O'Hegarty, Eoin O'Duffy, Gearóid O'Sullivan and Seán MacEoin. Agreement was reached that prisoners on both sides who were not being held on criminal charges would be released and that public buildings occupied by the anti-Treaty faction, other than the Four Courts, would be evacuated.

On 10 May the Committee of Ten reported its failure to find a consensus for national unity. It was asked to continue to deliberate but again reported failure on 16 May. A pact between Éamon de Valera and Michael Collins seemed to offer some hope for political unity. It envisaged a deferment of a vote on the acceptability of the Treaty and the creation of a government and Dáil in which pro- and anti-Treaty interests were represented.

Negotiations for army unity continued and produced drafts and counter-drafts of an agreement. A document put forward by Moylan commanded significant agreement. It was a measured proposal that sought to build an acceptable compromise to unify the army.[2] But the slide to war had become inexorable. There were too many tensions to contain. The architects of the Treaty were under pressure from the British cabinet to frame a constitution acceptable to both Britain and the anti-Treaty faction. It was an impossible task. The de Valera-Collins pact fell apart and the prospect of unity within the army was further undermined by a split in the anti-Treaty camp.

On 22 June, two IRA men fatally shot General Sir Henry Wilson outside his house in Eaton Place, London. The British cabinet had its own domestic pressures and ordered an attack on the Four Courts, which had been occupied by anti-Treaty forces. The attack was rescinded after wiser counsel prevailed but, goaded by Winston Churchill and General Macready, the Provisional Government launched its own artillery attack on the Four Courts on 28 June. The Civil War had begun.

22

THE CIVIL WAR

The artillery bombardment of the Four Courts drove the disparate anti-Treaty factions together. After the shelling started Liam Lynch convened a meeting of senior officers in Dublin's Clarence Hotel; a decision was taken to support the men under siege. A proclamation was drawn up by Lynch and signed by all the senior anti-Treaty officers available, including Liam Mellows, Rory O'Connor, Joe McKelvey, Ernie O'Malley, Seán Moylan, Michael Kilroy, Michael Barrett, Thomas Derrig, Pax Whelan, Liam Deasy, Peadar O'Donnell and P. J. Ruttledge. It was a call to arms by a formidable body.

Most anti-Treaty officers not in the Four Courts left Dublin to join their brigades. Deasy, Lynch, Moylan and Moss Twomey set off for Kingsbridge in two jaunting cars together with Con Moylan and Seán Culhane.[1] They caught a train from Kingsbridge to Newbridge. It seems the party then split up and drove along the back roads until they got to Mallow, arriving in the early hours of 29 June. The shelling of the Four Courts continued and culminated in the surrender of the garrison and the death of Cathal Brugha on O'Connell Street. Other Dublin enclaves held out for some days in an echo of Easter 1916.

The closing lines of Moylan's witness statement record his intention to write an account of the Civil War: 'A difficult story to tell for one who called both Mellows and Collins friend, who held them both in high esteem, to whom their deaths were an agony and by whom their

SEÁN MOYLAN: REBEL LEADER

memory is revered. It is a story of failure and disruption, of bitterness and antagonism, from it may be learned the method of eliminating these evils and avoiding them.'[2] He died before he wrote that account and much of the period is obscured by time and the reluctance of many to talk about these events.

In purely military terms the only sensible strategy for those opposing the Treaty was to advance in strength on Dublin and to do so in force. The anti-Treaty feeling was strongest in Cork and the Volunteers there were adequately armed, experienced and far outnumbered the pro-Treaty faction. They were, however, less well-armed than their opponents and it must have been obvious that this disparity would only get worse with the passage of time, with the British supplying the Free State army. Instead, Lynch's strategy was to create what amounted to a 'Munster Republic' along a line from Limerick to Waterford, which would make the implementation of the Treaty impossible. His policy was driven by non-military considerations, namely a desire to avoid waging war on former friends and comrades.

We pick up Moylan's trail in Ernie O'Malley's memoir when he describes the fortification of defensive positions in Limerick some weeks prior to the storming of the Four Courts:

> The western men arrived and were marched off to take over other hotels. Soon practically every hotel in the city was occupied. Seán Moylan of Cork came to see me. He offered to send engineers and explosives. We could blow in the gate of the castle or a portion of the wall and rush the buildings, using explosives in petrol tins with batteries attached. Extra Mulcahyites arrived. We marched and counter-marched to give the appearance of having more men than were actually there. Supplies of land mines had been prepared, the city had been surveyed and supplies of sandbags and barbed wire had been commandeered.[3]

A number of local non-aggression pacts had sprung up, for example, in Limerick. These local pacts lasted until the Free State government felt that there was no choice but to go on the offensive. By 28 June the Civil War was on, the anti-Treaty forces began to take a more aggressive approach. The following letter from Moylan gives a flavour of the times:

Irish Republican Army
Field General Head Quarters
New Barracks
Limerick

10.55 p.m. 6 July 1922

To O/C First Southern Division

(1) I must get one hundred riflemen and ten machine guns ... sent from Cork 1 army at once. The Staters are in force and I must hold the offensive.
(2) Cork 1 can send a bunch of right good men, so can Kerry. Let us have them. There is no use in fooling with the question any longer. Send on the men and let us get on with the war.
Hope the boys are ok.
What about sending a few hundred grenades?

Seán Moylan
Could Cork 3 send us fifty men? SM[4]

We know that Moylan served as Director of Operations, with Éamon de Valera as his adjutant, but what his title meant is less than clear. Lynch and most of his staff had extensive experience in guerrilla warfare but none had experience or training in commanding large bodies of men in a conventional war. This shortcoming permeated all officer ranks. The defensive posture the IRA adopted allowed the Provisional Government to take the initiative and to do so on a number of fronts. Government policy included censorship of press material coming into Ireland, control of the domestic press, internment, rule by decree and the suppression of the Supreme Court. To this armoury was added the vocal support of the Catholic Church.

On the military front the Provisional Government had certain obvious advantages. It had the active support of Britain, which supplied it with guns, ammunition, grenades, armoured cars and artillery. The 18-pounder artillery guns proved decisive in most of the set-piece encounters at Limerick, Waterford, Bruree and Kilmallock. It held the purse strings. It had the National Army, which had been recruiting relentlessly since December and by the end of July stood at a little under 14,000 soldiers. It was able to draw on experienced mercenaries as drill instructors and officers and was ready to embrace new weapons such as the armoured car and aircraft, and imaginative strategies such as sea landings at Clew Bay, Fenit, Cork, Youghal and Glandore to reinforce troops or to wrong foot the republicans.

Moylan becomes an increasingly shadowy figure. He was seen at New Ross in early July leading an anti-Treaty force of some 400 men. It appears he intended to link up with Ernie O'Malley, take Waterford and push up the coast to Dublin. This attack fizzled out for a variety of reasons: lack of logistical support, the absence of local Volunteers and low morale amongst republican troops. A letter from Moylan to O'Malley, dated 10 July, foreshadows the development of a guerrilla strategy: 'We are without a base, transport, food or intelligence. The local Volunteers seem to be practically non-existent.'[5] He brought his troops back to Buttevant Barracks, a withdrawal that later attracted criticism from O'Malley and Pax Whelan. It is a safe inference that Moylan withdrew because he did not think the operation was feasible and he was, as always, cautious with the lives of his men.

His next action attracted high praise. According to Liam Deasy, Moylan led a raid capturing the Provisional Government barracks at Caherconlish on or about 11 July. The *New York Times* described the raid: 'The barracks was captured after stiff engagement. Generals Hayes and Connolly and five staff officers were taken prisoner.'[6]

Moylan then appears to have returned to Limerick, where sporadic fighting on 19 July culminated in an artillery bombardment by the pro-Treaty forces. The fighting went on for two days. Many anti-Treaty troops surrendered after breaking their rifles or throwing the bolts away. The bulk of the republican troops, estimated at about 1,000, retreated south. Behind them the New Barracks was little more than a shell and the Strand Barracks was all but demolished. It was a controlled retreat, felling trees and blowing bridges as they went, and spreading out on all roads to Cork.

Contemporary press reports show Deasy in command and Moylan as Director of Operations as the republican forces dug in to Bruree and Kilmallock. An *Irish Times* reporter travelling with an advance guard of the National Army evoked something of the chaotic atmosphere: 'As I write, a captured Ford car has just been brought into the quarters of the advanced guard ... On the car is written "Vote for Seán Moylan" and in it are two prisoners.'[7]

We know very little about Moylan's movements in these weeks. We do know that D company of Newmarket was dug in around Bulgaden for nearly two weeks. It is likely given his longstanding connection with Newmarket company that Moylan was there or close by. Minor engagements followed at Ballycullane Cross, Thomastown and Bruff. After two days of fighting the National Army took Bruree on 30 July leaving Kilmallock outflanked on two sides.

The defence of Kilmallock was undermined by the National Army's sea landing in Kerry. Many Kerry Volunteers were ordered to return home to meet this new threat. The republicans were now heavily outnumbered by 2,000 National Army troops supported by artillery and armoured cars. On 4 August the republicans started to slip away under cover of a rearguard action by the Cork brigades. And on the morning of Saturday 5 August, General Murphy led the National Army troops into Kilmallock. Many collapsed by the roadside, exhausted, and slept by their rifles.[8] For the republicans, it was a retreat not a rout, but it was a defining moment in the Civil War and many Volunteers simply returned home.

A number of important buildings were burned by republican forces retreating ahead of the National Army. Many cut-stone barracks and fine houses were destroyed. When the order was given to evacuate Mitchelstown Castle this neo-gothic landmark was consigned to the flames. Other large houses in County Cork were more fortunate – Bowen's Court, just a short distance away, remained untouched. According to Elizabeth Bowen, the republicans occupied the house for some days, laid mines up the avenue, rested, read Kipling and left.[9] The Honourable Mrs Amy Lysaght, who grew up in Newmarket and was friendly with Moylan, recalled that even at the height of the war he made sure she could join the hunt and the Dower House on the Aldworth Estate where she lived with her parents survived unscathed and unthreatened while many similar houses were burned.[10] On 16 August the *Irish Independent* reported that republican forces had moved west and that de Valera had been in the district 'with Irregular leaders who occupied several mansions including Shanbally Castle. They had also occupied Cahir Park House but left after the occupation of Tipperary town by National troops; these places were not destroyed.'

We know something of Moylan's view on the destruction of historic buildings from his stance in later years when Shanbally Castle came to his attention again. His was one of the few political voices to object to the then Fianna Fáil government's decision to demolish what was in fact one of the largest and most striking examples of Georgian architecture in Ireland. A more compelling piece of evidence is found in Tom Doyle's account of the Civil War in Kerry, in which he describes the burning of the new section of the Great Southern Hotel by republican troops on or about 14 August: 'the older part of the hotel was spared destruction thanks to the intervention of Seán Moylan, the republican Director of Operations, who appreciated that the Great Southern was the lynchpin of Killarney's tourist industry'.[11]

It was a feature of this war that buildings were torched to deny Provisional Government forces the use of them as barracks, but many country houses were lost in this bitter struggle. In early August Otway Castle was burned out with only two pianos and a few small articles saved.[12] Buttevant Barracks was burned as the republicans withdrew, and on 12 August Lynch burned his headquarters at Fermoy Barracks before retreating into the hills. The second phase of the war had begun.

One of the first major casualties of the guerrilla campaign was Michael Collins, killed at Béal na mBláth on 22 August. It has been said that Collins was on a peace mission at the time of his death. He had received an overture from some prominent Cork citizens and, quite separately, from Dan Breen. Other senior republican figures favoured peace – de Valera was one, Florrie O'Donoghue another. Liam Deasy, it seems, was already convinced that the war was lost. Deasy and de Valera were both in the vicinity of Béal na mBláth on the day of the ambush but that appears to be happenstance. In any event Collins was one of the few men who had the charisma and contacts in Cork to bring about a settlement and when he died at the tail end of a hastily prepared ambush, any prospect of a halt to the fighting died with him.

Collins' well-documented last days provide a glimpse of this stage of the war. He made his way to Cork city, which had been abandoned by the republicans in mid-August. The *Cork Examiner* was on the side of the Provisional Government from the outset and the anti-Treaty forces smashed its printing presses before departing. Throughout the south, normal life had begun to grind to a halt. Food supplies were interrupted and two weeks previously the GPO had announced that mail would no longer be carried to Munster. The bridges at Mallow and Annacotty had been blown up. The Cork to Bandon road was blocked by felled trees. General Eoin O'Duffy had travelled some of the way with Collins before going on a tour of inspection to the Kanturk, Rathmore and Killarney areas, during which he was ambushed three times.

As the conventional phase of the war turned into a guerrilla struggle, the position of the republicans became even more precarious. The National Army knew their enemy, their names and where they lived, and in due course they knew the terrain, the tactics and the hideouts. More importantly, in most urban areas they enjoyed the broad support of the civilian population. Meanwhile the republicans had finite supplies of money and ammunition that could only be replenished by seizures from the pro-Treaty faction or by importing arms, which had become increasingly difficult.

In late August a newspaper reported 'the capture of Seán Moylan, the well-known Irregular leader with eighteen others at Nawd [*sic*] in Cork'.[13] The report is detailed, specific and wrong; Moylan seems to have slipped away.

Some information can be gleaned from the *Limerick War News*, a pro-Treaty propaganda sheet in circulation at the time. It records an attack at Newmarket on 7 September that was repulsed by the National Army:

> A very determined attack was made on the town of Newmarket by about 400 irregulars led by Seán Moylan on the night of 7 Inst. The attack commenced at 12 o'clock midnight and continued until 8 a.m. the following morning.
>
> A simultaneous attack was made on the barracks and two houses on the opposite side of the street held by the troops. Four men who occupied one of the houses were overpowered after their ammunition became exhausted but three men in another house, although attacked by Thompson guns, still refused to surrender.[14]

Another edition of the *Limerick War News* dated 18 September reads: 'News has just reached Limerick that Seán Moylan, the notorious Irregular leader, has been captured by the troops.'[15] Again the report was wrong but its language reflects the fortunes of war. Ten weeks previously Moylan had been a respected Dáil Deputy and O/C of Cork No. 4 Brigade. By mid-September he was classed as a 'notorious Irregular leader'.

We know that Moylan was back in Knockavorheen in mid-September, because Jim Riordan recalled Moylan lending him his old Spanish revolver when he went to Knocknagree fair. Later that day Riordan found himself hemmed in at the fair by Provisional

Government troops and was fortunate to be able to shoot his way out.[16]

The war was taking a depressing turn. The killing of republican prisoners provides a stark example. Dorothy Macardle records that between 1 August and 23 September twelve republican prisoners were shot dead in custody; ten more were shot dead whilst unarmed and six were shot dead on Ben Bulben in Sligo.[17]

Shortly afterwards Moylan was one of those who signed the Declaration by the Republican Army Executive reaffirming their determination to continue the struggle. On 25 October he was one of a number of republican Deputies who met at a secret location in Dublin, as the 'Second Dáil Éireann', to appoint a Council of State which included Moylan, Austin Stack, Robert Barton, Count Plunkett, J. J. O'Kelly, Laurence Ginnell, Seán T. O'Kelly, Kathleen O'Callaghan, Mary MacSwiney, P. J. Ruttledge, M. P. Colivet and Seán O'Mahoney.[18]

The Emergency Powers Act had been passed by the Provisional Government on 1 August. On 26 September, the Minister for Defence, Richard Mulcahy, put forward a motion to amend the act giving Military Courts authority to sit and impose the death sentence on civilians for possession of arms and kindred offences. It also provided for internment. Simultaneously, an amnesty was offered with a cut-off date of 15 October.

Despite this turn of events the ambush war in the south and west continued with vigour. Old tactics of blowing up bridges and trenching roads were revived. The pro-Treaty troops were in many places confined to barracks for fear of ambush.

In early November Moylan led an ambush against the National Army near Millstreet. It appears the republicans felled a tree across the road, blocking the path of the troops, who then sent for reinforcements from Macroom. Moylan and a number of republicans ambushed the reinforcements. The report is brief and states: 'Captain McDermott of the National Army was wounded and the others are known to have suffered heavy casualties.'[19]

The first four executions under the new Emergency Powers Act took place on 17 November; the same day that Erskine Childers was tried in secret by court-martial. Kevin O'Higgins, Minister for Home Affairs, was determined to see Childers' republican publicity machine shut down, come what may. He referred to Childers in the Dáil as 'the Englishman [who] keeps steadily, callously and ghoulishly on his career of striking at the heart of this nation'.[20] It is difficult to avoid any other conclusion but that the Provisional Government intended to see Childers dead. He was executed while awaiting an appeal against a refusal of an application of habeas corpus. The obvious illegality of the proceedings echoed what had taken place in the spring of the previous year when the British Army had been court-martialling and executing rebel prisoners.

The next wave of executions took place on 30 November. John Murphy, Patrick Farrelly and Joseph Spooner were shot by firing squad. The republican war effort became more uneven and fragmented. Columns were split because of the difficulty in finding accommodation and food for large numbers of men; others were reduced by capture or casualties. Many republicans were forced to sleep in dugouts as the winter closed in. The Free State practice of holding senior republican prisoners on suspended sentence of death grew, with the judgments to be implemented in the event of any attacks on the National Army.

The *Freeman's Journal* records the capture in December of Jeremiah Philpot, who was en route to the theatre to see *The Lady of the Rose*.[21] The report claims Philpot was Moylan's adjutant. This is one of those areas where it is difficult to separate myth from fact – Philpot may have been Moylan's adjutant but Moylan had left Ireland in the second week of November 1922.[22]

23

OVERSEAS

Moylan was in a position to get men out of Ellis Island, and nobody here knows anything about it.

IRA Chief-of-Staff, 23 April 1926[1]

We now know that Liam Lynch sent Moylan to the United States in November 1922 to raise money and buy arms. It is likely that had he stayed in Ireland, he would have been captured and executed. No doubt Lynch knew this too. And it appears that his health was again a worrying factor.

On 9 November *The Irish Times* reported on a 'concentration of republicans in Carriganimmy between Macroom and Millstreet under the command of Seán Moylan MP … after two hours' fighting the republicans retreated across country'. Tim Cronin of Kiskeam gives this account from 'the other side of the hill':

Before the attack on Millstreet Barracks. There was an 'armoured car' stuck out the road and Jack Henry Murphy and myself were told to see the 'steward' at Drishane who was very friendly to us and stay until further orders. It was a desperate night with rain and in spite of being clad with good trenchcoats we were wet clean through and the 'steward' seeing our condition brought us a drop of whiskey. He was in the act of pouring some when Seán Moylan came in. The 'steward'

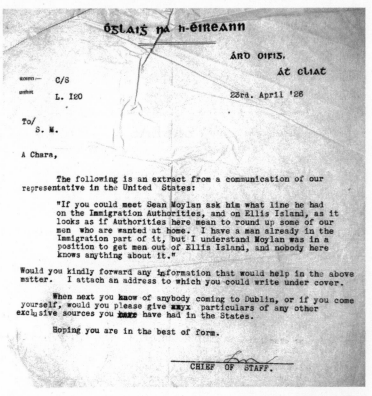

'I understand Moylan was in a position to get men out of Ellis island and nobody here knows anything about it'.

gave him the bottle saying 'you can do the honours now Seán' and as Jack Murphy said afterwards 'If it was cyanide it wouldn't harm you.'[2]

Moylan left Ireland the following day. According to family sources, he was picked up by a fishing boat off the coast of Kerry. He travelled to England, where at Rawtenstall in Lancashire on 2 December he married his fiancée, Nora Murphy of Kiskeam. There was a small Volunteer outfit in Manchester and Salford, and these contacts were used to get Moylan a false passport in the name of John Morris, motor mechanic, which was stamped by the British Foreign Office on 28

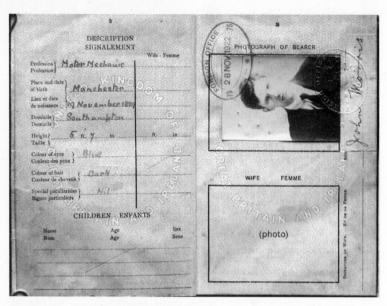

Moylan's false passport in the name of John Morris.

Pages from Moylan's false passport. Note the date stamp of 4 April when Moylan arrived in Hamburg and that he was still in Germany some weeks after Lynch's death.

November 1922.[3] Moylan and his new wife spent a few days together in London before he left for Southampton, from where he sailed to the United States to raise funds for the war effort. His passport was stamped at the American consulate office on 6 December 1922, the same day that Westminster legislation brought the Irish Free State into existence. Nora returned to her teaching post in the north of England.

Two days later Liam Mellows, Dick Barrett, Joe McKelvey and Rory O'Connor were shot by firing squad as a reprisal for the killing of Seán Hales. They had been in custody for five months. They were not the subject of any charge or judicial process. The killings were justified by the government as a deterrent to others.

The next reference to Moylan can be found in a letter dated 21 December 1922 from Lynch to Joe McGarrity, a wealthy businessman and Clan na Gael fundraiser for the republican cause: 'You have by now met Comdt Gen. Seán Moylan who has been sent by Army Council as Executive Representative to Clan ... Brigadier Leahy will give him some assistance. Both had to be allowed to travel owing to breakdown in health as a result of activities during both wars.'[4] Other letters passing between Lynch, Moylan and McGarrity show that there were plans to bring heavy weaponry into Ireland. McGarrity's handwritten notes confirm the long shopping list: 'four mountain batteries, four guns each ... four larger guns, extra parts, as much ammunitions as possible ...'[5] The artillery was the prize that might still make the difference in the war. McGarrity's notes also set out his calculations of the funds needed and how this money would be raised.

Moylan was precariously short of funds: 'The story about this being the land of the flowing is all rot. I'm always on the "bum" and shall be under the necessity of holding up a bank if the fellows here don't come across with ... cash.'[6] Nevertheless, he was developing a range of unusual skills: acquiring fake identity papers, using false addresses, corresponding via safe houses, moving men and large sums of money across frontiers and organising arms deals. He knew how to get men through Ellis Island and his knowledge in this area would be called on again in 1926, when Moss Twomey, acting Chief-of-Staff of the IRA, contacted him on behalf of Andy Cooney (IRA Chief-of-Staff 1925) who was then in America on a fundraising drive and in need of this covert information. Moylan also knew that letters were being intercepted by British intelligence, feared informants were at work and he was concerned about a threat to his life. His fears about detection were well founded. Letters between Lynch and Moylan had been passing through a safe house in London, but British intelligence intercepted some of this correspondence and sent it to the Provisional Government in Dublin. There was a strong interest in putting a stop to Moylan's activities.

Captured memos reveal Lynch's increasing impatience and urgent demands in the early months of 1923. He wrote to Moylan: 'A few pieces of artillery would save the situation, shells if procurable, Thompson ammunition is badly needed.'[7] 'Even one piece of artillery … moved around … would completely demoralise the enemy … and end the war.'[8] And on a personal note, he mentions Moylan's first cousins Con and Liam Moylan from Newmarket: 'Your cousin Liam is under sentence of death. I feel certain though this will not be carried out as enemies are using such [to] terrorise. But the action had the desired effect on Con who surrendered to save Liam.'[9]

On the Civil War generally, Lynch's letters to Moylan and to McGarrity are markedly unrealistic, indicating that victory was achievable and just around the corner. In fact by that stage the Provisional Government held all the towns and although the republicans made many rural areas impassable, their campaign was handicapped by lack of ammunition and depleted resources. As a result there were fewer ambush engagements and sniping coupled with sabotage became more common. There were many occasions when combatants recognised a comrade on the other side. Johnnie Jones, a Volunteer of the Newmarket battalion, recognised a friend in the midst of a group of National Army troops; he did not abandon the sniping operation but it caused him to direct his fire more carefully.[10] Many others switched sides, usually from pro- to anti-

Treaty. A number were executed for treason. The country was in an ugly, ungovernable stand-off.

By early 1923 some senior Volunteers were talking openly about the means to bring the war to an end. Florrie O'Donoghue was one. Others had to confront that issue along with the prospect of being executed imminently, for example Liam Deasy, who had been captured in mid-January. It brought about his famous invitation to other republicans to surrender. In a captured letter Moylan wrote: 'Deasy's attitude knocked me silly. I thought he'd be the last man to cave in. It wasn't a question of being able to win with us. It was that we were right, that we couldn't surrender being right. It wasn't cowardice on his part I know and I have feared greatly that the boys must have got hell in the south since I left.'[11] It is more than possible that cut off and far from home, Moylan did not know quite how desperate the situation was and may not have persisted in his mission had he known the full grim picture.

The prisons were another source of tragedy and atrocity. By the time of the ceasefire in spring 1923, there were almost 12,000 republican prisoners in custody. Many had been interned without trial. Many others had been captured in arms and were awaiting the firing squad. For families all over Ireland these were months of great anxiety and strain, never knowing when news might come that a loved one had been executed. One of these prisoners was Jim Riordan of Knockavorheen, but he managed to swap identities with a 'no charge' internee while a former comrade who had become a National Army officer turned a blind eye.[12]

Conditions varied widely from prison to prison. Food and hygiene had been poor since the start of the conflict. Mistreatment had been institutionalised, torture was common and the practice of firing into cells had become a blood sport.[13] For some reason prison conditions in Kerry were by far and away the hardest. Near Ballyseedy Castle there is a memorial to one of the worst atrocities committed by the National Army. The vindictiveness of this massacre may have its origins in a dispute that occurred shortly after the start of the Civil War. The republicans fined Pat O'Connor, an elderly pro-Treaty sympathiser, for allegedly passing information to the enemy; he refused to pay and his cattle were taken for sale. His outraged son Paddy subsequently joined the National Army. We can infer that this incident continued to fester and O'Connor was blamed for much of the torture and brutality inflicted on anti-Treaty prisoners in Kerry. A further downward spiral of bitterness and terror occurred with the execution of eleven prisoners on 20 January, four of them from Tralee Barracks. The republicans laid a trap-mine at Knocknagoshel on 6 March killing Lieutenant Paddy O'Connor, two officers of the Dublin brigade and two soldiers, in response to the torture of republican prisoners at Castleisland.[14] This led to savage reprisals by the National Army.

Within days nine prisoners were taken from the barracks in Tralee to Ballyseedy crossroads where they were tied to a mine on the roadside. The mine was detonated, killing eight of the men. A single prisoner was blown over the ditch where he lay with only minor injuries; in the carnage he was not missed. He escaped and was able to give the lie to the official story that the men had been killed by accident. There was an identical incident the same day, when prisoners were brought out of Killarney prison and tied to a mine that was blown up at Countess Bridge. Miraculously one man again survived. These atrocities involved prisoners from different prisons on the same date, which indicates a degree of planning and collusion. One other similar event took place a few nights later, when five prisoners were taken from the Bahaghs workhouse near Cahirciveen. They were shot in the legs to prevent escape and then blown up.

Documents released to the National Archives in 2008 disclosed that compensation claims subsequently made by the relatives of these men implicate a previously unknown section of the National Army called the 'Visiting Committee'. Maurice Riordan's claim states that his son was 'done to death by being dragged over a mine on the public road' and another from the father of Daniel Shea is supported by a covering letter from Inspector C. Reynolds of Cahirciveen, stating that 'this act was perpetrated by a number of men of the National

Army known as the "Visiting Committee" and was not an official reprisal'. But in 1923 the Provisional Government cleared the army of any wrongdoing, and all compensation claims associated with this horrific incident were rejected.[15] It was a low point in the Civil War. While torture of prisoners, particularly in Kerry, was widespread, much more commonly republicans, when taken in arms, were shot without any court-martial.

Elsewhere on 10 April, a party of men including Liam Lynch had been discovered in one of the many round-ups of the time and were pursued by the soldiers. They were comfortably outdistancing their pursuers when Lynch was shot and badly wounded on the slopes of Knockmealdown. He was carried down the mountainside by National Army troops and died that evening after expressing a wish to be buried with Michael Fitzgerald of Fermoy. Austin Stack, Dan Breen, Todd Andrews, Seán Gaynor and Frank Barrett were captured a few days later. Frank Aiken took over leadership of the IRA after Lynch's death and declared an end to armed resistance on 30 April.

Moylan's false passport shows a stamp at Hamburg on 4 April 1923.[16] Another letter to McGarrity indicates that he was in Germany involved in a massive arms purchase.[17] It calls to mind his earlier gun-running venture in Dublin, when he described the guns as: 'the rubbish that is produced in certain European ports for sale to revolutionaries'.[18] After five years of war he knew something about weapons and no doubt he went to Germany to ensure the quality of the arms. News from home must have filtered through and a letter bearing a Hamburg–Amerika line logo from Moylan to McGarrity, dated 24 April, tells its own story:

> Your man arrived and delivered his stuff all right. We have made … practically complete arrangements for securing our stuff and exporting it but owing to press reports and the apparent slump in our stock we decided it was better not to close the deal until we found out if our people could handle … your man left here for England where he is to get in touch with my wife … I trust all will be well but we certainly

have had severe reverses during the past few weeks … I am anxiously waiting for the return of our man. There is no use in my moving until I hear from him but I feel that I ought to be at home. If our fellas have got to take the gruel, I want to be with them … all will yet be well and we'll pull a victory out of the fire in spite of fate.[19]

After Lynch's death communications from Ireland ground to a halt, making it hard for Moylan to judge the political situation. Pa Murray, the republican O/C in Britain, was in much the same boat and wrote to Moylan on 8 May: 'they have not sent me one written word since Liam's death … I do not know how matters stand'.[20] Moylan's response says it all: 'I await a definite reply from Ireland together with some news as to conditions … Lynch certainly believed in keeping in touch with his outposts. I am sorry about his death. I'm damn glad he went down fighting … we shall have to go underground [and] keep up the irritation against the Free State'.[21] Two weeks later in a coded letter he wrote of Lynch as 'wonderful, brave and generous without any trace of materialism … he was a good comrade and a brave soldier'.[22]

The anxiety and uncertainty of Moylan's position in Germany was shared by his wife. She was one of the key contacts on the communications chain and the stress and strain eventually took its toll. Since their marriage they had spent only five days together. Moylan wrote and asked her to get a passport so she could travel over for a few weeks, but this did not happen. With news of the suspension of offensive operations filtering through to Germany, the arms deal did not progress.

The Civil War was a bitter blow for Moylan. Not only was it the end of all he had worked for, but the list of his friends and comrades killed in action or shot by firing squad was a long one. Cathal Brugha died under the guns of the army he had helped to establish. Rory O'Connor, Liam Mellows, Joe McKelvey, Dick Barrett and Erskine Childers were shot by firing squad. Liam Lynch had died on the slopes of Knockmealdown. And then there were the friends on the other side, whose deaths were no easier to bear: Michael Collins, Denis

Galvin and many others. It must have made a mockery of the deaths of other friends in the War of Independence, such as Paddy Clancy, Paddy McCarthy and Charlie O'Reilly.

It is generally accepted that over 3,000 people had been killed and many more were seriously wounded. The country was in a weak position, it owed colossal debts to Britain to pay off the sums judged owing after the Treaty, and much of the population was unemployed. The 1923 general election was fought against this backdrop. The new pro-Treaty party Cumann na nGaedheal put the blame for the state of the country squarely on the anti-Treaty faction. Most of the senior anti-Treaty figures were dead, on the run, in prison or had emigrated and were unable to answer the charge. There were numerous instances where the political opponents of the Provisional Government were beaten and intimidated. Éamon de Valera was seized by soldiers while addressing a crowd at Ennis. Some spectators were wounded in the incident and, although he later topped the poll, de Valera remained in prison for nearly a year without charge. It was truly said in the English newspapers that the new government elected itself at the point of a bayonet.[23]

Moylan was back in Cork in December 1923. He had been unwell, and, as he confided in letters to McGarrity, his wife had suffered a breakdown 'more or less'.[24] The Moylans travelled to the United States on another false passport in the name of John and Nora Harrison. The passport was issued on 27 December 1923 and the visa stamped at Southampton on 2 January 1924.[25] Moylan was en route to New York on another fundraising tour and it is likely that he took Nora with him because of her health and perhaps, the war having ended, this latest trip was less dangerous.

In a letter in early summer to Jim Riordan of Knockavorheen Moylan mentioned Denis Galvin of Meenskehy, who in 1921 had driven a bride to her wedding in the captured touring car. Galvin had gone over to the pro-Treaty side but had never made the emotional break with his former comrades. His torn loyalties may have saved Riordan's life when he was captured and spotted by Galvin on an

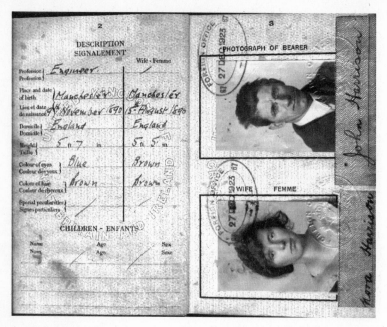

False passport for Seán and Nora Moylan in the name of John and Nora Harrison, which they used to travel to America in 1923.

identity parade in Limerick Gaol. They quietly acknowledged each other and the bonds of Tureengarriffe and Clonbanin transcended Civil War politics. 'Is it there you are Jim?' said Galvin. 'I won't breathe a word.'[26] Now he was dead. Moylan wrote 'poor devil' and wondered if anything had been done for his mother: 'I've always been sorry for him,' he said, 'and for the sake of old times we shouldn't let [her] be down and out.' For the rest of his life Moylan would voice a deep-seated concern for the men who served under him. He urged Riordan to let him know who needed financial help: 'I'm only half dressed myself too,' he wrote, 'but I wouldn't give it to say to anybody here that we're living well while the boys at home are on the rocks.'[27]

The Moylans were back in Kiskeam by early September 1924. By the end of the year Moylan's military career had ended in disgrace. We know this because of a curious letter to McGarrity, dated 29 January 1925, in which Moylan writes: 'he asked me if I was, as he had heard, reduced to the ranks, and if so, while he was in favour of discipline, he would try and do anything possible for me'.[28] What had happened? Moylan had served with distinction throughout the War of Independence and the Civil War and was one of Ireland's best-known military leaders. An answer is suggested in a letter emanating from IRA headquarters on 17 June 1924, which reads: 'I should be glad to learn the result of the "row", my personal opinion is that if Moylan is recalled or returns before someone goes out to replace him, the business in which we are interested will suffer considerably.'[29] 'The business' was fundraising. Moylan had many contacts in Clan na Gael and it is apparent that he liked the United States and was good at raising money. It seems from his correspondence, however, that two of the men sent over to support these activities were idle and in one case extremely disruptive. He was not given the backing he needed. It may well be that he acted against orders to remain in the United States and he was reduced to the ranks for this reason.

Seán and Nora had lived in Brooklyn in a small walk-up apartment with a fold-up 'tin lizzie bed' and the most basic of furnishings. Moylan liked New York but Nora less so. She plainly missed her mother, who had suffered her own losses – a brother died in a bar fight in New York and the deaths of two of her adult children: Nellie Rose to meningitis and John J. to Spanish flu. When Nora became pregnant with her first child she pressed to return home. It is likely that the fundraising 'row' and this personal crisis came to a head in the late summer of 1924. With the baby imminent, Moylan left New York and returned to Ireland with his wife. They arrived home in September 1924 just a few weeks before the birth of their first child, Peig.

24

In the Wilderness

For most of the 1920s the Moylans lived with Nora's parents at the Shamrock House in Kiskeam. Visits to Newmarket were frequent and Peig spent long periods in the care of her paternal grandmother. Moylan started work again as a jobbing carpenter and builder but the prospects were bleak. The era was marked by institutional discrimination against republicans and the bitterness of the Civil War permeated every aspect of life in Ireland.[1] Only a trickle of work came through: a few house renovations, a bridge – probably one he had previously demolished. Then he was given a contract of some substance by the Drishane nuns near Millstreet, perhaps implying that the superior, Mother Anthony from Bandon, sympathised with the Moylans' straightened circumstances. The nuns had their own republican connections through Terence MacSwiney, whose sister Kit and Aunt Kate were both members of the order.[2] The timing of the Drishane contract was impeccable: it got Moylan back on his feet and gave him a measure of financial stability.

Writing to Joe McGarrity in January 1925, Moylan expresses a growing disillusion with abstentionist politics and suggests a drift away from Sinn Féin and the IRA:

I think we'd do more towards the ultimate realisation of our ideals if we tried to help our people economically or rather showed them by precept or example how they might help themselves ... I believe money could be usefully spent on commissions of inquiry into fisheries and agriculture and co-operative societies and co-operative working brought about along the lines of the findings of these commissions. This would be, to my mind, peaceful penetration as opposed to what I call the stone wall-butting as presently practised.[3]

Letters to and from the United States continued and in March 1926 McGarrity wrote about money being wasted on political action

Letter from Joe McGarrity dated March 1926 (Moylan Papers).

going nowhere. He claimed that the oath of allegiance to the British monarch was not going to be removed and 'if necessary to keep in control, the Free State crowd will require that each candidate take [it] before his name can go on the ballot'.[4] McGarrity wrote again in July wishing for a return to happier days when they could 'talk the night away':

> I have cleared out of New York and opened a shebang in Atlantic City. On the mantelpiece as the patrons enter, General Moylan in plaster looks them over and considerable guessing is indulged in as to who the grim-looking fellow is. To those of the true National faith he is an Irish General, to others he may be Abe Lincoln at twenty-five or a soldier of the American Revolution ... you are likely to become a barbary pirate captured while rounding up the early settlers of Atlantic City.

McGarrity's preoccupation on divisions within the IRA was also expressed. He believed that whatever chance a united republican or near republican force would have of success, a divided one would have little hope. Just the same, he ended confidently: 'I have an abiding faith to see the job finished, and as Joxer says may it be a darlin' funeral.'[5]

Moylan was constantly in receipt of correspondence from Sinn Féin and the IRA, and was in contact with other irreconcilables such as Mary MacSwiney, Peadar O'Donnell, Austin Stack and Countess Markievicz. His personal papers include a travel voucher to enable him attend the Sinn Féin Árd Fheis in November 1925, but he did not go. He was invited to join the IRA Reserve List but did not respond. When Éamon de Valera formed his new political party in 1926 he hoped to persuade moderates like Moylan to stand for election. Moylan did not go forward but Constance Markievicz embraced the new republican party and presided at its first meeting. Despite a broken arm, she canvassed vigorously during the election campaign of 1927. Her arm was still in a sling when the Soldiers of Destiny won forty-four seats, but by mid-July she was dead. Moylan recalled a far-off day in 1919 when she paid a visit to Newmarket to address a rally. *Kiskeam versus The Empire* describes the ruse adopted to get her out of town under the noses of the RIC:

It was noted in the gathering that the Countess's build and appearance were very similar to those of a young Newmarket girl Madge McCartie … Madge donned the clothes of the Countess and accompanied by Meme [*sic*] Moylan paraded up the street of her native town and entered the Railway Hotel. Constance for her part had dressed up in men's wear and made her way out the back of Moylans' house, through the workshop window. [6]

Waiting in the field behind was Corney Lenihan, who drove her to Drominarigle in his pony and trap. On the Sunday morning word went back to Kiskeam to prepare for an important visitor:

There was pandemonium. Dan Guiney, Mike Daly, Jim Riordan, Dan Flynn and a host of others hastily erected a platform in the field … When all was ready, Con Sullivan of Drominarigle drove into town in his pony and trap accompanied by [Constance Markievicz], the most distinguished guest ever recorded in Kiskeam with perhaps the exception of Éamon de Valera himself.[7]

Those were heady days when anything seemed possible. Barely a decade later rural Ireland remained poverty-stricken and much of the optimism was gone. It was a bleak, forbidding time.

In 1928 Moylan received another overture from de Valera with an official notification of his selection for Seanad Éireann.[8] He did not go forward. There was much similar unanswered correspondence.

There were other problems in the area. Offenders who had felt the hand of the Republican Courts in the pre-Treaty period, and had been deported or received stiff sentences, now felt they could take their revenge on members of the IRA who no longer had any power or protection. Not far from Kiskeam was a crossroads which no ex-IRA

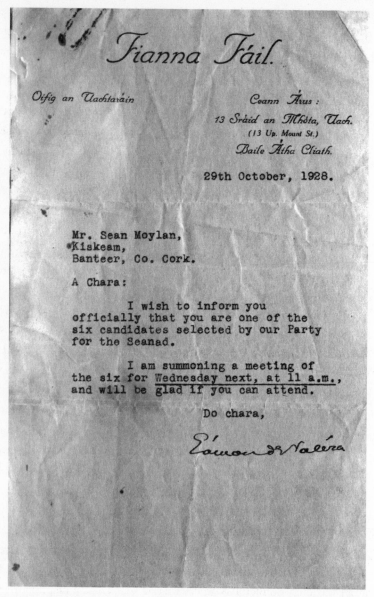

Letter from de Valera informing Moylan of his candidature for the Seanad.

man could pass at night without fear of assault or worse. One evening
Moylan was accosted by five or six men who advanced and knocked

him off his bicycle. He drew his old Spanish revolver and shot the ringleader through the shoulder. There were no further assaults and no repercussions. There is no evidence to suggest that he engineered the encounter but it is clear he was alive to the risk and perhaps invited the confrontation.

Living in the locality was a Volunteer named Edward Drew, who had served Moylan well during the War of Independence but whose allegiance was on the pro-Treaty side in the Civil War. After the war Drew and a number of his brothers joined the Civic Guards, which prompted local republicans to shoot at the family home. Moylan let it be known that the gunmen would be answerable to him if there was any repetition. There was none.[9] He appeared to recognise that times had moved on and these men needed to earn a living and build a future. The episode captures the almost tribal loyalties that existed during this period.

Another issue that intruded on Moylan's life at this time was the question of pensions. The Military Service Pensions Acts from 1924 onwards were intended to reward the soldiers of the Republic: an active service medal and a pension for those who had carried arms, a mere medal for those involved in the struggle who had not carried arms, a wound pension for those who had been injured in the course of the struggle, and what was euphemistically described as a special allowance for the holders of medals whose means were limited. For those who engaged in the War of Independence, their pensions and allowances were pitifully small and many former Volunteers got nothing.

Senior officers were called upon to authenticate the service record of the applicants. The line of demarcation between an active service medal and an ordinary medal was thin, and the line between those who had served in minor capacities and those who had not served at all was even thinner. No officer wished to exclude a neighbour or a neighbour's child. The applications were endless as the poverty in Ireland during this period was extreme. The public funds were operated by the Department of Defence, which was not very sympathetic. The initial nucleus of civil servants had served under the old regime and

Referee R.17.

OIFIG AN RÉITEÓRA,
(OFFICE OF THE REFEREE)
BEAIRICÍ UÍ GRÍOBHTHA,
(GRIFFITH BARRACKS)
CUAR-BHÓTHAR THEAS,
(SOUTH CIRCULAR ROAD)
BAILE ÁTHA CLIATH.
(DUBLIN)

Ref. No. 49   14 OCT 1936.

A Chara,

I am directed by the Referee to refer to your application under the terms of the Military Service Pensions Act, 1934, and in accordance with the provisions of Statutory Rules and Orders 1936, No. 61, I am to notify you that on the evidence submitted, the findings of the Referee in respect of your application are as follows :—

Service Period.	Duration of Active Service during each period, as established to the satisfaction of the Referee.	Appropriate pensionable service.
(1) Week commencing 23/4/16	Nil	Nil
(2) (a) 1/4/16 – 22/4/16 (b) 30/4/16 – 31/3/17	Nil	Nil
(3) 1/4/17 – 31/3/18	ENTIRE PERIOD	⅔ of 1 year
(4) 1/4/18 – 31/3/19	ENTIRE PERIOD	⅔ of 1 year
(5) 1/4/19 – 31/3/20	ENTIRE PERIOD	1 year
(6) 1/4/20 – 31/3/21	ENTIRE PERIOD	2 years
(7) 1/4/21 – 11/7/21	ENTIRE PERIOD	1 year
(8) 12/7/21 – 30/6/22	ENTIRE PERIOD	1 year
(9) 1/7/22 – 31/3/23	ENTIRE PERIOD	2 years
(10) 1/4/23 – 30/9/23	ENTIRE PERIOD	1 year

Grade of rank on 1st critical date   B   TOTAL— 9 years.
     ,,   ,,   ,,   2nd   A

I am also to inform you that if you desire to submit any additional evidence or to make any representations with a view to the revision of these findings, such evidence or representations must be submitted in writing to the Referee and must reach this office not later than   5 NOV 1936

The Referee will give full consideration to any evidence or representations so submitted, and after such consideration will make his report to the Minister. If no additional evidence or representation is furnished before the date indicated, the Referee will thereupon make his report to the Minister.

I am to add that the report of the Referee, when made, will, subject as mentioned in Section 9 of the Act, become final and conclusive and binding on all persons and tribunals whatsoever.

Mise, le meas,

M. Seán Moylan, T.D.
Kiskeam,
Banteer,
Co Cork

Rúnaí.

SP 3464 5000 3-36 EC F6321

Record of the IRA pension granted to Seán Moylan.

continued the colonial style of making limited funds go as far as possible and drafting regulations that only they could understand. A typical response was: 'there is no evidence that the disability from which you suffer is attributable to ... military service as claimed. In any event the degree of your disablement does not reach the minimum required by the Act for the grant of pension viz 80% in the case of disease.'[10]

If any members of the flying columns were wounded or became ill during the period of the struggle, there were limited opportunities for them to get medical treatment. They had to be cared for, nursed and looked after by Cumann na mBan and the many supporters, who freely supplied them with medicine, clothing and all the other necessities required. Mrs B. of Mallow had a Cumann na mBan medal and her husband had an active service medal, and when he died suddenly she applied for a special allowance from what she hoped was a grateful country. The response from the Department of Defence was:

I am directed by An tAire to state that one of the statutory conditions for the award of a special allowance in Mrs B.'s case is that she is duly awarded a service (1917–21) medal in respect of continuous membership of Cumann na mBan during the period of three months which ended 11 July 1921. A medal was issued to her some time ago but as a result of further enquiries in the matter it has not been established that the medal was duly awarded. Accordingly it is regretted that she is not eligible for a special allowance.

Mrs B.'s friends came to her assistance, as did Moylan, and eighteen months later the Department of Defence reversed its decision and awarded her a special allowance of just under £2 a week. She got nothing for the eighteen months in which they engaged in the re-examination of her case.[11]

Moylan was intensely loyal to the men he served with and the pensions issue would resurface throughout his time in public office.

In the late 1930s he was still in correspondence with Tom Barry in support of an applicant's claim.

Towards the end of the 1920s Moylan won a contract to build the new parish church in Kiskeam. It was consecrated in 1930 by the Bishop of Kerry, Dr O'Brien, and dedicated to the Sacred Heart. The parish priest, Father Jeremiah Brick, was inclined to let politics drift into his Sunday morning sermons and his opinions did not suit Moylan. To the delight of the Kiskeam congregation Moylan interrupted one of his homilies with the words: 'Stop your politics Father and preach the Gospel!'[12]

Politically, Moylan was gradually drawn towards the new Fianna Fáil party. One suspects that personal loyalty to de Valera was an important motivation. Many others of similar outlook were also swayed: Dan Breen, Seamus Robinson, Oscar Traynor, Frank Aiken, P. J. Ruttledge and Seán Lemass. Moylan was reluctantly attracted to the notion that once power had been achieved, some purposeful steps could be taken towards independence. He could not support Sinn Féin, whose members, out of principle, would never take up their seats. The country was divided by bitterness and beset by poverty and unemployment; economic and social reforms were desperately needed. This was the vacuum de Valera stepped into when he founded Fianna Fáil.

It took Moylan a long time to stand for election. He was reluctant to run against his lifelong friend, Dan Corkery of Macroom, who was then an independent republican TD in north Cork. When he finally stood for office in the February 1932 election, his campaign was fought in the shadow of the Civil War; his daughter Stephanie never forgot the fear, the late night disturbances and the shouts of 'Up Moylan' or 'To Hell with Moylan'.[13] He was successfully elected as a TD for north Cork.

Fianna Fáil was elected to government for a number of reasons. The party had very swiftly developed a strong local organisation. Moreover, the impact of the Wall Street crash tipped an already impoverished Ireland into the depths of recession. Cumann na nGaedheal was operating what we now know as a monetarist policy. Fianna Fáil was prepared to adopt a policy of public spending to get the country moving again. Voters were attracted by the political legacy of Michael Collins, which can be summarised as taking any small step leading to independence whenever the opportunity presented itself. One suspects that many were also reassured by de Valera's pledge that Fianna Fáil would not attempt to end partition by force thus tipping Ireland into another war. Finally, Fianna Fáil had the active support of the *Irish Press*, which ran a series of damaging stories on the government, while a leaked circular indicated that prominent unionists were engaged in raising funds for Cumann na nGaedheal. Like many political campaigns, the 1932 election was lost rather than won. And so, despite a devastatingly funny poster campaign against 'Senor de Valera', Fianna Fáil took power for the first time.[14]

In 1930 Moylan had been given a small stretch of land next to his in-laws. He built a house for his growing family using stones from the tumbled ruins of the old penal church that stood on what is now the lower part of Kiskeam cemetery. By that time the Moylans had five children: a son, Rick (born in 1926) and four daughters, Peig (1924), Mary (1927), Stephanie (1928) and Carmel (1930). Tragically, their young daughter Mary died in September 1932. The violence and tension in the months following the 1932 election were a terrifying and disruptive time for the Moylan children and Stephanie and Mary were sent to Kilmallock to the care of their maiden grand-aunts. The elderly Victorian aunts believed that children should be seen and not heard and failed to recognise the seriousness of Mary's sudden illness. She died of septicaemia following a perforated appendix. In a small country village like Kiskeam, on the fringe of Sliabh Luachra, the burden of grief was shared but the Moylans were heartbroken. Two years later their youngest child, Eileen, was born.

25

DÁIL CAREER 1932–1937

When Fianna Fáil came to power in 1932, the first party meeting was a turbulent affair. President Éamon de Valera was adamant about the urgency of getting rid of the oath of allegiance and the position of governor general. He spoke at length about the latter and the desirability of eliminating all vestiges of British rule. Moylan, who was strongly tipped for ministerial office, and his friend Dan Breen were much more concerned with the relief of poverty, which was endemic in their constituencies. Nonetheless, the party leader continued to explain in detail how essential it was to remove the governor general. When he had concluded he looked down at Breen and Moylan and said: 'Now gentlemen, what have you to say to that?' Breen said nothing but Moylan's reply was unprintable. This incident may explain why he did not become a Parliamentary Secretary until 1937 or a minister until 1943.[1]

There were many pressing difficulties in this period. The new Fianna Fáil administration had to deal with entrenched unemployment and poverty and also had to contend with the threat of a new civil war as both the IRA and the Blueshirts threatened to foment violence. Ireland at that time was a cauldron of anger and discontent. The Dáil mirrored the passions and tensions of the country. It could be a rough and even brutal forum and the Civil War was a recent and painful memory. The following passage from the Dáil record gives a flavour of events:

Mr Moylan: … men like my comrades and myself resent the fact of our being called gunmen. A gunman, sir, is a murderer. We are more used to being shot at than to shoot. It has been unfortunate for us that we have had to use guns and kill people. We never used guns against anybody who was not using them against us. For that reason we resent being called gunmen and we resent these men being called gunmen. Deputy Dillon and others like him who never handled a gun in defence of this country should keep their mouths shut when men and soldiers talk.[2]

De Valera, searching for an outright majority, called a snap general election for January 1933. Moylan's papers contain three telegrams dated 16 December 1932. The first, from the general secretary of Fianna Fáil, states: 'You are invited to speak at Tralee tomorrow at 2.30 p.m.' The second, from de Valera's secretary, reads: 'The President wishes you to be present at Tralee, tomorrow.' And the third, a clarion call from his lifelong friend Father Myles Allman, whose brother Dan was killed at Headford Junction, commands: 'Come Tralee tomorrow without fail.' The rally in Tralee on 17 December was a robust affair:

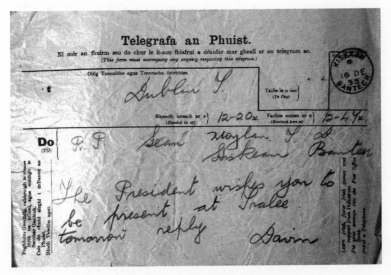

One of the telegrams asking Moylan to be at Tralee on 17 December 1932.

It was well known that every old IRA man in north Cork, Kerry and west Limerick together with every Blueshirt and every unreconstructed republican was in Tralee that day. It was a bruising, passionate meeting and every speaker was heckled and abused. Some of those present later spoke of the atmosphere of hate and anger that pervaded the meeting and made them fear, not for their safety but for their lives. Moylan was the last speaker and was greeted with jeers, abuse and indescribable noise. In a moment of silence he was able to shout: 'Who remembers Clonbanin?' The roar of assent that answered him silenced the hecklers and from there on the meeting was his. The speech he made that day was important politically, opposing a second civil war and backing de Valera:

'I come here among friends, among old comrades with whom I have tramped the roads of Kerry, and with whom I have lain beside in Kerry ditches. I do myself the honour of coupling my name with de Valera when we faced the music of the enemy's guns, and the policy he adopted, and the reason of our coming to Kerry is to prevent the women and children, aye, and the young manhood, of hearing ever again, the guns of the enemy of the nation in Kerry. Kerry has suffered too much. I have stood beside plots and beside republican monuments and watched the tears of mothers and sisters, and seen the fatherless children.'

And then he went on to deride the Blueshirt chief, Eoin O'Duffy:

'I ask myself what is all the shouting about? Who is this famous General O'Duffy? The title of General pre-supposes a military career and a military record, and we have it on the words of General O'Duffy that his is the greatest national military record of any man in Ireland. On his own words we have it. On what foundation was this great edifice of General O'Duffy's military career built up? In 1920 there was a police barrack captured in County Monaghan, at Ballytrain. The officer in charge of the IRA was Commandant Ernie O'Malley, whom some of you old soldiers here know. The total casualties were one RIC man who lost a toe and on the RIC man's big toe the famous edifice of O'Duffy's military career was built up.

'You have a government in power; you have a man leading that government of whom nobody has any need to speak of his national record. The names of Boland's Mills and Mount Street Bridge will go down in history as two of the most outstanding episodes in Irish history, and as we trusted him in 1916 so we trust him now. I was reared in a Fenian household with the Fenian tradition in my heart, and I am confident I am following the right leadership when I am following the leadership of Éamon de Valera.

'We did not altogether blame the Cosgrave government for governing this country. What we blamed them for was governing it in the interest of England. You [now] have a republican government in power, led by the outstanding republican leader of the country, governing the country in the interest of Irishmen. He says that we are at times softhearted, [and] I came here today to appeal, with you, to him to harden his heart a little bit. The Civil War was fought and left sorrow and bitterness in its wake. We want an assurance from President de Valera that there will be no more civil war, and I for one will back him to any length he goes in prevention of another civil war in this country.'[3]

Fianna Fáil won the election with a clear majority.

Not everyone was impressed with Moylan's transition to mainstream politics and around this time a well-known Cork republican and four others arrived at his home in Kiskeam to assassinate him. They searched his house, terrorised his wife and children, and then adjourned to the pub next door to wait for him to return. They did not know that the pub was his brother-in-law's, nor did they know that the message had gone out into the hills and that rifles were being unearthed. Very shortly the premises was surrounded by two dozen members of the old flying column. The incident was quickly over and was never repeated, but it is an illustration of the volatility of the times, the anger, the disappointment, the disillusion and the entrenched tradition of violence for political ends.

There were other, more welcome, visitors to the Moylan's house in Kiskeam, including Dan Breen, who taught Rick Moylan to fish and to poach. When in gregarious mood, Breen would show off his wounds and relate stories of the war to the Moylan children. He and Moylan had much in common, they shared a similar political outlook and both appear to have endured torn loyalties for some years.

In 1934, Moylan was on his way from Cork to the Dáil when he met four IRA prisoners who had been arrested for firing a volley of shots over the grave of their former comrade John (Flyer) Nyhan. The prisoners were being transported to Arbour Hill in Dublin and had embarked on a hunger strike for political status. Moylan gave them his public backing and stated he would resign his Dáil seat if their demands were not met. Press reports show that the prisoners were met by many sympathisers at Kingsbridge station, including Breen, staunch as always, though wisely silent. A letter dated Arbour Hill, 1 March 1934, speaks of Moylan's efforts on behalf of the prisoners:

Dear Seán,

Up to and even after the time I wrote yesterday, our demand for association had not been granted – that is why we went back on strike. However, after a few trips between here and Leinster House, I've discovered that Frank Aiken had actually granted the demand but that there was a blunder in the transmission to here, so we came off again.

I told Joe to see you today to explain the conditions which existed when I wrote you. At the same time, I offer you an apology for my lack of faith in you and for any recriminations in my letter. Of course I am sure you will understand my attitude when you learn that it was not until about 10 p.m. last night that we became aware that our demand for association was granted. Anyhow Seán, I want to thank you for what you have done for us. I would not like you to think that I am ungrateful. We are to be tried next Wednesday, I am hoping for the best. Hoping that this explanation will be satisfactory.

Sincerely, Peter Kearney[4]

Moylan's intervention on the prisoners' behalf coincided with the introduction of proposed new legislation to restrict the wearing of uniforms, badges, banners and other military paraphernalia. In the weeks that followed, the entrenched bitterness of Civil War politics dominated stormy Dáil debates and newspaper headlines, as the 'Wearing of Uniform (restriction) Bill' passed through the various stages of the Oireachtas. Moylan was committed to supporting Fianna Fáil but his efforts on behalf of the IRA men at a time when the government was determined to control the use of guns meant he was persona non grata with de Valera for some time.

Even in the 1940s, old IRA members, who had not conformed, continued to look to Moylan for help. One incident seems to mark the parting of the ways. It concerned a young IRA man, Charlie Kerins of Tralee, who was under sentence of death for the shooting of a detective in Dublin. It was only natural that representations would come to Moylan from Kerry. The reply which he wrote to Roger Kiely, his lifelong friend and his companion of flying column days, was the clearest indication that he had made the transition from guerrilla leader to politician:

A Chara,
I had already had a note from Donal McSweeney in the matter about which you wrote me. Since the matter of government intervention has been raised by the Kerry County Council and since no government decision in regard to the representations thus made has yet been made public, I can offer no opinion as to what the result will be.

All of us in this country concerned in political effort are somewhat the victims of historical circumstance and it may be argued that the present-day IRA are the victims of a historical circumstance which we in Fianna Fáil are in a measure responsible for creating. We are, however, also responsible for the creation of circumstances in this country which preclude the necessity for the utilisation of force. There is no help that can be given to reasoning individuals who will not accept that point of view. The community must protect itself and they who are responsible for the protection of the community must too have safeguards provided for them, otherwise we have chaos. Courts are provided for an examination of such cases as that of Kerins and for deciding on them.

The Court in this case has given its decision. What the government can or will do in relation to an appeal for mercy I cannot prophesy but no government can admit that the trial court was not properly constituted or that its decision was prejudiced.

We in this country are faced with a number of difficulties and with problems which, if we don't solve, we cannot survive as a nation. It is a government's duty to secure the well-being and security of the State and if it is unwilling or incapable of taking action to that end it is unfit to govern. If the view of the general public is that the government in this matter is not doing its impartial duty there is always the remedy in the hands of the people.

It is a responsible and awe-inspiring thing to be charged with the necessity for bringing any young life to a tragic end and it is with a full conception of that responsibility and after the gravest consideration that the government will make its decision in this case.

Is mise le meas,

Seán Moylan[5]

Charlie Kerins was executed.

A review of internal Fianna Fáil records of the period shows that the issues Moylan raised related to creating a better and fairer pension system, both for military service pensions and pensions for widows and orphans.[6] There was a strong streak of idealism in him. He was familiar with poverty, having seen much of it while he was on the run and having experienced the scarcity of work after the Civil War. He continued to run his contracting business and believed he should pay his workmen a little more than the average wage. Not long after being elected he discovered, and he was not the first person to do so, that politics and a one-man business do not go hand-in-hand. The affairs of the nation and the constituency left no room for anything else. With no one to oversee the business, he went broke. His papers are littered with sheriff's notices and solicitors' letters demanding money. It began to be rumoured that he would have to retire from the Dáil and that there would be a by-election in north Cork.[7]

On Saturday 23 March 1935, the *Southern Star* announced the forthcoming resignation of Seán Moylan on the grounds of ill health. It may be that the real issue was financial insolvency. In any event, his friends rallied round, his finances were put back on an even keel and his resignation never came about. For the rest of his life, however, part of Moylan's annual income went towards paying off his debts, which was a difficult situation for a married man with five children to rear and educate.

The year ended on a seasonal note. In December 1935 the editor of the *Cork County Chronicle* invited Moylan to write a new year's message to his constituents. Wryly reflecting on the life of a politician he replied:

These messages are generally composed of two ingredients, seasonal greetings and some light moral platitudes with a liberal seasoning of butter sauce. The current wearers of the toga do not desire to advise. It is only the veriest threat of political extinction that forces a TD onto the platform or into the press. He believes that the only voice to be heard from the pulpit is the healing voice of Christian charity. Furthermore, the modern politician has very little of the 'plamas' of his predecessor. He is in fact inclined to call a spade a bloody spade and leave it at that. In these circumstances then, what manner of message shall be mine? Instead of stressing the good wishes which I extend to all my constituents, instead of promising at no far distant date an Irish Utopia, instead of telling them what fine fellows they all are, I wish to make a plea to them for the politician. In God's name, during the year 1935 make up your minds to give him a dog's chance. Mae West may have said 'come up and see me some time' but none of your representatives has as his slogan 'come up and see me anytime'. The day of the deputation and the personal interview is gone. A twopenny stamp is a first class substitute for a two pound railway ticket or motor drive. Put it in writing and you will save money. Stick to the facts and you will save time. A politician is, to the people, a necessary evil. So is a general election to a politician. At the election, you have an effective method of expressing your opinion of him. In the meanwhile, give him a chance to carry out the service you elected him to perform. If you do so, the expression, a 'Happy New Year' will be less a platitude and more an actuality when the time again comes round to renew the ancient wish.

Seán Moylan[8]

The editor did not publish the message, perhaps believing that Moylan's plain speaking did not quite strike the right tone of festive goodwill.

While Moylan was a Dáil Deputy, and later a government minister, there was a constant stream of gifts sent to the house by grateful constituents or those who hoped for a favour or assistance. It might be a turkey or a goose or a bottle of whiskey. All gifts were returned. On a few occasions when whiskey was sent with no address from the sender, his children remember the sound of bottles being smashed on the back garden wall. He represented all his constituents with unstinting fairness and would not allow himself to be compromised.

The family was never well off or even comfortable. Moylan did not own a car and for the first twelve years of his political life he travelled to Dublin by train, living in digs when the Dáil was in session. Books were his lifelong passion, nurtured from a young age in his grandfather's house. There was, he said, the foundations of a great library in every household in Ireland: the *Penny Catechism*, the *Creamery Yearbook* and *Old Moore's Almanac*. He filled his bookshelves with American and European histories, with the works of Victor Hugo, Charles Dickens and the emerging accounts of the War of Independence. These he would read and re-read like old friends. In later years he took down *The Pickwick Papers* and introduced his grandchildren to the adventures of the rascally Mr Jingle and the well-upholstered Mr Pickwick. There is no doubt that his health continued to trouble him; although there were periods when he was manifestly in good health. He must be one of the few Dáil Deputies to have been seriously injured at a sporting event that took place inside Leinster House when he slipped during a long jump competition and broke a bone in his back.

Moylan was an enigmatic and difficult character. Shortly after his youngest child, Eileen, was born, he was out walking in Kiskeam with the next youngest, Carmel. He now had a son and four daughters, which some of the older generation would have viewed as a heavy burden; indeed there was a saying at the time: 'Did you have a boy or a child?' Carmel recalls that a man approached with the words 'I'm sorry for your trouble' and was promptly floored by Moylan. He found himself in hot water for similar reasons when he punched a fellow Deputy on the steps of Leinster House – the man had just alleged in the Dáil that someone had shot themselves in the foot to get a pension.

In the late 1930s Moylan emerged as a much more polished Dáil performer. In the summer of 1937 he became Parliamentary Secretary at the Department of Industry and Commerce. The long delay in his promotion owed much to his robust speech, which was legendary, and his refusal to compromise, which was both a strength and failing. This was a happy and productive time in his life. The oath of allegiance was dispensed with and a new Irish Constitution came into force in December 1937. One suspects that Moylan must have wondered if Michael Collins had been right after all: that the Treaty was a stepping stone to real independence and therefore the Civil War had been fought for nothing. If this thought troubled him in the small hours he never shared it. He never spoke in detail of the Civil War and expressed no regrets for fighting the war.

26

THE BOTHY FIRE

It is hard to believe that Moylan's Commission comes to the coast to undo this desertion.

Peadar O'Donnell[1]

On Saturday 16 September 1937, ten young men were burned to death in a bothy fire near the remote Scottish village of Kirkintilloch. They were all from Achill Sound and the neighbouring townlands of north-west Mayo. Amongst the dead were three sets of brothers aged between thirteen and twenty-three years. Throughout the summer, with spirits buoyed by the music of their melodeons and mouth organs, this group of young men had followed the work from one farm to another until they arrived at Kirkintilloch. They were typical of the islanders who migrated for a number of months each year to earn a wage and relieve the economic hardship at home. Like many seasonal workers in Scotland, they slept in a bothy. On the night of the fire, the door was locked from the outside and the windows were covered with wire netting. It was an avoidable tragedy and it was not the first to afflict the people of the Gaeltacht community. Another migration disaster had occurred in November 1935 when nineteen 'tattie hokers' drowned as the boat bringing them home foundered within sight of their homes on Arranmore Island.

At Kirkintilloch arrangements for the funerals were stalled when the bereaved families back home sent a telegram: '*Beir abhaile ár marbh*'

– Bring home our dead.[2] The local railway, which had been shut down, was re-opened to transport the bodies back to Achill.

Ireland had endured centuries of forced migration and the tragedy at Kirkintilloch carried echoes of other times. The event captured the emotions of the nation. Subscription funds to support the survivors and bereaved families were set up and the public began to look afresh at the fact that so many people from the west and in particular the Gaeltacht areas were forced to leave the country to find poorly paid employment elsewhere. It was not just the fact that they had to migrate, but the living conditions they endured. These seasonal workers were housed in small huts and slept on beds consisting of inverted potato boxes covered with straw palliasses and blankets.

Moylan was appointed by the Tánaiste, Seán Lemass, to chair a government commission, which later became known as the Moylan Commission. Its terms of reference were to examine the problem of seasonal migration of labour to Britain from certain congested districts, to make recommendations as to the improvement of the conditions under which migrants were recruited and employed, and to prevent abuses in the future. The morning after the terms of reference were published, the veteran socialist campaigner Peadar O'Donnell phoned Moylan at his office. He was delighted and hopeful that something positive would finally be done for migrant farm workers.[3] Years later he said that Moylan's was the most insistent voice in his demands for relief from the chronic hardship endured by the people of the west. Government efforts, however, could not prevent the slow decline and Moylan reflected sadly to O'Donnell that 'the girls were the first to go, their … instinct telling them to flee from where there was no hope of life'.[4]

It seems that Moylan quickly ripped up the terms of reference and embarked on a much wider review of poverty in the west of Ireland. The commission was obliged to accept that widespread economic hardship forced people to search for seasonal work in Britain. In these circumstances they were vulnerable to exploitation by unscrupulous employers or gangmasters. Despite a raft of legislation in the intervening years, the exploitation of migrant workers continues to endure: 2004 saw the death of twenty-one migrant cockle pickers in Morecambe Bay in England. In Ireland the economic boom of the 'Celtic Tiger' years saw an influx of migrant workers with the same attendant opportunities for unscrupulous work practices. In 2005 the plight of exploited Turkish construction workers was taken up in the Dáil by Socialist TD Joe Higgins. These workers, he maintained, put in an eighty-hour week and were paid less than half the legal minimum wage. Plainly the protection of workers and the fairness of work practices is an ongoing issue for governments and requires constant vigilance.

The Moylan Commission quickly recognised that nothing could be done to prevent seasonal migration or to regulate the employment and living conditions of workers abroad. It focused therefore on the underlying problems, which boiled down to the very high number of people in the west who derived their living from the land. There was plenty of bog and a large number of poor arable farms but a chronic shortage of good land. The position was made worse by the fact that many holdings were made up of a patchwork of unconnected fields. Even by the standards of the time, families lived in dire poverty.

The commission completed its report in 1938.[5] The main recommendations included a programme of resettlement for the congested areas of the west of Ireland, with 150,000 acres set aside for this purpose; a reclamation programme of waste land and cutaway bogs; and the development of tourism and the introduction of new industries in the west (although the commission highlighted the need to protect the Irish language). The report was received with the usual squabbling over what could be done and how much it would cost. Eventually the government introduced some limited employment schemes and made available 150,000 acres of untenanted land in other counties for resettlement and relief of the congested areas.

Moylan's pragmatic but scholarly approach to the problems of migrant labour echo his 1925 letter to Joe McGarrity in which he expressed the view that progress in agriculture could best be achieved through commissions of inquiry. It also foreshadowed his time as Minister for Lands and his brief tenure as Minister for Agriculture in which policy would be led by academic research and good science.

Addressing poverty in the west of Ireland was a challenge for politicians who wished to respect the traditions of the Gaeltacht as well as relieve hardship. Striking the balance with sustainable development underpinned much of the rest of Moylan's life in politics and the distribution of land through the Land Commission was overtaken by the pressing need to move Ireland towards agricultural economic efficiency and competitiveness.

27

WORLD'S FAIR – SEÁN KEATING

Our waggon is still hitched to a star… the star of international goodwill … the star of peace.

President Franklin D. Roosevelt, 30 April 1939, World's Fair

One of Moylan's responsibilities at the Department of Industry and Commerce was the organisation of the Irish pavilion at the New York World's Fair. This major international event, scheduled to take place in the summer of 1939, carried an optimistic dedication to 'The World of Tomorrow'.[1]

The architect Michael Scott received this important commission and created what was recognised internationally as an outstanding building of steel and glass, winning him a silver medal for the project. Seán Keating later praised Scott's ingenuity in developing a design that showed 'more brains than money'.[2] The government was very anxious that the pavilion should have a distinctly Irish character and Scott accommodated this request with a shamrock-shaped internal floor plan. When the World's Fair opened, the Irish pavilion was a popular drop off point for tour guides and quickly became known as the 'shamrock building'. While the national emblem would become a clichéd motif in later years, in 1939 it offered a sense of familiarity and had great appeal for the Irish-American visitors. The opening of the pavilion on Saturday 13 May 1939, was an emotional occasion; a

Inscription from John Keating to Seán Moylan on the reverse of a photograph of the World's Fair mural.

nineteen-gun salute was fired as the Irish dignitaries arrived. Ireland's new constitution had come into effect in December 1937 and Éire's presence in New York was seen as something of a homecoming for the many visitors whose links with Ireland went back generations.

A mural by Seán Keating was displayed in the mural hall along with another equally remarkable painting by his contemporary at the School of Art, Maurice McGonigal. Keating's mural depicted elements of the agricultural, sporting and industrial life of Ireland and projected a modern country with the fledgling Aer Lingus Teoranta displayed prominently in the foreground. Because of its immense proportions – eighty feet long by thirty-four feet high – the mural was painted in the riding stables at Collins Barracks in Dublin. For Moylan, who walked everywhere, the distance between Leinster House and the barracks was just a pleasant stroll, and he watched the mural take shape over a number of months. The influence and friendship between Moylan and Keating had endured from earlier years and was recorded in a generous dedication written on the reverse of a photograph of the mural: 'To the man who had the idea from the man that worked it out, John Keating to Seán Moylan 1939'.[3]

In New York a great deal of political manoeuvring went on behind the scenes with Ireland first being offered a site with the rest of the British Empire. Éamon de Valera was having none of it and diplomatic posturing ensured that Ireland was awarded a prime location for the country's first appearance as an independent nation at such an event.

Because of IRA bombings in Britain and the worsening political climate in Europe, de Valera postponed his plans to visit the Fair. In his place the Tánaiste, Seán T. O'Kelly, set sail from Cobh on board the SS *Washington* to attend the opening ceremonies on 13 May. Moylan was already in New York to oversee the final preparations; before he docked on 23 April he wrote to his wife from the SS *President Roosevelt*. The letter contains an oblique reference to events in Nazi Germany:

> Dear Nora,
>
> We are only 370 miles from New York and land DV [*Deo Volante*] about midday tomorrow … The deck is like the ground floor of the Tower of Babel with the mixture of tongues. Quite a number of those on board can speak no English. One German girl told me that coming out of Germany she was allowed bring only forty dollars. This is to carry her to Frisco. She doesn't look or act in any way Jewish but there must be some strain otherwise she would not have to leave … I shall write at once when I land.
>
> Love to you and the gang.
>
> Seán[4]

US Customs permission granted to Seán Moylan to board the SS Washington. An Tánaiste, Seán T. O'Kelly, travelled from Cobh to New York on board this vessel to attend the opening ceremonies of the Irish Pavilion.

The trip was a chance for Moylan to revisit the city in which he had lived for many months in the more difficult circumstances of 1923 and 1924. He made no contact with his old friend Joe McGarrity, who had strenuously opposed Fianna Fáil's entry into the Dáil as a sell-out of his republican ideals. Their friendship had withered in the late 1920s after Moylan abandoned the IRA and Sinn Féin. McGarrity remained a lifelong adherent of the armed struggle and supported the 1939 IRA bombing campaign in Britain.

The connections between Keating and Moylan also had their origins in the 1920s, in particular, Moylan's court-martial in the summer of 1921 when he was defended by Albert Wood, KC. Moylan met Wood again in Dublin just after he was released from Spike Island to take part in the Treaty debates. A few days later Wood took him to visit the National Gallery. Moylan takes up the story:

> He was a great lover of pictures and sculpture and I, who had never been in the National Gallery before, spent under his guidance, a most pleasurable and educative afternoon. On the following day, he said to me, 'I would like to have a picture of you and would be glad if you would permit yourself to be painted by Seán Keating in the clothes you wore in the dock in Cork.' I agreed and Keating tackled the job in the following week.[5]

In conversation during these sittings, Keating became familiar with the background and attitude of the fighting men of north Cork. Moylan records: 'Wood was a constant visitor to the studio while the work was in progress. Among the various discussions we had, Wood put forward the idea that it would be something of historic value to make a picture of a group of men who had been concerned in the fighting. I arranged the matter and brought a dozen men to Dublin.'[6] The men from north Cork were put up in the Clarence Hotel; it was a welcome luxury after many months dodging the forces of the 6th Division.

Keating's memory of the events, written in 1951, recalls that he was working in his studio at the Metropolitan School of Art, 'a very British Institution, when a porter rushed in breathless and pop-eyed to say the hall is full of men with guns and they're looking for you!'[7] Never before or since, Keating said, 'have I so impressed a porter as when I answered nonchalantly, all right, bring them up'.[8] However, that wasn't the end of it, 'when the Department of Education had dried its pants' he was ordered off the premises.[9] He got permission to work on the painting in the Mansion House but this arrangement was not satisfactory as the light in the room they gave him was entirely unsuitable. In any event, it did not last long and Keating found himself ejected again. He returned to the School of Art and set about making a second painting entitled 'Men of the South'.

A new approach was needed as Moylan declined to be included in this second picture. He believed at the time that 'the Truce was transient, that the fighting would be resumed and that, under such circumstances, it was unwise that the pictures and photographs of leaders should be available to the British'.[10] Looking back, he said this was not much of a reason, but at a time of general chaos and political tension, when many saw the Truce as no more than a breathing space, it was perhaps a prudent decision.

Keating devised a new composition and, to avoid upsetting the college authorities, he arranged to have one rifle and some equipment smuggled in. The men visited his studio one by one and so the picture evolved. He later observed critically that this new painting was not as coherent as the first because of this piecemeal approach. He believed the original 'had a quality of verve and dash that would probably have been lost had I been permitted to carry it out in a calm atmosphere so perhaps from the point of view of a historical document, it has the qualities more descriptive of the time and circumstances than had it been done out of a mood of reflection and deliberation'.[11]

The painting was exhibited at the Royal Hibernian Academy in 1922 and was well received. It was hoped that Cork Corporation or Cork County Council would find the £250 to purchase this picture of 'the boys'. The 'Men of the South' was acquired in 1923 by the Gibson

Bequest Committee and now hangs in the Crawford Municipal Gallery in Cork. In Moylan's place, on the rear right-hand side of the canvas, is a strapping young man with the physique and manner of a war leader.

There is a sense in Keating's later letters to the Bureau of Military History that he thought the men of the south themselves were badly treated or forgotten. Moylan disagreed:

It is true that they are men whose lives have consisted since of hard effort and that some of them had to leave the country to make a living, but I don't think that any of them would be grateful to Keating for his sympathy. Revolutionaries, by their very mentality, are precluded from living comfortable lives. Soft living would make them uncomfortable, and it is my opinion that from the day of the inception of the Volunteer movement until now, there have been no happier lives in Ireland than the lives of those men.[12]

He continued, 'I have an idea that Keating, with his sensitive artistic mind, was slightly afraid of them.' This may be so, although he did find common ground with the schoolteacher Roger Kiely. Breeding said Moylan 'goes a long way, and that is true of these men. They all came from families in which there was a tradition of resistance to British rule in Ireland.'[13]

In Moylan's colourful profile of the Volunteers who posed for '1921, An IRA Column' and 'Men of the South', what stands out is the united patriotism and comradeship of these men whose faces were carved from the rock of experience:

Denis Mullane's father was a Fenian. An uncle of his was a Fenian organiser. History and tradition have queer interminglings and unexpected effects. In Mullane's farm at Freemount, Co. Cork, there are four graves – the graves of O'Sullivan Bere's soldiers, killed at a fort near there during his march to Leitrim. Who knows what an effect the story of O'Sullivan Bere's march might have had on a young mind?

Michael O'Sullivan was one of the most outstanding fighters in all Cork. Nervous, gentle and imaginative, any fears he might have had at the beginning, he had completely crushed until he had developed into the most fearless fighter I knew. His father was a captain of the Moonlighters. Among the Moonlighters, there were many men whose characters were not very estimable. It is a recurrent phenomenon in all such movements that evil men take advantage of disturbance. O'Sullivan's father was a gentle, unselfish type, entirely sincere in his efforts to secure a reducing of British strength in Ireland.

James Riordan was a big hefty man and was concerned in all the fighting in north Cork. The Riordans came originally from the North as Gallowglasses and Riordan displayed all the fighting capacities of his forebears. Yet, he was a gentle, disciplined man, fierce only when the fighting was to be done.

Dan Brown [sic] was a good soldier. Always he seems to me to have the grimmest face of all those in the picture. Perhaps this is due to the fact that he was a clerical student, destined to be a parish priest in his early days.

James Cashman was very young, only a boy, a very fine athlete and a most enthusiastic Volunteer. He is a first cousin of my wife. I am glad to say that all the aggressiveness has been confined to the male members of the family.

John Jones was then seventeen and had had his first fight at sixteen. He went to Oregon, USA, after the Civil War and is now farming in Cork.[14]

The solidarity and friendship of these IRA men would later extend to familial relationships. Jim Riordan married Moylan's sister-in-law Nancy Murphy of the Shamrock House in Kiskeam and Tom McNamara, a Volunteer comrade from the Newmarket company, married his youngest sister, Gret.

The early unfinished painting, which had given the porters at the School of Art so much anxiety, languished for some years in Keating's studio in Rathfarnham, Dublin, before being purchased for the

Douglas Hyde Collection in 1944. It is recorded in the collection catalogue as '1921, An IRA Column'.[15]

Reflecting on the work he completed in 1921, Keating observed, 'It has been said that art originates from emotions recollected in tranquillity'.[16] In painting this picture, 'I had many intruding emotions, no need to recollect and no tranquillity ... one too easily forgets what is too painful to remember. Mr Churchill's loan of that convenient artillery damaged more than the stones of the Four Courts.'[17] Keating felt that history belonged to posterity and should be documented in paint as well as print. He had hoped to do a series of paintings recording the birth of a nation, but the Department of Education turned down his offer, probably believing that the sooner the bitterness of the Civil War was forgotten the better. His iconic paintings, '1921, An IRA Column' and 'Men of the South', depict a group of ordinary men from Duhallow and the environs of north Cork who pitted their formidable courage against the might of the British Empire. It is one of the few pictorial examples of those troubled years created by an artist with an enduring international reputation.

Keating's preoccupation with the pre-Treaty period was still being played out in the 1940s. He visited Kiskeam, at Moylan's invitation, where he worked on preparatory sketches for 'Republican Court', now hanging in the officers' mess at Collins Barracks, Cork. The scene for the painting was set in Culloty's kitchen at Knockavorheen. In this painting, Keating successfully married his political message with the social details of the period. The salt cupboard in the fire hearth wall, the picture of the Sacred Heart, the dresser loaded with meat plates and the settle bed, all speak of a way of life long since gone but still part of the fabric of a country village in the 1940s. The reconstructed Sinn Féin court in the painting includes Thady Moynihan, Michael T. Cronin, Michael Mockie Cronin, Jim Riordan and Timothy Cronin all sitting at a court session. Standing at either end of the room are Riordan's first cousins, Paddy and Seán Culloty.[18]

While Keating was working on this project he stayed with Moylan's sister Mamie at the old Moylan home in Newmarket. His daily lift was assured by Jim Bourke, the driver of the creamery lorry. On its way to Kiskeam the lorry passed Glasakinleen Creamery where a local who spotted Keating in the cab beside Bourke remarked for the interest of the bystanders that 'the little man went back to Kiskeam again yesterday'.[19] Such events mattered in the daily gossip of the creamery yard, where strangers were observed with intense curiosity. In the evenings Keating hitched a lift on the mail car returning to the post office in Newmarket. He visited Roger Kiely and renewed their friendship of earlier times. Perhaps he thought Kiely should have got a better deal in life than trying to drill into the heads of the local children the fact that there were no f's in enough. Moylan took another view. The brigade he said could 'all look back on a great adventure successfully pursued … they had a tremendous advantage in life over those who accepted comfort and security as against effort on behalf of their nation'.[20] Mamie Moylan's memory of Keating's visit to Newmarket and Kiskeam was coloured by her belief that he blocked her bathroom basin with his whiskers.[21] That aside, she offered a hospitable house and he was assured of a comfortable bed and an early wake-up call to the sounds of a creamery town passing under his bedroom window each morning.

Moylan returned from the World's Fair in the summer of 1939. The Irish pavilion had been a success but events at home were developing rapidly. Months earlier de Valera had given clear signals regarding his position on neutrality. Despite Churchill's objections, control of the Treaty ports had been returned to Ireland and would not become a bargaining tool. De Valera's postponed visit to the United States was rescheduled for October but that trip was cancelled when Germany invaded Poland on 2 September 1939. The changed European political landscape foreshadowed a war that soon engulfed most of the world.

28

Director of Air Raid Precautions
1939–1942

> *If there was a silver lining in the cloud which hung over the North Strand, it was displayed in the courage and efficiency of the ARP and allied services.*
>
> Seán Moylan, 1 June 1942[1]

The fire hose suddenly and unexpectedly shot out a jet of water. At hundreds of pounds per square inch the pressure pitched a man into the air. The teenager holding the hose was George Murphy of Wexford. The year was about 1940 and the occasion was a public demonstration of the efficiency of the local air raid precautions (ARP). The drenched man was his commander, he was not happy and Murphy was not promoted. Another drill involved a bombing emergency with casualties and a serious leg injury: 'On the way to the scene of the "carnage" the ambulance had a front wheel blow out which caused delays until a replacement wheel and jack could be found.' When the ambulance filled with nurses eventually arrived at the scene they found a note pinned to the 'injured' man's kitchen cabinet. He had gone to the pub.[2]

All over Ireland ARP wardens were drilling with varying degrees of efficiency. Moylan's involvement can be traced to his return from New York in June 1939. There were family matters and urgent constituency affairs to attend to, but there were other pressing issues forcing their way onto the political scene. Since early 1938 there had been a growing realisation that a major European war was inevitable and that Irish cities might well be bombed. At the time there was no appreciation of the scale of the carnage that would take place.

An ARP Act passed in 1939 was set up on a statutory basis for air raid protection in all major cities. In August 1939, at short notice, Éamon de Valera recalled Moylan from his family holiday in Dunquin on the Dingle Peninsula. As a result of their discussions Moylan was appointed to head the ARP service. He also held the briefs of Parliamentary Secretary for the Ministries of Defence and of Industry and Commerce. It was a busy time for him. The outbreak of the Second World War was imminent. The primary concerns were the threat to the safety of citizens and the prospect of large-scale damage. Another linked concern was that Ireland might, by some unforeseen event, be drawn into the conflict.

The bitter legacy of the Civil War was still evident in Ireland and Moylan seems to have seized on the Emergency as a means of promoting national unity. He attended many of the ARP wardens' meetings and supported their civic endeavours. By the end of 1940 there were 4,500 wardens and the fire and hospital services were geared up to respond to the potential threat. The first bombs had already dropped.

On the afternoon of 26 August 1940, a German aircraft was seen over Wexford. It was observed to circle above Campile and fall to about 200 feet before dropping a line of bombs on the creamery below. Kitty and Mary Kent and Kathleen Hurley died. The creamery and other buildings sustained extensive damage. At Scurlogue Bush, ten miles away, another bomb destroyed a large tract of wheat, potatoes and turnips. An 'Irish stew' of vegetables flew in the window of James Hawkins' house and the only item left standing in his bedroom was a statue of the Little Flower.[3] Two days later *The Irish Times* devoted its editorial to the outrage: 'A German plane released bombs over Wexford on Monday afternoon and through this dreadful happening, Ireland has experienced for the first time the meaning in all its horror of an aerial bombardment'; no accusations were made against those responsible, but the poignant consequences were a stark reminder that it 'might have been Dublin or Cork … and the number of dead might be not three but 300'.[4] It was a prophetic observation.

As day broke on 2 January 1941, a line of bombs fell over Mount Leinster; the isolated home of the Shannon family at Knockroe in County Carlow suffered a direct hit. Mary Ellen and Bridget Shannon and their sixteen-year-old niece Kathleen were killed, Michael and James Shannon were badly injured. On this bitterly cold morning a cluster of bombs also fell on the south Dublin suburbs of Donore and Terenure, destroying a district that had been home to Ireland's tiny Jewish community for many years. By a miracle there were no fatalities but the irony was not lost on the local people who rallied round to help. Many houses, five churches and a synagogue sustained considerable damage. In County Kildare on the same morning over thirty bombs strafed the Curragh plains; incredibly there was no damage or loss of life.

At 1:30 a.m. on Whit Saturday, 31 May 1941, a German bomb fell on Dublin's Summerhill and North Circular Road, galvanising the fire services and ARP wardens into action. Close by, the familiar landscape of the North Strand was about to implode. At 2:05 a.m. a devastating 500-pound bomb tore through the heart of this close-knit community. Twenty-eight people were killed instantly, more died in the following days and a few were never located. Scores suffered injuries and hundreds more were made homeless. 'A muffled peal of bells rang out at Christ Church Cathedral on Sunday morning in sympathy with the victims.'[5] The immediacy of the crisis was reinforced in Moylan's mind when the front door of his Dublin lodgings was blown in. For many, the raid was interpreted either as a device to bring Ireland into the war or as retaliation for the assistance given by the Dublin Fire Brigade to the city of Belfast during the blitz of the previous month.

The lord mayor threw open the doors of the Mansion House and the homeless were given emergency shelter across the city. On Saturday an *Irish Times* correspondent toured 'Dublin's Via Dolorosa' where 'not a single smile could be seen along the bomb-straddled path of havoc', but his memory was not one of pulverised homes but of the little stories he heard everywhere 'of the courage, self-sacrifice and good-neighbourliness' shown by the people who lived in the North Strand.[6]

As the relief effort gathered momentum, Dublin Corporation secured 800 mattresses and 2,400 blankets from the ARP Department of Defence stores 'on a repayment basis' at 'sixteen shillings and eight pence per mattress and twelve shillings and eleven pence per blanket'.[7] The departmental letters are typed on both sides of poor quality paper, everything was rationed and the sense of austerity is palpable. One also senses a shared determination to get things done. Correspondence in the Dublin City Archive shows Moylan chasing the city manager to take action: 'public morale demands that this matter should be dealt with swiftly and efficiently'. His letter of 13 June deplored the slow progress of repairs in the area: 'I visited the North Strand on the twelfth instant and to say that I was amazed and shocked at the lack of progress is to put it lightly.'[8] The repairs rumbled on for months. For the workmen involved in the reconstruction, the sense of urgency was questionable: 'they seemed to enjoy themselves immensely, it was the best day's work they ever had'.[9] In the aftermath of the bombings, gas masks, which had been in short supply, were distributed with renewed zeal. Some, like the ARP warden on Donore Road, made great efforts to train his neighbours on how to put on the masks and instructed his fellow citizens on how to dispose of imaginary incendiary devices in a bucket of water. For others, including the impoverished tenement mammies in inner-city Dublin, the gas masks were examined for their financial opportunities, 'but you couldn't pawn Government property'.[10]

One other drama occurred in Dublin on that fateful Whit Saturday morning. It captured the imagination of the Moylan children and provoked much discussion. The blast of the bomb near the Dog Pond pumping station in the Phoenix Park caused wild chatter and mayhem in the monkey house at Dublin Zoo, the bison ran amok and the poor distressed elephant was in such a state she trumpeted madly with fright and could only be consoled by her keeper and good friend, Cedric Flood.[11]

On the first anniversary of the North Strand bombings, the ARP organisations held an anniversary parade from the bombed area to the Central Model School on Marlborough Street near the Pro Cathedral. In taking the salute, Moylan remembered all those who had died the previous year:

> On this day, exactly a year ago, a number of citizens were hurled into eternity and a larger number received injuries, the marks of which they would carry all their lives … when the bombs began to fall there were no grievances in the allied organisations that tackled the work of rescue, healing and restoration, only a desire to carry out [their] duties.[12]

His regard for the ARP volunteers was sincere and it was reciprocated.

In July the Dáil Committee on Finance debated the compensation costs 'in connection with the injuries to property caused by the dropping of bombs from foreign aircraft'.[13] The meticulous calculations applied to some claimants did not help one old lady who had put her teeth into a glass of water on the night of the bombing as she always did. 'When the bomb came the false teeth went' but her compensation was reduced on the grounds that 'she had the teeth a number of years and a depreciated value should apply'.[14] As for the man whose overcoat was stolen when he went to the assistance of the fire brigade on the morning of 31 May 1941, his claim would be 'sympathetically considered' within the scope of the Damage to Property Compensation Act.[15]

Despite the damage, injuries and loss of life, the large-scale bombing that so many had feared never materialised. The prospect of invasion by Germany continued to loom large, at least until Dunkirk. Later, as the Battle of the Atlantic gathered pace, plans were being laid in Britain for an invasion of Cork and the Treaty ports; a full division had been earmarked for the operation. Field Marshal Montgomery, who had been assigned to lead the invasion, later wrote in his autobiography: 'it might have been quite a party'.[16] It was not to be.

29

DÁIL CAREER 1943–1957

Plain perhaps, sometimes blunt in speech, sparing in words, by a vivid phrase he exposed the kernel of a problem and secured for his views an acceptance more complete than could have been obtained by lengthier argument.

Éamon de Valera, 19 November 1957[1]

Following the June 1943 general election, de Valera appointed Moylan to his first cabinet post; he would be Minister for Lands for the next five years. With his new responsibilities it became increasingly difficult to meet family obligations in Kiskeam. Moylan and his wife moved to Dublin and rented a house in Clontarf. This was the family home for the rest of their lives.

The Moylans conveyed a lifelong passion for learning to all their children and encouraged lively debate at the kitchen table. It was a bookish house, the tattered remains of an anthology of poetry illustrated by Harry Clarke bears testament to much use. The inscription on this volume reads: 'To make permanent a memory, Christmas 1921, Albert E. Wood', recalling a far off time when Moylan spoke with passion at Earlsfort Terrace during the Treaty debates.[2]

In 1944 his mother Nora died. After the funeral, he reminisced about her success at the Aldworth Auction in 1921 when the contents of Newmarket Court were sold. One of Nora's bids was for a watercolour of a lady on horseback. It was knocked down to her for one shilling. In later years she liked to comment on the provenance of her purchase suggesting that the horsewoman in the picture was Lady Mary Aldworth. Nora was an artistic woman with a fine singing voice, she appreciated beautiful things and her influence undoubtedly shaped her eldest son. The Black and Tan years had been difficult for both of them – a photograph from August 1921 shows her drained and care-worn. Perhaps for this reason the painting had certain resonances for Seán; he brought it back to Dublin and hung it on his sitting-room wall. Moylan's sister Mamie and her husband continued to live in the family home in Newmarket and his hospitable Moylan aunts enjoyed rude good health for many more years. His links with Newmarket remained strong until his death.

Government policy on land redistribution throughout the 1920s and 1930s had been driven by the need to alleviate poverty and congestion. It was administered by the Land Commission under a series of statutes. The policy had become a sacred cow for both major parties. One of Moylan's first acts was to challenge the received wisdom. In a memo to de Valera in September 1943 he questioned the merits of continued land distribution.[3] Briefly, the basis of his challenge was that the practice of giving land away created a culture of dependency and those receiving land had no proven record of competence as farmers. Moreover, the farms created were often subsistence holdings for small farmers and did not generate excess cash, and finally the size of the holdings were not conducive to modern farming techniques. Underpinning these arguments was the notion that agriculture was Ireland's greatest asset and it was necessary for this indigenous industry to compete internationally to generate wealth for the nation. The debate about land policy rumbled on for years. The proponents of the new philosophy had to tread carefully because the demand for land distribution made any u-turn politically contentious. In the mid-1940s Moylan was still a new boy in the cabinet. In addition, his outlook on land reform had begun to diverge from mainstream opinion.

As the following letter to his old friend Roger Kiely makes clear, the job also had its lighter moments. The letter is in relation to the vacant sub post office in Cullen in north Cork and the possible appointees show that the life of a politician had not changed since Abraham Lincoln's day:

A Ruaidhrí, A Chara,
Please regard this note of mine to you as an entirely personal and confidential one. I want your advice about the Cullen Post Office. There are eleven candidates. The official report states that the last five are regarded for various reasons as being unsuitable. Therefore they may be ruled out. There has been a good deal of pressure brought to bear on me from various sources with a view to having Mrs Ellen O'Keeffe appointed. Mrs O'Keeffe is the wife of a Home Assistance Officer and, as such, is completely ruled out. The reasons given me – the regulation which rules out such applicants – are quite sound and understandable and I agree personally that it is a regulation that should be enforced. Mr Mulcahy and Mr B. Cronin are also ruled out. The only candidates that might be considered are Messrs Dineen, McSweeney and Murphy. Personally I favour giving the position to Matthew Murphy. I think as a businessman he would be entirely suitable and reliable. There is, of course, a suggestion that he is of the opinion that Sinn Féin is still the legitimate government of this country and, from that point of view, his appointment would be a reason for legitimate criticism by all political parties in the Dáil. The suggestion has been made that he might utilise the office, as little as it is, against the ordinary working of the government in this country. I doubt that he would do so, of course. There is a technical objection also to his appointment – his house is somewhat outside the village. I don't think that this technical objection is sustainable.

Before I decide to make a recommendation to the Minister for Posts, which recommendation will naturally influence him in his final choice, I would like to have your personal considered view as to what the best thing to do in the matter would be. In the middle of the American Civil War Lincoln was met by a friend on coming out of his office in an exhausted and dejected condition. The friend asked him if there was bad war news, 'No,' he said, 'but I've been listening to a deputation about the filling of a Post Office vacancy worth a couple of hundred dollars a year.' I am in about the same position with regard to the Cullen Post Office.

Yours sincerely,

Seán Moylan[4]

One of Moylan's last acts as Minister for Lands was to initiate a report into the lives of the Blasket Islanders in October 1947, a few months before Fianna Fáil lost office. This tiny Irish-speaking community off the Dingle Peninsula earned a living by lobster fishing and sheep rearing. Theirs was a solitary and arduous life. There was no doctor, nurse or priest on the islands. There were no industries and only a fraction of the land was arable. Contact with the mainland was by currach, but the rough seas in the Blasket Sound often left the islanders cut off in bad weather. The community began to decline in the late 1930s as remittances from Britain and the United States brought news of a more comfortable life elsewhere. Given the alternatives, women did not wish to marry into this impoverished and isolated way of life. By 1947 the population was reduced to fifty-one islanders, twenty-three of whom were single men.[5] They were living in hovels, in circumstances of desperate poverty and isolation and were eager to be resettled. The government report instigated by Moylan did the rounds but the general election of February 1948 intervened and prevented any action on the issue.

Moylan had developed a formidable reputation as a speaker on the stump; funny or passionate as the occasion required. He was in demand to speak at by-elections and could work the crowd, bringing them with him. Jack Lynch remembers canvassing for Pa McGrath in the 1946 Cork by-election. A meeting was not going well, even the hecklers had lost interest. Moylan, as Director of Elections, rearranged the speaking order and stepped up to the podium, throwing a few hurley metaphors into the crowd and saving the day for Fianna Fáil.[6] He was used to speaking from a wall or sometimes on the tailgate of a lorry. On one occasion he grew impatient with a speaker who had, he thought, taken up too much time. To the growing amusement of the crowd he edged slowly across the tailgate until the speaker was tipped off the side.

One of Moylan's anecdotes from the 1948 election campaign gives a flavour of the period and a sense of a mature man looking back over his life. He had been on the stump in Ballylanders and there was the usual adjournment to a local pub. The minister was introduced to the old lady of the house and made some reference to the fact that there was a big crowd and that the kitchen door was firmly shut. She said: 'Oh indeed! I always lock the kitchen door when there is a crowd from Kilmallock in town. They stole a pig's head from me in 1904.'[7] Moylan then recalled the day that he, as a fifteen-year-old boy, had gone to a feis in Ballylanders with the Kilmallock Brass Band. While he never admitted to much in the way of musical accomplishment, on that day he was given the cymbals, commonly known as the 'brass plates'. The band had travelled on the long car, assembling outside Ballylanders, playing into the village, playing out to the feis, playing many times at the feis, playing back into the village in the evening and all were suffering from extreme thirst and hunger. They went into the pub, which was very full, and made themselves comfortable in the kitchen. One of the band looked in the pot hanging over the open fire. It contained a well-cooked pig's head. They slipped the head into the mouth of the biggest of their instruments and played their way out of the village. Having marched a suitable distance, the famished musicians crouched by the side of the road and devoured their booty.[8]

There was plenty of time for reflection in the years that followed. Moylan retained his seat in the 1948 election but Fianna Fáil went into Opposition. That year his son Rick received his Law degree and in the mid-1950s set up a legal practice in Mallow. His Fenian ancestors would surely have wondered at the trajectory of a family and of a country where such possibilities could be achieved. Moylan now had time to enjoy his first grandchild and family life took a slower pace. A spry middle-aged man in a suit, the picture of middle-class respectability, he walked to Leinster House most weekday mornings and back home in the late afternoon to St Lawrence Road, Clontarf. It was not a typical suburban house. Hundreds of books lined the homemade shelves and against the mantelpiece lay a Lee Enfield rifle. On the sitting-room wall, facing the fireplace, hung a picture of '1921, An IRA Column'. Moylan's long-standing association with Seán Keating reflected his sense of history and the part played by the people of north Cork.

The Bureau of Military History had been set up in 1947 in response to a growing sense of urgency that the crucial events of the period from 1916 to 1921 should be recorded. Many of the people in the Volunteer movement had died or were coming to the end of their lives. Moylan was frequently called upon to deliver the final oration at funerals. In Opposition, with time to reflect, he would sit by the fire in his front room, with the rifle at his elbow and the Volunteers looking down, and conjure up old memories. It was in these circumstances that he started to write the memoir that he later presented to the Bureau of Military History.[9]

When Fianna Fáil was returned to power in 1951 Moylan was appointed Minister for Education. According to Eileen Magner's eloquent account of Moylan's time in office he briefed senior civil servants on his views in his usual terse and sometimes epigrammatic manner. He opened with these words: 'There are many mistaken beliefs current about Éamon de Valera, one of them being that he is a man totally lacking in a sense of humour. But the fact that I stand before you as Minister for Education is testimony to his sense of humour.'[10] This reluctance was not borne out of an indifference to education: Jack Lynch once described him as 'one of the most widely read men that ever graced Irish public life'.[11] But as Moylan said to one of his senior civil servants: 'I would give my eyes to be Minister of Agriculture.'[12] It was in that post he believed he could do most good for his country.

Moylan had the reputation of being an effective and determined minister. Kevin Devlin's article in the *Sunday Press*, on 8 November

1953, outlined the minister's plans for accelerating the appallingly slow school rebuilding programme. At the time, almost ten per cent of the country's primary schools were structurally defective to the point of being derelict and in urgent need of replacement. Moylan tackled the project with energy and obtained government consent to double the building targets to 100 new primary schools per year. A principal teacher recalled the minister's visit to his school in Listowel: 'Taking a penknife from his pocket, he thrust the blade through the window frame, right up to the hilt. The timber was rotten to the core. He smiled, then turned to me and asked if we wanted a library in a new school.'[13] Moylan was not a professional said Devlin, but he won tributes from the teaching profession and the staff of his department who 'responded to the quickening of a new spirit … an educational idealism built on the rock of uncommon common sense'.

It is in the area of vocational education, however, that Moylan is best remembered. Over a two-year period, thirty vocational schools were built as he set out to give a solid foundation to the training of craft skills. In rural communities he also promoted closer contact between the work of the school and that of the farm through the newly established Macra na Tuatha scheme for junior farmers' clubs. He injected a new sense of purpose into the old maxim that 'education was preparation for life' and saw the teaching of children as a 'drawing out' rather than a 'hammering in'. Acknowledging that learning extended beyond the curriculum, Moylan implemented an imaginative programme that allowed every primary school teacher a 'hobbies half-day' to teach any subject of special interest they wished in order to broaden the horizons of their young pupils.[14]

Although it was outside his remit, Moylan intervened in the affairs of the Blasket Islanders again in late 1952 when there was only a single child on the islands.[15] The cabinet minutes of 7 November 1952 show Moylan pushing hard for the relocation of the islanders and some foot-dragging and strife among his cabinet colleagues over which department would bear the costs. Moylan had found a precedent in the Land Commission's resettlement of the islanders of Iniskea in

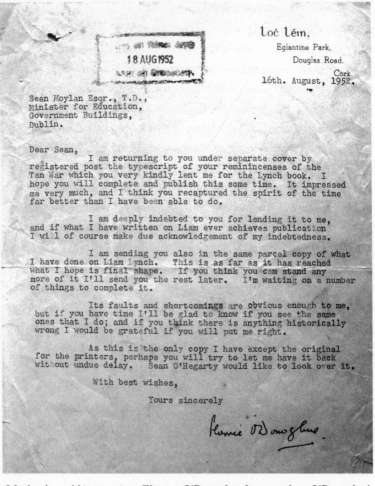

Moylan loaned his memoir to Florence O'Donoghue for research on O'Donoghue's biography of Liam Lynch, No Other Law.

1931, which laid the expenditure for the resettlement of the Blasket islanders firmly at their door. He argued that it was now a 'national and humanitarian' issue.[16] At last the cabinet agreed to act. By the end of 1953 this tiny community was resettled in and around Dunquin on farmland overlooking the Atlantic Ocean, with their homeland on the horizon. They continued to speak Irish as their first language.

Their livelihood remained dependent on fishing and their sheep still grazed on the islands. It is likely that Moylan's former Irish teacher from Dunquin, Seán na Cóta Kavanagh, would have approved.

There is one shadow that hangs over Moylan's tenure as Minister for Education. It arises out of a question raised on 23 April 1954, the day of the dissolution of the Fourteenth Dáil, and concerns a boy who had been beaten at the Artane Industrial School and sustained a broken arm. In investigating the circumstances of the case, Captain Peadar Cowan, TD, established that a fourteen-year-old boy had suffered a broken arm as a result of an incident at the school. The boy had been punished for misbehaviour following an altercation with another student and was given a number of slaps on the hand from the punishment leather. He was ordered to submit to further punishment from the edge of the strap and refused to do so. The Christian Brother in charge sent for another teacher and the boy grabbed a sweeping brush which he held in front of him. The second Brother snatched the brush and struck the boy on the head, back and arm. He was taken to hospital two days later and his arm was set in plaster. The mother of the boy was not informed and did not see her son for more than a week and only then after Cowan contacted the superior of the school on her behalf. Cowan sent a telegram to Moylan asking him to investigate the matter and informing him of his intention to raise the matter in the Dáil. The following is an extract from the Dáil minutes:

> *Deputy Cowan*: I think the House and the country will want to have from the Minister an assurance that an incident such as has occurred in this case will not be permitted to occur again. I am informed that the Brother who injured the boy was barely past 21 years of age ... the country will want an assurance ... that punishment, if it is to be inflicted on those sent to industrial schools, will be inflicted by some person of experience and responsibility. If punishment were to be imposed in a fit of hot temper, it would be exceptionally bad, and, in fact, as in this case, it would be dangerous. I regret very much that I have had to mention or raise this matter in this House. I

have lived for many years convenient to Artane Schools. For many years, whenever I was asked, I have been a subscriber to the funds of the schools. I have seen their boys week after week passing my house, looking exceptionally fit, well clothed and happy. All of us have seen their magnificent band playing on big occasions in Croke Park and it would be regrettable that an incident, such as I have mentioned in this case, should be permitted under any circumstances to occur in a school of that kind. I myself personally am satisfied that it is an isolated instance. I am satisfied that the superiors will take appropriate action against the Brother concerned. The very fact that the incident did occur shows how necessary it is that this House, through the machinery of the Department of Education and through the Minister charged with that responsibility, should have the closest supervision of schools such as this, where children, many of them without parents at all, are sent to be brought up. This incident, when I heard it yesterday morning and heard the details subsequently, profoundly shocked me. I am perfectly certain that the fact that it has been raised in this House, that the Minister has investigated it, will ensure that no similar incident will occur in the future. It will be a guarantee to the parents and relatives of children who are in these industrial schools that this House and the Minister and the staff of the Department will jealously guard and protect those children while they are under the care of the State in these institutions.

Minister for Education (Mr Moylan): I think Deputy Cowan has been quite reasonable in admitting that this is an isolated incident and that in general his appreciation of the work of the Artane School and of the condition of the children there has not lessened. The boy was hit and his arm was broken. I would be as much concerned as the Deputy is if I thought it was anything other than a very isolated incident and in one sense what might be called an accident. I would not tolerate cruelty to any boy or misuse of any boy in any institution. I visited Artane and found the boys were healthy and well cared for. I visited the schools there and it struck me that there was great evidence of very earnest endeavour, even of notable achievement, in the schools. It would be very difficult to improve the conditions under which the schools operate, certainly without a very substantial subvention from this House for the upkeep of the schools and for the development of what may be essential and necessary there. I would like to remind the House that the community provided the lands in Artane, the building and the equipment from their own resources; and they did this in a Christian endeavour to ameliorate certain conditions, the development of which had not been provided for in any way by anyone. I cannot conceive any deliberate ill-treatment of boys by a community motivated by the ideals of its founder. I cannot conceive any sadism emanating from men who were trained to a life of sacrifice and of austerity. They are also trained to have great devotion to a very high purpose. The point is that accidents will happen in the best regulated families and in this family there are about 800 boys. Many of them were sent to Artane because of the difficulties of their character and because of a good deal of unruliness of conduct. These boys are difficult to control at times. Maybe it is essential now and again that children should be punished. I am not all at one with the people who claim that children should never be punished, but I think the punishment should be administered, as Deputy Cowan says, by a responsible person in conditions of calm judgment. I do not know how the edge of the strap is used, but I will make an inquiry into that. I think it would be an evil thing for the school, for the character of the children, for the future of the children, that any misuse should arise in any school like Artane. Because of the unfortunate background of many of these boys, possibly due to evil social conditions, Deputies must realise how careful the handling of them as a group must be and how far from easy it is to ensure the working of such an institution. I deeply regret that there should be such a happening and I appreciate the anxiety of the boy's mother. Apart from my high regard for the Brothers concerned, the community concerned, there is also a very constant system of inspection for all such institutions. I personally have visited practically all of them and I make personal and constant inquiry as to what is happening in them. I know in that particular school how deep is the anxiety for the children's spiritual and physical welfare. This is an isolated incident; it can only happen again as an accident.[17]

A few points are worth noting. First, corporal punishment was a widespread practice in all schools in Ireland at the time and was often used at home, as indicated by common maxims that ruled the upbringing of children in the 1950s: 'spare the rod and spoil the child' and 'children should be seen and not heard'. These were almost universally held perceptions and it is not difficult to see how excesses occurred even to the point of brutality. Second, the Catholic Church retained a very powerful influence on Irish society. One only has to look at the way in which a government was fractured and brought down by the influence of the hierarchy over the proposed mother and child health service in 1951. Likewise, the ban on Catholic students attending Trinity College without a dispensation from the Archbishop of Dublin continued until 1970. There was a deference shown to the clergy in every aspect of Irish life, from throwing in the ball at GAA matches in Croke Park to regulating people's pastimes in case dancing became an occasion of sin; indeed dance halls were regarded by some as the 'vestibule of hell'. By contemporary standards, the Church's grip was pervasive and nobody saw this as either unusual or undesirable.

Moylan was appointed Minister for Education in succession to a line of distinguished and revered politicians, Professor Eoin MacNeill, Thomas Derrig, Éamon de Valera and Richard Mulcahy. To single him out for criticism would be erroneous. Unlike some of the other holders of this office, he was not a past pupil of the Christian Brothers; his education had been at Drominarigle in north Cork where the principal, Dan O'Keeffe, was to remain his lifelong friend. Nor was Moylan an obvious choice for the education portfolio, as his interests lay in land reform and agriculture. During his tenure, he inspected schools up and down the country and the newspapers of the day are littered with photographs recording these events. He visited Artane and found the boys well cared for. In an environment where such visits were scheduled in advance, the school had ample time to prepare and the boys' band which was synonymous with Artane would have added colour to such an important occasion.

During the adjournment debate, Moylan put on record his wish to improve conditions at the school, but said it could not be done without substantial additional funds from the public purse. In the post-war years Ireland was in a deep financial crisis and many children from poverty-stricken areas went to school unwashed, ill-nourished and badly dressed. It was not uncommon for newspaper boys to appear without shoes on the streets of the capital. Against widespread unemployment and mass emigration, it would have been a difficult task to win support for additional monies for Artane or other institutions which appeared to be well run.

The 2009 report of the Ryan Commission makes it clear that the Department of Education received a belated report on the broken arm incident. The Inspector of Industrial Schools wrote to the superior at Artane criticising the school's behaviour in not allowing the boy's mother immediate access. He further drew the superior's attention to the circular relating to 'Discipline and Punishment in Certified Schools' and recommended that this be brought to the notice of the Brothers 'from time to time'.[18] It is apparent that there were systems in place, but they were not robust enough to deal with problems when they occurred.

Moylan retained his seat in the May 1954 general election, but Fianna Fáil was removed from office. It is notable that the incoming inter-party government did not pursue the Artane matter raised in the Dáil two months previously and that Moylan did not raise the issue from the Opposition benches.

Moylan ran his last election campaign in 1957. In his own three-seater constituency of north Cork, Fianna Fáil pursued the unfulfilled ambition of taking two seats out of three. Moylan allocated one-third of the constituency to himself and two-thirds to his running mate, Batt Donegan. Unsurprisingly he was defeated and Donegan was elected. Moylan's friends listened with pride as he offered his vote of thanks to the returning officer. Speaking in Irish he said:

Many people seem to believe that the best way to propose a vote of thanks to a returning officer is to utilise it for a peg on which to hang a complaint or a grievance. I have no complaint, and I have no grievance. We men who came into Irish politics in the revolutionary period took victory with humility and defeat with good grace. I have the very good consolation in my personal defeat in being replaced by a man of high honour and principle and in whom the people will have confidence, and who will, I believe, represent them as diligently as I tried to do. Naturally it would be hypocrisy on my part if I did not tell you that I must feel a certain sense of personal disappointment but, after all, the Fianna Fáil vote is really the majority vote in this constituency still.

I thank the people of north Cork who continued me in representation in the Dáil for so many years. I thank the people who voted for me in this election, and I thank the many diligent workers who supported Fianna Fáil in the election. Leaving Irish politics, I do so in the personal belief that during my political career I did nothing that was dishonourable or dishonest. I tried to serve the people honestly and to speak courageously, and now all I can say is *nunc dimittis*.[19]

Seán MacBride also lost his seat in 1957. He wrote to Moylan recalling their meetings at Strasbourg where both served as Irish representatives to the Council of Europe. Moylan joined the Irish delegation in 1956 and was in Strasbourg attending an assembly meeting just weeks prior to the general election. Now he was out of office; private post-mortems were shared with his family.

He was staying outside Mallow with his daughter Stephanie and son-in-law Kevin O'Callaghan, and from their window he gazed at the sugar-beet factory in the valley below: a symbol of progress and prosperity. It was a moment of reflection on what seemed the final chapter of his life. His family had grown up. His brother Ned had died the year before. Many of the Volunteers he had served with had died and most of the officers of the 1st Southern Division had passed away. Within weeks Ernie O'Malley was also gone. On 28 March, as his funeral approached Glasnevin cemetery in Dublin, 'men who had been his comrades in rural Ireland … and who knew him as a

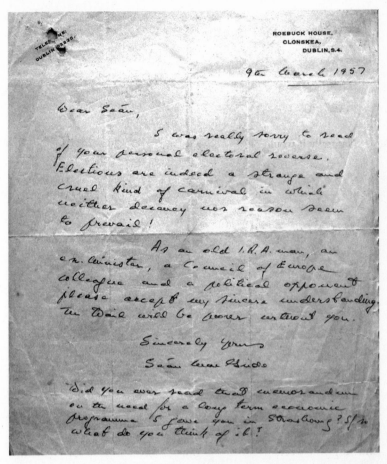

Letter from Seán MacBride to Moylan about the electoral defeat, which finishes:
'The Dáil will be poorer without you'.

gallant soldier, tried to remember "Ernie" as he was thirty-five years ago. Here the men of old companies and battalions and brigades and columns and the women who aided them in war and wound' stood by as Moylan stepped forward to deliver O'Malley's graveside oration. He spoke of 'a fragrant memory of ancient comradeship' for a soldier 'who carried the gospel of national freedom into every corner of the country, inspiring men by his example and steeling their courage by his contempt of danger'. Moylan recalled the old days of danger and nights of hardship, but across those darksome memories, was the courage of his comrade-in-arms.[20]

Throughout his life, Moylan spoke of the sincerity and sacrifice displayed by the men in the Volunteer movement. Looking back to the Civil War, we see a brief glimpse of his thoughts written in the mid 1950s:

In any country where the ordinary conditions of liberty obtained, those men would have been good citizens, taking their places in any movement directed to the national betterment. They were neither adventurers nor professional soldiers to whom revolution was the breath of life, they were men who left their peaceful avocations in a patriotic desire to serve their country, they expected neither reward or recognition ... whatever capacity they displayed in the difficult and unusual conditions which their country's history had thrust upon them, they were almost wholly simple men, of no political experience or knowledge, no familiarity with historical facts that might have guided them. Had they been trusted, had the bare bitter truth been told to them, I am of the belief that the Civil War, which no man wanted, might have been avoided.[21]

Moylan had mellowed, retirement beckoned and he seemed resigned to that. Perhaps then he might have written that history of the Civil War. Was it inevitable he reflected?

Who can say! But if an ideal is alluded, if men are urged to arm and strive, to every and ultimate sacrifice in its service, the more earnest, high-minded and honourable among them will find it difficult to accept anything less than the full recognition of that for which they fought. If at and during a cessation of hostilities, they are ordered not merely to stand to arms as a factor in the bargaining powers of diplomats, but are urged to believe that the work of the diplomats is merely a ruse to enable them to re-align, strengthen and train their forces to a continuance of the struggle to reach the ideal, it is difficult to expect that they shall be satisfied with a bargain which leaves their country in a state of subservience with a territorial division, the justice of which has not been and cannot be recognised.[22]

Moylan's written assessment of the period was not to be. The Taoiseach co-opted him to Seanad Éireann and nominated him as Minister for Agriculture; he was the first government minister to be appointed from the Senate. In the Dáil, the constitutionality of his selection was debated and opposed by Independent TD Jack McQuillan and the north Cork Labour Deputy Patrick McAuliffe, but his appointment was a popular choice and the motion was carried without a division of the House.[23] Writing in the *Sunday Independent* on 24 March 1957, T. P. Kilfeather spoke of the two Seán Moylans. The first was 'a man like a don, the lens of his glasses … thoughtful, introspective [and] quietly humorous'. He interviewed Moylan at his home in Clontarf where a fire roared up the chimney and the room was lined with books, as was the next room and the rooms upstairs. Moylan had a huge collection, although library is perhaps too grand a word; the books were just part of his life as were the paintings and reproductions on his sitting-room walls which reflected an 'appreciation of something more than the dilettante in art'. That was one of the dual Seán Moylans. The other said Kilfeather was as rugged as a boulder of Irish granite. 'His voice with its rasping quality … has never been known to call a spade an agricultural implement … this is the blunt Seán Moylan to whom de Valera has given the task of directing the efforts of those engaged in the biggest industry in the country and if there is one man who is not dismayed by the responsibility which has been given to him, he is Seán Moylan, book-lover and straight-talking man of dynamic action.'

Moylan had coveted the Agriculture portfolio for years. De Valera expressed only one reservation: 'that the man should not overwork himself and kill himself because it is a very difficult task'.[24] It was a prescient remark.

Moylan's opening speech as Minister demonstrated three key principles: that Irish agriculture was a national resource; that Ireland needed to compete with international competitors; and that the reform of agriculture would be led by sound science and research. In the months that followed he had a busy itinerary. He attended the sheep-shearing championships at Tinahely on the Wicklow Mountains, where he emphasised that Ireland's methods of production and marketing must be prepared to buttress the national economy through new ventures and the development of trade in less well-known products. The same message was evident in his speech at the Bandon & Fermoy Mart in June: 'The marketing conditions of a former age,' he declared, 'were entirely unsuitable to the trade of the present day where changes in production methods had brought competition in the international markets to the keenest edge … Governments can make laws to ensure that only completely disease-free animals are placed on the market. But legislation does not formulate public taste.' He signalled this point once more in his address to the National Council of Macra na Feirme in July 1957. We must 'put our products before the purchasing public in the best condition, with a guarantee of quality and by way of the most attractive methods' and again he spoke of the need for agricultural reform to be led by specialised training and scientific enquiry.[25] In the summer he was back on Spike Island to unveil a memorial to Paddy White, who had been shot dead while a prisoner. Fort Westmoreland had been renamed Fort Mitchel and Moylan was returning as Minister for Agriculture of an independent Republic. He used the opportunity to refute suggestions by historical revisionists that the War of Independence need not have been fought (see Appendix III). His firmly held beliefs echo a private memoir he wrote in 1944 about Volunteer Martin Savage who died at Ashtown in 1919 (see Appendix I):

> Today we live under different conditions, brought about by the efforts of Savage and his comrades, when to the quality of selflessness must be added that of wise statecraft. But wisdom in any form is of no avail if we cannot breed men like Savage whose lack of concern for personal well-being and security in the service of the nation overrode all natural human weakness and desire … we have still among us as a

reminder of the past and as a touchstone of achievement, men who fought at Ashtown twenty-five years ago, who fought while fighting was to be done and continue still to serve the nation.[26]

Moylan died in office on 16 November. A state funeral took him to a little cemetery in Kiskeam not far from his 1920 brigade headquarters at Riordan's of Knockavorheen in the immediate hinterland of the village. At Cahir the funeral was met by veterans of the War of Independence, including his lifelong friend Dan Breen. On quiet country roads old Volunteers stood holding their caps and saluted a former soldier. The cortège drove through Mitchelstown, Mallow, Kanturk and Newmarket, where crowds stood in silence and watched the final journey of a man who in other days had fought for Ireland. In Kiskeam the people, who loved and respected him for all that he was, gathered in their thousands. De Valera paid tribute to a man who 'was the soul of integrity.'[27]

The achievements in his life were many. The part he played in the War of Independence was considerable. His contribution was to train, arm and maintain a battalion of Volunteers in the teeth of military occupation by the British Empire. He led a series of ambushes in which his men sustained no fatalities, nor indeed were there any civilian fatalities. The manner in which he conducted the fight was notable. British Army captives were disarmed and released; wounded prisoners received first aid. His conduct on capture and during court-martial set him apart.

During his time as a Civil War leader, his actions were never tainted by any of the atrocities that marked this period. His service as a Dáil Deputy, a Senator and a government minister spanned twenty-five years in which he made a significant contribution to land policy and the development of Irish agriculture as a national resource.

If he had a regret, it might have been failing to prevent the Civil War or failing to bring it to a swift conclusion. But if he had such thoughts he never expressed them publicly. If there was a lost opportunity, then he might have regretted that he did not have the chance to spend some years at the Department of Agriculture.

People had different memories of Moylan: as a politician, a father, a grandfather or a soldier. He was a complex figure. His courtesy to ordinary people was notable, but so was his legendary forthrightness in expressing his views. He was a formidable opponent, a remarkable orator and older readers will remember his poetic exchanges with the unrepentant blueshirt Ned Buckley of Knocknagree, whose satire lampooned Moylan and many others. Among his constituents, whether they were his supporters or not, he had the reputation of being a hard-working Deputy.

Perhaps the best measure of his worth is that he was respected by his opponents. He had friends on all sides of the political divide. Tom Barry observed: 'He was a brave and able field commander, a tireless military worker for the Republic and a wise counsellor at Brigade, Divisional and Executive meetings, who never hesitated to take his own line and speak out his mind. He had a hatred of sham and slogans which obscured realities. His sense of humour was the strongest of all the Volunteers I met.'[28] Likewise, Lieutenant General M. J. Costello, who thought Moylan wrong in the Civil War and was not a close friend or colleague, acknowledged his patriotism and his moral courage: 'He was honest and not afraid to show it.'[29]

Members of the Gloucestershire Regiment, which served in Ireland during 1921 and 1922, followed the significant milestones of Moylan's career. The regimental magazine, *Back Badge*, recorded his death in December 1957 with an article on the events that had taken place in Kiskeam thirty-six years previously.[30] As for the press, they had him marked down, somewhat bizarrely for a politician, as a man who did not court political popularity.[31]

Everyone who knew Moylan had their own image of the man. The following extract is a reminder that the Republic was established with great personal sacrifice by men and women who are barely remembered by new generations. It is taken from Moylan's witness statement and relates to the early hours of a January morning in 1921.

It is a fitting way to end the story of a man who made the journey from soldier to democrat to statesman:

> I left Kiskeam after dark on the fourteenth. I had a number of calls to make during the night and finally arrived at the ambush position about four a.m. It had been raining heavily. The rain had now ceased but it was bitter cold. I crept under a hedge and went to sleep for a few hours. When I awoke there was a slight drift of snow. It was not yet daylight and the boys had begun to gather. Inside an hour we were all in position.[32]

Appendix I

Martin Savage – A Memory

Escaping from prison in 1919 I was, as a result of a hunger strike and of the conditions under which I had to live in the immediately previous years, in poor physical shape. The attention of the Crown forces in my own district made it impossible for me to receive the medical care I needed, so I decided to come to Dublin.

I arrived in early September. I knew nobody in Dublin but Patrick O'Keeffe, the Deputy for my constituency; to him I went.[1]

Even in those far off days, it is of significance to remember that the much criticised Deputy was, as he still is, the medium through which many individual troubles are solved. And mine was an individual trouble. Those who nowadays believe that the IRA was then, as it later became, a highly integrated organisation fully informed of the activities, movements and needs of its units, capable of protecting and providing for the wants of its wounded, are basing their views on lack of information. They will realise the truth of this if they will remember that only in the spring of 1921 was it that the army was divisionalised; an organisational system created as a result of experience and because of desperate need. I told the Deputy the story of my need for medical attention, of my complete lack of financial resources and of my belief in my capacity to hold down any job he might be able to secure for me while I was getting back into shape. He gave me a note to Senator Thomas Foran then Chairman of the ITGWU.[2] Senator Foran phoned that lovable character, the late Mr Michael Somerville, first mentioning with confidence the name of a horse that was being tried out that day at the Curragh and then casually suggesting that he was sending along a friend. I saw Mr Somerville and as a result started work next morning with a firm of building contractors. The kindly sympathy of the leaders of Dublin trade unionism of the time, of the Dublin worker and his strong national spirit remain a bright memory in the life of one who has had his fill of disillusion.

Other pleasant memories of my short sojourn in Dublin are of the quiet of a September day in Howth, spent with the late Tomás MacCurtain, Lord Mayor of Cork, who had come to town for a discussion with IRA headquarters. We talked at length of proposals for activities and re-organisation to be undertaken on my recovery: of the brilliant teaching of Margaret Brown at the Leinster College where I went to perfect my Irish: of interesting lectures at Bolton Street where one night Piaras Béaslaí, fresh from his escape at Strangeways, made a dramatic appearance.

But my most vivid memory is that of a dull December afternoon, the happenings of which electrified the country. I was working in the Phoenix Park, and in the early afternoon I noticed considerable activity in the RIC depot; armed policemen falling in, orders being shouted, the rumble of lorries and a general air of intense excitement. Some instinct warned me. I dropped everything and got out of the park. Not too soon; as I passed by Infirmary Road, I met British troops moving towards the park and in a few moments, every exit was held by armed men.

Excited speculation was rife in the tram. Rumour took many forms and it was several hours before I learned the truth. Lord French and his escorts had been attacked at Ashtown, they had escaped, one of the attackers was killed; his name was Martin Savage. Thus I heard the name of one who was probably the first of those in the post-1916 period who laid down their lives in the attempt to shelter the flame of Irish National aspiration.[3]

Twenty-five years today have passed, of hope and disillusion, of struggle and storm, of suffering and success and the end is not yet come. But I remember my feelings on hearing of the death of Martin Savage; a feeling of pride in his courage, of appreciation of his motives, of admiration for an unselfish sacrifice, and even of envy that his opportunity had not been mine. These were the feelings, generated by the courageous effort of a hitherto unknown man, that were universal in the Ireland of my youth, that raised Irishmen to a place of self-immolation and achievement never surpassed in the history of our country.

Today we live under different conditions, brought about by the efforts of Savage and his comrades, when to the quality of selflessness must be added that of wise statecraft. But wisdom in any form is of no avail if we cannot breed men like Savage whose lack of concern for personal well-being and security in the service of the nation overrode all natural human weakness and desire. We do breed them, and we have still among us as a reminder of the past and as a touchstone of achievement, men who fought at Ashtown twenty-five years ago, who fought while fighting was to be done and continue still to serve the nation.

Today in a bookshop in Nassau Street I saw one of these, who 'had stood on many a field of blood and fought with many a foe his greying head bent over a book.' The book was Dr Dixon's 'Michael Dwyer'. Over his shoulder I read the words: 'writers in the press of the period and historians with few exceptions have been bitterly hostile to the cause for which Dwyer fought and when they have condescended to mention him at all, have laboured to portray him as a mere bandit or midnight marauder'.

We who remember 1919 know how true the statement is. Those who are forgetful of, or misread the past, are the doubting critics of today, the defeatists of tomorrow.

But Michael Dwyer and Martin Savage and the long roll of our soldier dead are the strong links in the unbreakable chain of our national tradition. So is our nation strong. May we here highly resolve that these dead shall not have died in vain.

Seán Moylan, 1944

Appendix II

Transcript of Voice Recording for the Bureau of Military History

I have met them at close of day.[1]

The abstract principle that freedom is the birthright of a nation is generally conceded; the putting into effect of abstract principles is not highly regarded in this workaday world. And so, nations with a lust for power have enslaved weaker ones. Ireland was the victim of English conquest, but the finality of that conquest was never recognised by the Irish people. Time and again, that recognition has been emphasised in revolt. Always there has been the minority who insisted that submission was slavish; always the majority who consciously or subconsciously believed in the doctrine preached, but who were awed to silence and inaction.

It was a doctrine that gave no thought to economics. It was the expression of a psychological need, the need that men feel for a recognition of their manhood; an expression of that unquestioning belief that man, endowed with an immortal soul is, because of that fundamental fact, the equal of his fellows and not to be exploited, derided or enslaved.

The insurrection of Easter Week was a protest made, not so much in the hope of an immediate adoption of the ideas on which it was based, as on the belief that the sacrificial promulgation of those ideas would eventually bear fruit, would induce acceptance of the principles of the insurrectionists.

Those who promote revolution seek an immediate effect, expect that their efforts will result in radical change. It is my view that what began as an insurrection in Easter Week evolved, and swiftly, into a revolution. Everywhere in Ireland was the old leaven of Fenian tradition. Deep in the hearts of all Irishmen of my generation was a sense of racial solidarity. Even those who looked with dismay on Easter Week were proud of the courage of their compatriots, bitterly resentful of the execution of prisoners. Irish history has made insurrection inevitable; the conditions and mentality created thereby produced a revolution.

The gravel was raked smoothly over the prison graves of the dead of Easter Week; the fighting men were tucked away securely in British jails; Sir John Maxwell could report that quiet was restored, rebellion quelled and that the King's Irish subjects repudiated and abhorred the action of the rebels. But the gravel, smooth over quicklime graves, was deceptive; for the replacement of each man in prison there were countless others, now fiercely earnest and clear of purpose. The quiet was ominous.

Into this quiet the prison gates were opened and the prisoners streamed back to an enthusiastic welcome. Insurrection was to become revolution and those who were to make it were never again to lead quiet, uneventful lives. They were to travel many a weary mile, to make good friends and bitter enemies, to develop endless patience and tolerance, to know wounds and hunger and weariness of spirit, to spend themselves in a fight, the end of which most of them were not destined to see.

The army that they organised had one outstanding quality, that of suitability to its purpose. Critics of every effort and of every accomplishment are manifold, and the Irish army, its efforts and accomplishments, has not escaped criticism and odious comparison. But it had a particular piece of work to do in circumstances unique and extraordinary. It cannot be said that it was created as a result of clearly conceived plans, that its campaign was related to a well-considered strategy; that it was directed and controlled by a centralised headquarters, had its needs supplied by a well-organised quartermaster's department. I consider it to have been, it was indeed, the spearpoint of an uprising of a people. It had its roots in an age-long tradition of resistance. It was shaped and conditioned by a long-continued underground organisation forced on a subject race who refused to accept subjection and was brought into being by the inspiration of Easter Week.

I do not say that there was no direction by headquarters. There certainly was. But it was a general rather than a specific direction. Headquarters was a co-ordinating body which left each brigade to its own resources, to make the most of the opportunities offered, which kept brigades informed as to the general situation and of any developments of enemy tactics.

The military effort was so mingled with developments on the political side; the work of the soldier so gradually shaded into the work of politics; there was such a complete fusion of thought and action within the nation that it was difficult to say where the ever-widening circle of activity ceased to absorb the community. It was a concentrated effort in which each citizen subordinated his private interests to the welfare of the community and the Irish Republican Army, adequate to its task, was wholly suitable to this background.

The central figures of each Irish National movement are re-membered and honoured; the memory of the many men of capacity and patriotic outlook, who worked so selflessly in the background of each such movement, is dim and clouded and unappreciated. And this remains true even though the grave of the first 'Unknown Soldier' is in Ireland.

Let me, therefore, pay a tribute to the rank and file of the Irish Republican Army. Never has there been in any country a generation of men who reached a higher plane of courage and self-sacrifice; who displayed a greater effectiveness against overwhelming odds; who walked so proudly into the valley of the shadow of death, as those men who served Ireland in her revolutionary years.

Those who most successfully make war are those who weld

their nation into a single-minded unit, clear on its objective and determined to achieve it. The creation of such a unit was Ireland's supreme accomplishment.

Future generations of Irishmen will be able to view the work done by their forbears in true perspective and can formulate a considered judgment thereon. I put my trust in their verdict and hope, as we in our time have done, that they will experience, but in peace and freedom, the loyalty of good comradeship, the compelling force of unselfish purpose and the inspiring example of true leadership.

Seán Moylan, 14 December 1950
Bureau of Military History, 1913–1921
No. V.R.7

Appendix III

Speech at Spike Island to commemorate Patrick White

There is an honourable pride among those of the Irish Republican Army who survive, in courage displayed, capacity shown, results achieved. Among them no men have greater reason for that pride than have the men of the East Clare Brigade. Established in the initiatory period of the Volunteer movement its name is written in letters of light on every page of Ireland's revolutionary record. It is not surprising that we call Clare the Banner County. In every advance Clare has been the pennant that led the nation's march. The work of the Irish Volunteers could not have been specifically directed by an army headquarters, nor was brigade leadership sufficient to the particular purpose. The circumstances were such as demanded a looseness of organisation. A combination of distinct units finding their coherence in a common purpose. Of these units the company captains were the leaders and the driving force: whatever success was achieved would have been impossible without their efforts, their steadfastness, their persistence, the loyalty that bound them to a common cause. The man who we honour today was one of these, associated from his early years with patriotic endeavour, a pioneer Volunteer, captain of the Meelick Company of the East Clare Brigade. Here, where his body fell, we of the Cork Brigade pay our tribute to his memory. His spirit has gone back to Corca Baiscin, to the stony hills of Clare, to become part of Clare's tradition, that tradition that ensures that in the nation's need

Clare will stand in her defence as stern as the Cliffs of Moher, as strong as the Shannon, as enduring as the sea.

In these days of greater material well-being the voice of cynicism is sometimes raised. Men who pose as thinkers have by some process of disillusion arrived at the idea that 1916 and the events that logically followed from it were at best an error, at worst a crime. Because under drawback and difficulties we have not under national government arrived at the millennium, they seem to preach that our continued acceptance of foreign rule would have been better for the Irish people. How has the welfare of this country been promoted by alien rule? There is no need to recall the evils imposed on this nation by alien rule, the rule described by Canon Sheehan in one of his books as that of 'the whip and the sop' blundering alien administration acting often in good will, irritated by its failure at placation, attributing that failure to the intransigency of the people and attempting to redeem its errors by punitive measures. The social and political order that must be the basis of community life did not exist and could not have emerged from such conditions. Lack of respect for law, irresponsibility, indiscipline, all the factors of moral deterioration are rooted in their existence. Where they obtain, government and people co-exist in severance, in distrust, in apprehension and insecurity. A man's personality is his most precious possession; it distinguishes him from the unreasoning beast. He may, of his free will, accept authority rightfully imposed, while recognising its imperfections. He may for the general good, obey regulations which limit his freedom of action: he may respect conventions which he believes to be outworn in the desire to preserve the intangibles embodied in a national or cultural tradition. But there is a limit to his acquiescence. It is impossible for him to display it to the same extent under the rule of the alien.

An American writing of the American occupation of Japan says: 'If you come to think of it the people of an occupied country can have no sincere feeling towards the conqueror except to wish him gone. No matter how laudable are his intentions, nor even how useful he may sometimes be, his presence is odious; he is a blot on the landscape and

A page of the handwritten speech Moylan made at Spike Island.

a constant reminder of disgrace and defeat and of the fact that one is nothing but a second-class citizen in one's own land.'

The leaders of 1916 were deeply thoughtful men and scholarly. They were men who in their characters were the antitheses of those who regard force as a solution of national problems. They pursued the ideal of national freedom, not in egoistic fury, not in any sense of personal frustration but because they believed it to be essential to their nation's survival, its progress and development. The action they took was implicitly in that belief. They knew what they were doing; they had counted the cost; they entertained no hope of personal survival. They sacrificed their lives in an endeavour to accomplish their aims as did many of those who followed them in Ireland's revolutionary years.

Human nature is the same the world over: all men are our brothers. But no matter how perfervidly internationalism is preached and nationalism condemned, the fact remains that nations are distinct entities. There is a vast difference in the traditions, customs and outlook of different peoples. The social order is promoted only by government that understands, appreciates or makes allowance for the existence of these. Such a government, no matter what its form takes, must be one that springs from the people – a native government. Political order is essential for the support of enduring human communities. Its acceptance and maintenance depends on the confidence and goodwill of the community; depends too, on the moral courage they bring to its support.

Patriotism, said Pearse, is in great measure a memory of heroic dead men. If it is to be something other than an unreasoning emotion, it must be based on an understanding of the reason for their sacrifice and effort, on an appreciation of the ideals pursued and the results envisaged. True patriotism may entail a venturous courage or may be displayed in the submission to a daily grind. It must be directed to a specific end, the value of which must have been thoughtfully assessed. It must utilise means that are morally justifiable and that offer some assurance of success. It is not implicit in an invitation of historic deeds, no matter how heroic, since it must take cognition of changed conditions and changed circumstances.

This is our country to love and to serve. Captain Patrick White and his comrades served it in their turn to the limit of their ability, to the ultimate in sacrificial effort. It remains for us to complete their work. This we cannot do without a reasoned acceptance of discipline, without a recognition of the view that the national problems of today cannot be set in terms that are obsolete. Those who so set it impede the progress of the nation. Courage, energy and enthusiasm are dissipated by the blind arrogant and egotistical pride of absolutism, the failure of which are strewn over all the pages of history. Those who would serve the nation, are concerned for the welfare of the people and the future of the country, should remember that nothing is so important as integrity of purpose and personal integrity in defence of that purpose.

I do not depreciate or undervalue the effect of the work of the efforts of the Irish Republican Army in Ireland's revolutionary years. But I would urge that there was in those years a concatenation of circumstances that wisely used, ensured the measure of success we achieved. Until such circumstances repeat themselves or until we can mould them to our purpose, we can make no spectacular advance.

There is a wide field of endeavour open to those who would serve Ireland. Let us utilise it with integrity of purpose and with uncomplaining courage or let us cease paying lip service to the memory of heroic dead men.

Seán Moylan,
Sunday 25 August 1957

NOTES

1 The Ties that Bind

1   Adams, Patience Pollard, 'Account of Attack on Kilmallock Barracks', *History Ireland*, vol. 11, no. 1, 2003, p. 6.

2   Joyce, Mannix, 'Who Carried a Fenian Gun', *The Capuchin Annual* 1968, p. 195.

3   Adams *op. cit.*, p. 6.

4   Seán Moylan, Bureau of Military History Witness Statement No. 838 (Moylan Witness Statement) p. 10.

5   Allen, Larkin and O'Brien were hanged in November 1867 for the murder of Sergeant Charles Brett, who died in Manchester during the rescue of two leading IRB men. The condemned men's final prayer 'God Save Ireland' was set to music. The lyrics first appeared in *The Nation* on 7 December 1867.

6   Bureau of Military History Witness Statement No. 838 (Moylan Witness Statement) p. 6.

7   Peig O'Brien (née Moylan), voice recording, n.d.

8   The 1911 Census returns show Seán and his siblings Joe, Mamie and Gret speaking both Irish and English. Likewise his first cousin Con Moylan and his aunt, Mary Raleigh, in Kilmallock. His brother Ned had emigrated to America prior to the taking of the 1911 census.

9   Richard Moylan, unfinished biography of Seán Moylan, n.d.

10 Moylan Witness Statement *op. cit.*, p. 11.

11 GAA Committee, *Our Proud Heritage: The History of Kilmallock GAA from 1884–1976* (The Kerryman Ltd, Tralee, 1977) p. 47.

12 *Ibid.*, p. 52.

13 *Ibid.*, p. 47.

14 Paddy O'Brien, Bureau of Military History Witness Statement No. 764, p. 4.

15 William Reardon, Bureau of Military History Witness Statement No. 1185, p. 1.

16 Moylan Witness Statement *op. cit.*, pp. 52–53.

17 Dan Flynn, Bureau of Military History Witness Statement No. 1240, p. 2.

18 Moylan Witness Statement *op. cit.*, p. 6.

19 Macardle, Dorothy, *The Irish Republic* (Corgi, London, 1968) p. 237.

20 Moylan family papers held by the author.

2   1919

1   Seán Moylan, Bureau of Military History Witness Statement No. 838 (Moylan Witness Statement) pp. 65–67.

2   Moylan family papers held by the author.

3   Moylan Witness Statement *op. cit.*, p. 68.

4   General Prisons Board Records, CR132, National Archives of Ireland. See also DORA prisoners' correspondence NA GPB Box 3.

5   Moylan Witness Statement *op. cit.*, p. 65.

6   Townshend, Charles, *The British Campaign in Ireland 1919–1921* (Oxford University Press, London, 1975) p. 221.

7   Moylan Witness Statement *op. cit.*, p. 70.

8   General Prisons Board Records, CR132.

9   Moylan Witness Statement *op. cit.*, p. 72.

10 Moylan family papers held by the author.

11 6th Division Record of the Rebellion, Strickland papers, p. 17. Major General E. P. Strickland was commander of the 6th Division and governor of the military law area. His immediate superior was General Sir Nevil Macready, Commander-in-Chief of the British forces in Ireland.

12 *Ibid.*, p. 18.

13 O'Donoghue, Florence, *No Other Law* (Irish Press Ltd, Dublin, 1954) p. 50.

14 Moylan Witness Statement *op. cit.*, p. 65.

15 Moylan family papers held by the author. See Appendix 1.

3   The Road to Recovery

1   Macardle, Dorothy, *The Irish Republic* (Corgi, London, 1968) p. 309.
2   William Reardon, Bureau of Military History Witness Statement No. 1185, p. 23.
3   Jones, Thomas, *Whitehall Diary. Volume III (1918–1925)* (Oxford University Press, London, 1971) p. 21 [Record of Cabinet Meeting, 31 May 1920].
4   Hansard, HC Debates, 25 March 1920, vol. 127, col. 574.
5   Seán Moylan, Bureau of Military History Witness Statement No. 838 (Moylan Witness Statement) p. 82.
6   *Ibid.*, pp. 82–83.
7   6th Division Record of the Rebellion, Strickland papers, p. 24.
8   Moylan Witness Statement *op. cit.,* p. 173. Although Moylan describes the attack on Kilmallock RIC Barracks he does not say that he was there or, as is sometimes asserted by historians, that he led the raid. Kilmallock was outside Moylan's area of operations and it is clear from *The War in Clare* (Brennan, 1980) that Moylan was not involved in this raid.
9   Moylan Witness Statement *op. cit.,* p. 40.
10   Strickland papers *op. cit.,* p. 34.
11   Smyth quoted in Gaughan, J. Anthony, *Memoirs of Constable Jeremiah Mee, RIC* (Anvil Books, Dublin, 1975) p. 104. Mee's note of the meeting was written up and checked by a number of other constables before being published. The full text of Smyth's speech is simply breathtaking and should be read.
12   Moylan Witness Statement *op. cit.,* p. 174.
13   Hansard, HC Debates, 1 July 1920, vol. 131, col. 619–20.

4   The General Lucas Affair

1   Seán Moylan, Bureau of Military History Witness Statement No. 838 (Moylan Witness Statement) p. 88.
2   *Ibid.*
3   *Ibid.*, pp. 88–89.
4   *Ibid.*, p. 89.
5   Ryan, Meda, *The Real Chief, Liam Lynch* (Mercier Press, Cork, 2005) p. 50.

6 Moylan Witness Statement *op. cit.*, p. 90.

7 *New York Times*, Monday 28 June 1920.

8 John (Jack) O'Connell, Bureau of Military History Witness Statement No. 1211, p. 5.

9 'An Irishman's Diary', Nichevo, *The Irish Times*, Saturday 15 December 1945.

10 Hansard, HC Debates, 28 June 1920, vol. 131, col. 30–31.

11 O'Donoghue, Florence, *No Other Law* (Irish Press Ltd, Dublin, 1954) p. 79.

12 Hansard, HC Debates, 29 June 1920, vol. 131, col. 245.

13 Major General Strickland, personal diary, 27 June 1920, Imperial War Museum.

14 Macready, General Sir Nevil, *Annals of an Active Life* (Hutchinson, London, 1924) vol. 2, p. 472.

15 Brennan, Michael, *The War in Clare 1911–1921. Personal Memoirs of the Irish War of Independence* (Four Courts Press and Irish Academic Press, Dublin, 1980) p. 54.

16 Major General Strickland, personal diary, 21 July 1920, Imperial War Museum.

17 Brennan *op. cit.*, p. 56.

5 Getting Guns

1 Dwyer, T. Ryle, *Tans, Terror and Troubles* (Mercier Press, Cork, 2001) p. 205.

2 Burrows, J. W. *Essex Units in the War 1914–1919, Volume 1: The First Battalion* (John H. Burrows, Southend, 1927) p. 274.

3 Seán Moylan, Bureau of Military History Witness Statement No. 838 (Moylan Witness Statement) p. 96. Ned Moylan shared his good fortune and used what remained of the reward money to pay his way through law school. He was admitted to the Colorado Bar in 1928 and practised there with success for many years.

4 Moylan Witness Statement *op. cit.*, p. 96.

5 *Ibid.*, p. 101.

6 *Ibid.*, p. 102.

7 *Ibid.*

8 Patrick O'Brien, Bureau of Military History Witness Statement No.

764, p. 22.

9   O'Malley, Ernie, *On Another Man's Wound* (Rich & Cowan Ltd, London, 1937) p. 195.

10 *Ibid.*

6   Spiral of Violence

1   Callwell, C. E., *Field Marshal Sir Henry Wilson, Volume 2: His Life and Diaries* (Cassell & Co, London, 1927) p. 263.

2   Self, Robert C. (ed.), *The Austen Chamberlain Diary Letters: The Correspondence of Sir Austen Chamberlain with His Sisters Hilda and Ida (1916–1937)* (Cambridge University Press, Cambridge, 1995) p. 150.

3   Burrows, J. W., *Essex Units in the War 1914–1919, Volume 1: The First Battalion* (John H. Burrows, Southend, 1927) p. 272.

4   Deasy, Liam, *Towards Ireland Free* (Mercier Press, Dublin and Cork, 1973) p. 213.

5   6th Division Record of the Rebellion, Strickland papers, p. 57.

6   *Ibid.*, p. 50.

7   Shea, Patrick, *Voices and the Sound of Drums* (Blackstaff Press, Belfast, 1981) p. 45.

8   Hopkinson, Michael, *Green against Green, The Irish Civil War* (Gill & Macmillan, Dublin, 2004) p. 50.

9   Jeffrey, Keith, *Field Marshal Sir Henry Wilson, a Political Soldier* (Oxford University Press, Oxford, 2008) p. 263.

10 O'Casey, Seán, *Autobiographies, Volume II: Inishfallen Fare Thee Well* (Macmillan, London, 1981) pp. 40–41.

11 Jeffrey (2008) *op. cit.*, pp. 265–266.

12 Seán Moylan, Bureau of Military History Witness Statement No. 838 (Moylan Witness Statement) p. 117.

13 *Ibid.*, p. 119.

14 Paddy O'Brien, Bureau of Military History Witness Statement No. 764, p. 26.

15 George Power, Bureau of Military History Witness Statement No. 451, p. 13.

16 Meagher, Jim, *The War of Independence in North Cork. The Story of Charleville No. 2 Cork Brigade* (Charleville and District Historical and Archaeological Society, Charleville, 2004) p. 68.

17 Strickland papers *op. cit.*, p. 47; the 6th Division Record of the Rebellion may be suspect on this point.

18 Dan Flynn, Bureau of Military History Witness Statement No. 1240, p. 7.

19 O'Malley, Ernie, *On Another Man's Wound* (Rich & Cowan Ltd, London, 1937) p. 189.

20 17th Lancers Regimental Diary, p. 147. Lieutenant McCreery had commanded the Lancers in Mallow at the time of the raid on Mallow Barracks.

7 Meelin

1 Florence O'Donoghue papers, MS31266, National Library of Ireland.

2 *Ibid.*

3 6th Division Record of the Rebellion, Strickland papers, p. 69.

4 Seán Moylan, Bureau of Military History Witness Statement No. 838 (Moylan Witness Statement) p. 158.

5 *Ibid.*

6 *Ibid.*, p. 159.

7 *Ibid.*, pp. 159–160.

8 Tim Cronin, Bureau of Military History Witness Statement No. 1134, pp. 4–5.

9 *The Irish Times*, Thursday 6 January 1921.

10 *Ibid.*

11 Strickland papers *op. cit.*, p. 73.

12 Moylan Witness Statement *op. cit.*, p. 160.

13 O'Donoghue, Florence, *No Other Law* (Irish Press Ltd, Dublin, 1954) p. 130.

14 *The Irish Times*, Thursday 6 January 1921.

15 Brennan, Michael, *The War in Clare, 1911–1921, Personal Memoirs of the Irish War of Independence* (Four Courts Press and Irish Academic Press, Dublin, 1980) p. 45.

8 Meenegorman

1 6th Division Record of the Rebellion, Strickland papers, p. 70.

2   Seán Moylan, Bureau of Military History Witness Statement No. 838 (Moylan Witness Statement) pp. 161–162.

3   *Ibid.*, pp. 162–164.

4   Macardle, Dorothy, *The Irish Republic* (Corgi, London, 1968) p. 383

5   Strickland papers *op. cit.*, p. 70.

6   Deasy, Liam, *Towards Ireland Free* (Mercier Press, Dublin and Cork, 1973) p. 346.

9   **Tureengarriffe**

1   Seán Moylan, Bureau of Military History Witness Statement No. 838 (Moylan Witness Statement) p. 165.

2   *Ibid.*, pp. 166–167.

3   Ó Ríordáin, J. J., *Kiskeam versus The Empire* (The Kerryman Ltd, Tralee, 1985) p. 53.

4   Moylan Witness Statement *op. cit.*, pp. 167–168.

5   Tim Cronin, Bureau of Military History Witness Statement No. 1134, p. 5.

6   Moylan Witness Statement *op. cit.*, p. 168.

7   *Ibid.*

8   James Cashman, Bureau of Military History Witness Statement No. 1270, p. 8.

9   Dan Guiney, Bureau of Military History Witness Statement No. 1347, pp. 9–10.

10 Ó Ríordáin *op. cit.*, p. 55.

11 *Ibid.*, p. 54.

12 Tim Cronin, Bureau of Military History Witness Statement No. 1134, p. 10.

13 *Cork Examiner*, Saturday 4 June 1921.

14 Abbott, Richard, *Police Casualties in Ireland 1919–1922* (Mercier Press, Cork, 2000) p. 191.

15 Cornelius Murphy was captured on 4 January on a visit to his parents. He was in possession of two revolvers. He declined representation and was court-martialled on 17 January. He was convicted of being in possession of arms. The military court made a recommendation for mercy in view of what they termed his limited education and intellect, but a sentence of death was confirmed by General Macready.

16 Typed rough notes kept by Lieutenant R. M. Grazebrook, Soldiers of Gloucestershire Museum. The content of the notes suggests they were written up early in 1921, perhaps only days or at most weeks after the ambush.

17 6th Division Record of the Rebellion, Strickland papers, p. 73.

18 Hopkinson, Michael (ed.) *The Last Days of Dublin Castle: The Diaries of Mark Sturgis* (Irish Academic Press, Dublin, 1999) p. 117.

19 *The Irish Times*, Monday 31 January 1921.

20 *Cork Examiner*, Tuesday 1 February 1921.

21 Strickland papers *op. cit.*, p. 73.

22 *Ibid.*, p. 75.

23 *Cork Examiner*, Tuesday 1 February 1921.

24 O'Donoghue, Florence, *No Other Law* (Irish Press Ltd, Dublin, 1954) pp. 132–133.

10 February 1921

1 PRO/WO/71/376, National Archives Kew.

2 Con Meaney, Bureau of Military History Witness Statement No. 787, p. 12.

3 Seán Moylan, Bureau of Military History Witness Statement No. 838 (Moylan Witness Statement) pp. 186–187.

4 *Ibid.*, p. 187. The official report quoted in Moylan's witness statement was published in the *Irish Independent* on 8 February 1921.

5 Hansard, HC Debates, 24 February 1921, vol. 138, col. 1115–1116.

6 Dan Flynn, Bureau of Military History Witness Statement No. 1240, p. 10.

7 Kennedy, Seán, *They Loved Dear Old Ireland* (private printing, 1974) p. 26.

8 Moylan Witness Statement *op. cit.*, p. 152.

9 Paddy O'Brien, Bureau of Military History Witness Statement No. 764, p. 61.

10 Moylan Witness Statement *op. cit.*, pp. 184–185.

11 *Ibid.*, p. 23.

12 6th Division Record of the Rebellion, Strickland papers, p. 73.

13 Paddy O'Higgins, Bureau of Military History Witness Statement No. 1467, p. 5.

14   Moylan Witness Statement *op. cit.*, p. 174.

15   *Ibid.*, p. 181.

16   *Ibid.*

17   *Ibid.*, p. 182.

18   Ó Ríordáin, J. J., *Kiskeam versus The Empire* (The Kerryman Ltd, Tralee, 1985) p. 62.

19   Second Battalion of the Hampshires, war diary, Hampshire Regimental Museum, Winchester.

11   Clonbanin

1   Seán Moylan, Bureau of Military History Witness Statement No. 838 (Moylan Witness Statement) pp. 193–194.

2   6th Division Record of the Rebellion, Strickland papers, p. 88. Moylan's comprehensive report contains a detailed analysis of the incident and provides fascinating insights on tactics.

3   Con Meaney, Bureau of Military History Witness Statement No. 787, p. 18.

4   Strickland papers *op. cit.*, p. 85.

5   Moylan Witness Statement *op. cit.*, p. 195.

6   *Ibid.*, p. 196.

7   *Ibid.*, pp. 197–198.

8   Patrick O'Brien, Bureau of Military History Witness Statement No. 764, p. 38.

9   Meagher, Jim, *The War of Independence in North Cork. The Story of Charleville No. 2 Cork Brigade* (Charleville and District Historical and Archaeological Society, Charleville, 2004) p. 47.

10   Moylan Witness Statement *op. cit.*, p. 198.

11   Strickland papers *op. cit.*, p. 86.

12   Moylan Witness Statement *op. cit.*, pp. 198–199.

13   Ó Ríordáin, J. J., *Kiskeam versus The Empire* (The Kerryman Ltd, Tralee 1985) p. 67.

14   Moylan Witness Statement *op. cit.*, p. 199.

15   James Cashman, Bureau of Military History Witness Statement No. 1270, p. 12.

16   Lieutenant R. M. Grazebrook, diary, Soldiers of Gloucestershire Museum, p. 19.

17 Moylan Witness Statement *op. cit.*, p. 200.

18 Strickland papers *op. cit.*, p. 88.

19 *The Irish Times*, Monday 7 March 1921.

20 Strickland papers *op. cit.*, p. 90.

21 *The Irish Times*, Thursday 10 March 1921.

22 *Lillywhite's Gazette*, September 1921, Queen's Lancashire Regimental Museum.

23 Macready, General Sir Nevil, *Annals of an Active Life* (Hutchinson, London, 1924) vol. 2, p. 463.

24 O'Donoghue, Florence, *No Other Law* (Irish Press Ltd, Dublin, 1954) p. 133.

25 Moylan Witness Statement *op. cit.*, p. 202.

26 *Ibid.*, p. 209.

27 Strickland papers *op. cit.*, p. 90.

28 Jeremiah Murphy, Michael Courtney and Denis Mulchinock, Bureau of Military History Witness Statement No. 744, pp. 15–16.

29 Strickland papers *op. cit.*, p. 96.

30 Moylan Witness Statement *op. cit.*, p. 215.

12 The Gun and Promotion

1   Annie Barrett, Bureau of Military History Witness Statement No. 1133, pp. 5–6.

2   Seán Moylan, Bureau of Military History Witness Statement No. 838 (Moylan Witness Statement) p. 216.

3   *Ibid.*, p. 219.

4   *Ibid.*, p. 220.

5   *Ibid.*, pp. 220–221.

6   *Ibid.*, p. 233.

7   Ó Ríordáin, J. J., *Kiskeam versus The Empire* (The Kerryman Ltd, Tralee 1985) p. 82.

8   Moylan Witness Statement *op. cit.*, pp. 224–225.

9   *Ibid.*, p. 226.

10 Barry, Tom, *Guerrilla Days in Ireland* (Mercier Press, Cork, 1955) p. 157.

11 O'Donoghue, Florence, *No Other Law* (Irish Press Ltd, Dublin, 1954) p. 144.

12 Barry, Tom, *The Reality of the Anglo-Irish War 1920–21 in West Cork. Refutations, Corrections and Comments on Liam Deasy's Towards Ireland Free* (Anvil Press, Tralee, 1974) p. 43.

13 Moylan Witness Statement *op. cit.*, p. 225.

13 Cork No. 2 Brigade O/C

1   Seán Moylan, Bureau of Military History Witness Statement No. 838 (Moylan Witness Statement) p. 227.

2   George Power, Bureau of Military History Witness Statement No. 451, p. 19.

3   *Ibid.*, p. 20; Power took over Cork No. 2 Brigade after the capture of Moylan and estimated that the strength of the brigade was 5,000 at the time of the Truce.

4   Ó Ríordáin, J. J., *Kiskeam versus The Empire* (The Kerryman Ltd, Tralee, 1985) p. 85.

5   Moylan Witness Statement *op. cit.*, pp. 230–232.

6   Abbott, Richard, *Police Casualties in Ireland 1919–1922* (Mercier Press, Cork, 2000) p. 230.

7   Ó Ríordáin, *op. cit.*, p. 95.

14 The Arrival of the Gloucestershire Regiment

1   *Cork Examiner*, Saturday 4 June 1921.

2   Lieutenant R. M. Grazebrook, diary, Soldiers of Gloucestershire Museum, p. 15.

3   *Ibid.*, p. 16.

4   *Ibid.*

5   *Ibid.*, p. 17.

6   Captain A. H. Richards, memoir, Soldiers of Gloucestershire Museum, p. 1.

7   Seán Moylan, Bureau of Military History Witness Statement No. 838 (Moylan Witness Statement) p. 247.

8   Richards *op. cit.*, p. 2.

9   Moylan Witness Statement *op. cit.*, p. 248.

10 Ó Ríordáin, J. J., *Kiskeam versus The Empire* (The Kerryman Ltd, Tralee, 1985).

11 Grazebrook *op. cit.*, p. 18.

12   *Ibid.*, p. 31.

13   Moylan Witness Statement *op. cit.*, p. 244.

14   Grazebrook *op. cit.*, p. 30.

15   Moylan Witness Statement *op. cit.*, pp. 235–236.

16   *Ibid.*, p. 236.

17   *Ibid.*, p. 236.

18   *Ibid.*, p. 237.

19   *Ibid.*, p. 237.

20   *Ibid.*, p. 237.

21   *Ibid.*, p. 239.

22   Grazebrook *op. cit.*, p. 30.

23   *Ibid.*, p. 31.

24   6th Division Record of the Rebellion, Strickland papers, p. 101.

25   Patrick O'Brien, Bureau of Military History Witness Statement No. 764, pp. 46–48. Dan O'Brien was executed on 16 May 1921 after a drumhead court-martial. O'Regan had sustained ten bullet wounds and was so badly injured that he was unfit to be court-martialled; he was saved by the Truce.

15 Capture

1   Lieutenant R. M. Grazebrook, diary, Soldiers of Gloucestershire Museum, p. 33.

2   6th Division Record of the Rebellion, Strickland papers, p. 107

3   Grazebrook *op. cit.*, p. 36.

4   *Ibid.*, p. 40.

5   O'Donoghue, Florence, *No Other Law* (Irish Press Ltd, Dublin, 1954) p. 169.

6   Bureau of Military History Witness Statement No. 838 (Moylan Witness Statement) pp. 248–250.

7   Ó Ríordáin, J. J., *Kiskeam versus The Empire* (The Kerryman Ltd, Tralee 1985) p. 90.

8   Grazebrook, *op. cit.*, p. 38.

9   Moylan Witness Statement *op. cit.*, p. 250.

10   Grazebrook *op. cit.*, p. 40.

11   Patrick Casey was captured in an engagement with the Green Howards at Shraharla Bridge not far from Kildorrery on 1 May

1921. Following drumhead court-martial he was executed at Victoria Barracks in Cork the following day. Drumhead courts-martial were used against soldiers in the field who deserted, mutinied or displayed cowardice in the face of the enemy. The legality of their use against civilians remains highly suspect. There can be no reason other than denying those captured legal representation or the opportunity to take a case to the civil courts.

12 Grazebrook *op. cit.*, p. 40.

13 *Ibid.*, p. 40. Grazebrook was a careful and inveterate note taker and used Moylan's typewriter to write his account; years later he referred to the brand new portable Corona as 'a pleasant trophy of the chase' (*Back Badge*, December 1957, p. 266). Corporal John Meadows of the Gloucestershire Regiment was Moylan's personal escort for the return to Kanturk workhouse. He was also present at Moylan's court-martial at Victoria Barracks. He had not been back to Ireland since 1922 and wrote to Moylan in 1956: 'I am hoping to come to Dublin … may I be permitted to come and see you?' (Moylan family papers held by the author).

14 Moylan Witness Statement *op. cit.*, p. 251.

15 Grazebrook *op. cit.*, p. 40. No polling took place for the Second Dáil as all candidates were returned unopposed.

16 Moylan Witness Statement *op. cit.*, pp. 252–253.

17 Moylan Witness Statement *op. cit.*, p. 253.

18 Grazebrook *op. cit.*, p. 40.

19 Report by C. F. N. Macready, general officer commanding-in-chief, on the situation in Ireland for week ending 28 May 1921, PRO/CAB/24/125, National Archives, Kew. In his witness statement written almost thirty years later, Moylan records that fourteen men were captured (including himself). Macready's report says thirteen.

16 A Writ of Habeas Corpus

1 Seán Moylan, Bureau of Military History Witness Statement No. 838 (Moylan Witness Statement) p. 253.

2 *Ibid.*, p. 254.

3 *Ibid.*

4 *Ibid.*

5   *Ibid.*

6   The account of Dan O'Brien's court-martial comes from PRO/ WO/71/383, National Archives, Kew. The legality of Con Murphy's court-martial and execution was raised in the Commons at Westminster on 24 February 1921. The point was made that the acts alleged against Murphy would not attract the death penalty under civil law. The question was brushed aside by the Chief Secretary Sir Hamar Greenwood.

7   Moylan Witness Statement *op. cit.*, p. 255.

8   *Ibid.*, p. 255.

9   *Ibid.*, p. 256.

10 *Ibid.*, p. 257.

11 Moylan, Richard, unfinished biography of Seán Moylan, n.d.

12 *Ibid.*

13 *Ibid.*

14 *Ibid.*

15 Moylan Witness Statement *op. cit.*, p. 257.

16 Moylan, Richard *op. cit.*

17 *Ibid.*

18 *Ibid.*

19 Moylan Witness Statement *op. cit.*, pp. 257–258.

20 *Ibid.*, pp. 258–259.

21 Moylan, Richard *op. cit.*, Years later, Barry Sullivan presented Seán Moylan with his case notes on *Moylan J. R. v Major General E.P. Strickland.* This extract is taken from Sullivan's notes.

22 Moylan, Richard *op. cit.*

23 *Ibid.*

17 The Court-Martial

1   Seán Moylan, Bureau of Military History Witness Statement No. 838 (Moylan Witness Statement) p. 259.

2   *Cork Examiner*, Tuesday 31 May 1921.

3   Moylan, Richard, unfinished biography of Seán Moylan, n.d.

4   *Cork Examiner*, Tuesday 31 May 1921.

5   *Ibid.* In *Portrait of Seán Moylan* painted by Keating in 1921, Moylan is wearing the greatcoat mentioned by the fifth witness.

6   Hansard HC Debates, 1 June 1921, vol. 142, col. 1047–1048. The Hansard debate indicates that the court-martial took place on 31 May 1921. Barry Sullivan, solicitor, recorded that the proceedings took place on 'Monday 30 May, 1921, [when] they did bring the plaintiff before a so-called Military Court not authorised by statute or common law.'

7   Lieutenant R. M. Grazebrook, diary, Soldiers of Gloucestershire Museum, p. 40.

8   Hansard HC Debates, 2 June 1921, vol. 142, col. 1223.

9   *Ibid.*

10 *The Irish Times*, Monday 6 June 1921.

11 Moylan Witness Statement *op. cit.*, p. 260.

12 The execution of three British soldiers is described by Ernie O'Malley in *On Another Man's Wound* (Rich & Cowan Ltd, London, 1937) pp. 327–332. See also Frank O'Connor, *Guests of the Nation* (Poolbeg Press, Dublin, 1985) pp. 5–18.

13 *R v Clifford and Sullivan* [1921] 2 A.C.570 (H.L. (I)).

14 *Cork Examiner*, Friday 10 June 1921.

15 *Egan v Macready and others* [1921] 1 I.R. 265. Dorothy Macardle suggests that the decisive decision in favour of the prisoners was delivered by the House of Lords in *R v Clifford and Sullivan*. With respect to Ms Macardle, whose work is a monument of carefully researched detail, this is incorrect. The Lords ruled against the prisoners Clifford and Sullivan by a majority of 4:1. A passage in General Macready's autobiography (*Annals of an Active Life*, vol. 2, Hutchinson, London, 1924) suggests that in early June Westminster ordered the military to defer any further executions until a legal appeal was heard. This could only be *Clifford and Sullivan*. The importance of *Clifford and Sullivan* appears to be that the army held off executions from the date when the case went from the Court of Appeal (early June) to the date judgment was given by the Lords (late July) by which time the Truce had been signed and O'Connor MR delivered the landmark ruling in *Egan v Macready and others*. The Attorney General for Ireland, Charles Andrew O'Connor, was appointed Master of the Rolls in 1912. This title was abolished by the Free State in 1924 under the Courts of Justice Act at which time O'Connor was appointed to the Supreme Court.

16 *Egan v Macready and others* [1921] 1 I.R. 265 and at 280.

17 Barry, Tom, *Guerrilla Days in Ireland* (Mercier Press, Cork, 1955) p. 164.

18 Owen Harold, Bureau of Military History Witness Statement No. 991, p. 12.

19 *R v Murphy* [1921] 2 I.R. 190.

20 *R v Allen* [1921] 2 I.R. 241.

21 Meagher, Jim, *The War of Independence in North Cork. The Story of Charleville No. 2 Cork Brigade* (Charleville and District Historical and Archaeological Society, Charleville, 2004) p. 60.

18 Spike Island

1 John Mitchel, *Jail Journal* (University Press of Ireland, 1982) p. 8.

2 John L. O'Sullivan recounts his experience in Griffith, K. and O'Grady, T., *Curious Journey. An Oral History of Ireland's Unfinished Revolution* (Hutchinson, London, 1982) p. 207.

3 Hansard, HC Debates, 21 June 1921, vol. 143, col. 1106. The internee who was shot dead was Patrick White, a captain in the Meelick company, East Clare Brigade. According to Hansard, White had been reaching through the wire, although, as the government spokesman confirmed, 'His motive appears to have been innocent, but it had been necessary to instruct sentries to fire immediately on any person attempting to break through or tamper with the wire.' Three other prisoners were killed in a similar way in Ballykinlar, including Tadgh Barry from Cork.

4 Seán Moylan, Bureau of Military History Witness Statement No. 838 (Moylan Witness Statement) p. 205.

5 Coogan, Tim Pat, *Michael Collins: a Biography* (Hutchinson, London 1990) p. 178.

6 Letter courtesy of Mrs Katty Sheahan, Newmarket.

7 Lieutenant R. M. Grazebrook, diary, Soldiers of Gloucestershire Museum. Grazebrook's diary appears to be a very candid and honest account of his service in Ireland. It does not seem likely that he had any personal involvement in this matter.

8 Hopkinson, Michael (ed.) *The Last Days of Dublin Castle: The Diaries of Mark Sturgis* (Irish Academic Press, Dublin, 1999) p. 211.

9   Moylan family papers held by the author.

10   Hopkinson, Michael, *The Irish War of Independence* (Gill & Macmillan,
Dublin, 2004) p. 107. This is a curious error since Moylan names
Lynch a number of times in his statement to the Bureau of Military
History. In the McGarrity papers he wrote of Lynch warmly and
with respect. No one knowing Lynch and his record could describe
him as a pen pusher. Hopkinson's error is repeated in *Green against
Green* (Gill & Macmillan, Dublin, 2004) p. 12. This time Tom Barry
is also alleged to have regarded Lynch in the same way. This does not
accord with Barry's observations about Lynch in *Guerrilla Days in
Ireland* (Mercier Press, Cork, 1955).

11   Moylan Witness Statement *op. cit.*, pp. 271–272.

12   Hart, Peter, *The IRA and Its Enemies: Violence and Community in Cork
1916–1923* (Clarendon Press, Oxford, 1998) p. 112.

19 The Truce and the Treaty

1   A report by General Macready to the cabinet at Westminster contains
a breakdown of rebel forces. There are factual errors in the report but
its importance lies in the fact that such reports were being prepared
lest there was a resumption of hostilities. One reads: 'There are at
present two units known as Cork IV Brigade; one is commanded
by Brig. Commandant Seán Moylan TD who has a large following
and supports the republican party.' PRO CAB/24/136, National
Archives, Kew, 6 April 1922.

2   6th Division Record of the Rebellion, Strickland papers, p. 130.

3   PRO CAB/118/26/295, National Archives, Kew.

4   Macardle, Dorothy, *The Irish Republic* (Corgi, London, 1968) p. 491.

5   Captain A. H. Richards, memoir, Soldiers of Gloucestershire Museum.

6   *Ibid.*

7   Moylan family papers held by the author.

8   Béaslaí, Piaras, *Michael Collins and the Making of a New Ireland*, vol. II
(Talbot Press, Dublin, 1926) p. 268. The IRA intelligence system in
Cork was very good and there is no reason to doubt the report. Also,
the substance of the report reflects cabinet committee discussions in
the summer; see Macardle *op. cit.*, p. 420.

9   The members of the Irish delegation were Michael Collins, Arthur

Griffith (chairperson), Robert Barton, George Gavan Duffy and Eamonn Duggan. Secretarial assistance was provided by Finian Lynch, Diarmuid O'Hegarty, John Chartres and Erskine Childers.

10 'An Irishman's Diary', Nichevo, *The Irish Times*, Saturday 15 December 1945.

11 *Official Report, Debate on the Treaty Between Great Britain and Ireland* (Stationery Office, Dublin, n.d.) p. 146.

12 Seán Moylan, Bureau of Military History Witness Statement No. 838 (Moylan Witness Statement) p. 277.

13 *Ibid.*, p. 155.

14 O'Keefe Institute, *Newmarket Court 1725–1994* (Duhallow Heritage Project, Duhallow, 1994) pp. 49–51.

15 Lynch, Michael, *Behold Aherlow: The Glen from Bansha to Galbally* (Rectory Press, Portlaw, 2002) p. 143.

16 Hogan, David, *The Four Glorious Years* (Irish Press Ltd, Dublin, 1953) p. 375. (Hogan was a pseudonym used by Frank B. Gallagher.)

17 Hogan, *op. cit.*, p. 370.

18 Moylan family papers held by the author.

19 *Freeman's Journal*, Thursday 9 February 1922 and *Southern Star*, Saturday 18 February 1922.

20 Memo entitled 'Suggestions by Seán Moylan', 21 April 1922, Mulcahy papers P7/B/152, University College Dublin Archive.

21 Peadar O'Donnell's recollection was set out in an interview with Eileen Magner on 30 September 1981 for her thesis: 'Seán Moylan: Some Aspects of His Parliamentary Career 1932–1948', 1982 MA Thesis, DM1588, University College Cork, p. 7.

22 *Irish Independent*, Thursday 20 April 1922.

20 On the Edge of Anarchy

1 *Back Badge*, spring 1957, p. 249.

2 Hart, Peter, *The IRA and Its Enemies: Violence and Community in Cork 1916–1923* (Clarendon Press, Oxford, 1998) pp. 312–314.

3 *Official Report, Debate on the Treaty Between Great Britain and Ireland* (Stationery Office, Dublin, n.d.) p. 146.

4 Macardle, Dorothy, *The Irish Republic* (Corgi, London, 1968) p. 420. Moylan would not have been privy to Churchill's observations in

cabinet, but the substance of British Army plans was known to the republican leadership.

5   Hansard HL Debate autumn recess, 19 August 1921, vol. 43, col. 1047.

6   Ryan, Meda, *Tom Barry, IRA Freedom Fighter* (Mercier Press, Cork, 2005) p. 215.

7   Personal interview with Carmel Enright, née Moylan.

8   *Irish Press*, Tuesday 19 November 1957; *Kerryman*, Saturday 23 November 1957.

9   Hart, *op. cit.*, p. 288, fn. 112.

10 Ryan, *op. cit.*, p. 213.

11 Hart, *op. cit.*, and for a rebuttal see Ryan *op. cit.*

12 Ryan *op. cit.*, p. 215.

13 Dáil Debates, vol. S2, col. 340, 28 April 1922, Department of Defence, questions.

21 The Slide to War

1   Dáil Debates, vol. S2, col. 363, 3 May 1922, The National Situation – Army Officers' Deputation.

2   O'Donoghue, Florence, *No Other Law* (Irish Press Ltd, Dublin, 1954) p. 242.

22 The Civil War

1   Deasy, Liam, *Brother against Brother* (Mercier Press, Cork, 1998) p. 48.

2   Seán Moylan, Bureau of Military History Witness Statement No. 838 (Moylan Witness Statement) pp. 277–278.

3   O'Malley, Ernie, *The Singing Flame* (Anvil Books, Dublin, 1997) p. 61.

4   Autograph Letter Signed (ALS), Manuscript Department, National Library.

5   Hopkinson, Michael, *Green against Green, The Irish Civil War* (Gill & Macmillan, Dublin, 2004) p. 144.

6   *New York Times*, Friday 14 July 1922.

7   *The Irish Times*, Tuesday 25 July 1922.

8   Seoighe, Mainchin, *The Story of Kilmallock* (Kilmallock Historical

Society, Kilmallock, 1987) p. 293.

9   Bowen, Elizabeth, *Bowen's Court* (Longmans, London, 1964) pp. 441–442.

10 Charles Lysaght in correspondence with the author recalls The Honourable Mrs Amy Lysaght late of Newmarket and Ballybunion.

11 Doyle, Tom, *The Civil War in Kerry* (Mercier Press, Cork, 2008) pp. 139–140; *Freeman's Journal*, Wednesday 16 August 1922.

12 *Freeman's Journal*, Saturday 5 August 1922.

13 *Ibid.*, Wednesday 30 August 1922.

14 *Limerick War News*, National Library, LOLB200.

15 *Ibid.*

16 Ó Ríordáin, J. J., *Kiskeam versus The Empire* (The Kerryman Ltd, Tralee, 1985) p. 120.

17 Macardle, Dorothy, *The Irish Republic* (Corgi, London, 1968) p. 731.

18 The republican Deputies attending this secret meeting had rejected the June 1922 elections and took the position that the Second Dáil which had been elected in 1921 had not been properly dissolved.

19 *Freeman's Journal*, Thursday 9 November 1922.

20 The *Irish Press*, Friday 6 November 1970 (extract taken from Longford-O'Neill biography).

21 *Freeman's Journal*, Saturday 30 December 1922.

22 Tim Cronin's handwritten memories of the Civil War, courtesy of Fr J. J. Ó Ríordáin.

23 Overseas

1 Letter from the Chief-of-Staff, IRA, to Seán Moylan, 23 April 1926, requesting information on the immigration authorities in America and querying how he got men through Ellis Island. Moylan family papers held by the author.

2 Tim Cronin's handwritten memories of the Civil War, courtesy of Fr J. J. Ó Ríordáin.

3 Moylan family papers held by the author.

4 Cronin, Seán, *The McGarrity Papers* (Clan na Gael, New York, 1992) p. 132.

5 McGarrity papers, 17466/1, National Library of Ireland.

6   Fitzgerald papers, P80/791/13, University College Dublin Archive.

7   *Ibid.*, P80/791/3.

8   *Ibid.*, P80/791/1.

9   *Ibid.*, P80/791/2.

10   Ó Ríordáin, J. J., *Kiskeam versus The Empire* (The Kerryman Ltd, Tralee, 1985) p. 123.

11   Fitzgerald papers P80/791/13, University College Dublin Archive.

12   Ó Ríordáin *op. cit.*, p. 126.

13   For a description of the prison crisis, see Peadar O'Donnell, *The Gates Flew Open* (Mercier Press, Cork, 1965). One of the earlier episodes of firing into cells is described (pp. 10–11). In this incident guards fired repeatedly into the cell windows and Liam Mellows had to be pulled away to safety by other prisoners. See also Ó Ríordáin *op. cit.*, and O'Malley, Ernie, *The Singing Flame* (Anvil Books, Dublin, 1997).

14   O'Connor, Seamus, *Tomorrow Was Another Day* (ROC Publications, Dublin, 1987) pp. 88–90. See also Doyle, Tom, *The Civil War in Kerry* (Mercier Press, Cork, 2008) pp. 270–271. Seamus O'Connor escaped to Manchester after the ceasefire and from there to the United States. He met Moylan at a Clan na Gael meeting in 1924, p. 124.

15   *The Irish Times*, Wednesday 31 December 2008. See also National Archives, Department of Justice File H197/52.

16   Moylan family papers held by the author.

17   McGarrity papers, 17466/1, National Library of Ireland. 'How did you know I was here? Nobody in Ireland should know that I left New York and was working from this end.'

18   Seán Moylan, Bureau of Military History Witness Statement No. 838 (Moylan Witness Statement) p. 96.

19   McGarrity papers, 17466/1, National Library of Ireland.

20   *Ibid.*

21   *Ibid.*

22   *Ibid.*

23   Macardle, Dorothy, *The Irish Republic* (Corgi, London, 1968) p. 789.

24   McGarrity papers, 17466/1, National Library of Ireland.

25   Moylan family papers held by the author.

26 Fr J. J. Ó Ríordáin CSsR, personal correspondence with the author.

27 Letter from Seán Moylan to Jim Riordan, courtesy of Fr J. J. Ó Ríordáin.

28 McGarrity papers, 17466/1, National Library of Ireland.

29 Moss Twomey papers, P69/145/200, University College Dublin Archive; see also P69/249, 252, 253, 255.

24 In the Wilderness

1   Macardle, Dorothy, *The Irish Republic* (Corgi, London, 1968) p. 804.

2   MacSwiney Brugha, Máire, *History's Daughter* (O'Brien Press, Dublin, 2005) p. 145.

3   McGarrity papers, 17466/1, National Library of Ireland.

4   Moylan family papers held by the author.

5   McGarrity papers, 17466/1, National Library of Ireland, in which McGarrity makes reference to Joxer Daly from Seán O'Casey's play *The Plough and the Stars*..

6   Ó Ríordáin, J. J., *Kiskeam versus The Empire* (The Kerryman Ltd, Tralee 1985) p. 28.

7   *Ibid.*

8   Moylan family papers held by the author.

9   'An Irishwoman's Diary', Edel Morgan, *The Irish Times*, Monday 13 December 1999.

10 Moylan, Richard, unfinished biography of Seán Moylan, n.d.

11 *Ibid.*

12 Ó Ríordáin, J. J., personal correspondence with author.

13 Personal interview with Anna Kirby, memories of her mother Stephanie O'Callaghan (née Moylan).

14 *The Irish Times* (Weekend Review), Saturday 16 May 2009 and NLI Ephemera Collection POL/1930–40/1, Cumann na nGaedheal 1932 election poster: 'Devvys Circus, Absolutely the greatest road show in Ireland today – Senor de Valera world famous illusionist, oath swallower and escapologist. See his renowned act. Escaping from the strait-jacket of the Republic. Everyone Mystified! Stupendous Attraction! Monsieur Lemass: See him cross from the Treaty to the Republic on the tightrope every night'.

25 Dáil Career 1932–1937

1 Moylan, Richard, unfinished biography of Seán Moylan, n.d.
2 Dáil Debates, vol. 50, col. 1195, 7 February 1934, Committee on Finance, Vote 64, Army.
3 Moylan, Richard *op. cit.*
4 Moylan family papers held by the author. The prisoners on the train were Cornelius and Michael Crowley, Peter Kearney and Stephen O'Neill. The report is contained in the *Irish Press*, Thursday 22 February 1934.
5 Moylan, Richard *op. cit.*
6 Fianna Fáil Archive, University College Dublin Archive.
7 Moylan, Richard *op. cit.*
8 *Ibid.*

26 The Bothy Fire

1 O'Donnell, Peadar, *The Bothy Fire and All That* (Irish People Publications, Dublin, 1937) p. 19. This booklet includes O'Donnell's article on the Arranmore drowning, which occurred on 9 November 1935.
2 *Mayo News*, Tuesday 11 September 2007, see article by Anton McNulty: 'When Dreams Went Up in Flames'.
3 Magner, Eileen, 'Seán Moylan: Some Aspects of His Parliamentary Career 1932–1948', 1982 MA Thesis, Ref: DM1588, University College Cork, p. 17: 1981 interview with Pat Murphy, Private Secretary to Seán Moylan 1937–1941.
4 *Ibid.*, p. 212.
5 *Report of Inter-Departmental Committee on Seasonal Migration to Great Britain, 1937–1938.* Courtesy of the Department of the Taioseach.

27 World's Fair – Seán Keating

1 Sheaff, Nicholas, 'The Shamrock Building', *Irish Arts Review*, vol. 1, no. 1, (1984) p. 26. The plans for the Shamrock Building are preserved in the Irish Architectural Archive, Dublin.
2 Contemporary newspaper cutting of Moylan and Keating at the 1939 New York World's Fair, courtesy of Dr Éimear O'Connor, Irish Art Research Centre, Trinity College, Dublin.

3   Moylan family papers held by the author. Keating signed his correspondence John Keating and Seán Keating.

4   Moylan, Richard, unfinished biography of Seán Moylan, n.d.

5   Seán Moylan, Bureau of Military History Witness Statement No. 505, p. 2.

6   *Ibid.*

7   John Keating to M. McDunphy, letter, 3 January 1951, ref. P2409, inserted with Bureau of Military History Witness Statement No. 505 (Moylan).

8   *Ibid.*

9   John Keating to M. McDunphy, letter, 22 January 1951, p. 1, inserted with Bureau of Military History Witness Statement No. 505 (Moylan).

10 Seán Moylan, Bureau of Military History Witness Statement No. 505, p. 6.

11 John Keating to M. McDunphy, letter, 22 January 1951 *op. cit.*, pp. 2–3.

12 Moylan Witness Statement No. 505 *op. cit.*, pp. 3–4.

13 *Ibid.*, p. 4.

14 *Ibid.*, pp. 4–5.

15 A catalogue of the collection of historical pictures established in 1944 by Dr Douglas Hyde, President of Ireland, is inserted with Bureau of Military History Witness Statement No. 505 (Moylan). The catalogue entry for '1921, An IRA Column' by Seán Keating RHA is on p. 58, ref. 138.

16 John Keating to M. McDunphy, letter, 22 January 1951 *op. cit.*, p. 3.

17 Ibid. Michael Collins accepted Churchill's offer of artillery for use by the National Army against the anti-Treaty republicans barricaded in the Four Courts.

18 Identification of the sitters for 'Republican Court' and background information on the painting is attributed to Fr J. J. Ó Ríordáin CSsR. His father James O'Riordan, who was known throughout his life as Jim Riordan, appears in '1921, An IRA Column', 'Men of the South' and 'Republican Court'.

19 Ó Ríordáin, J. J., personal correspondence with author.

20 Seán Moylan, Bureau of Military History Witness Statement No.

505, p. 4.

21 Eileen Bryan-Brown (née Moylan), personal correspondence with the author.

28 Director of Air Raid Precautions 1939–1942

1 The *Irish Independent*, Monday 1 June 1942.

2 Murphy, George, Archive of Second World War Memories gathered by the BBC (Reference: A1927307 2003).

3 *The People* (Wexford), Saturday 31 August 1940.

4 *The Irish Times*, Wednesday 28 August 1940.

5 *The Irish Times*, Monday 2 June 1941.

6 *Ibid*.

7 Dublin City Library and Archive, North Strand and Donore Road Bombing, records, CMD/1941/2.

8 *Ibid*.

9 Dublin City Library and Archive, North Strand Bombing, oral history transcriptions, B1/29/92, p. 53.

10 Kearns, Kevin C., *Dublin Tenement Life, An Oral History* (Gill & Macmillan, Dublin, 1994) p. 168, oral testimony of Mary Chaney.

11 *The Irish Times*, Monday 2 June 1941.

12 *Ibid.*, Monday 1 June 1942.

13 Dáil Debates, vol. 88, 16 July 1942, Committee on Finance, Vote 75 – Damage to Property (Neutrality) Compensation.

14 *Ibid*.

15 *Ibid*.

16 Montgomery, Bernard Law, *The Memoirs of Field-Marshal Montgomery* (Collins, London 1958) p. 383.

29 Dáil Career 1943–1957

1 Moylan family papers held by the author. An Taoiseach, Éamon de Valera: graveside tribute to Seán Moylan, 19 November 1957.

2 Moylan family papers held by the author.

3 Magner, Eileen, 'Seán Moylan: Some Aspects of His Parliamentary Career 1932–1948', 1982 MA Thesis, Ref: DM1588, University College Cork, pp. 180–182. For a full account see National Archives S12890A Moylan to An Taoiseach, 1 September 1943.

4   Moylan, Richard, unfinished biography of Seán Moylan, n.d.

5   Keogh, Dermot, 'Leaving the Blaskets 1953: Willing or Enforced Departures?' in Keogh, Dermot, O'Shea, Finbarr and Quinlan, Carmel (eds), *The Lost Decade, Ireland in the 1950s* (Mercier Press, Cork, 2004) pp. 50–73.

6   Jack Lynch speaking at the Annual Seán Moylan Commemoration in Kiskeam, 15 November 1981.

7   Moylan, Richard *op. cit.*

8   *Ibid.*

9   In the second half of the 1940s Moylan wrote his memoir on the Irish Volunteers' activities in north Cork. He loaned it to Florrie O'Donoghue for research on *No Other Law* (Irish Press Ltd, Dublin, 1954). An engaging letter exists from O'Donoghue to Moylan: 'I am sending you what I have done on Liam Lynch … If you think you can stand any more of it I'll send you the rest later.' And correspondence in 1948 from Tom Barry to Moylan concerning *Guerrilla Days in Ireland* (Mercier Press, Cork, 1955) records: 'It is good to know that leaders of the movement like yourself consider that I have written a true account of the days we knew over twenty-seven years ago … tell your son who is so interested that I will autograph his copy for him if he wants it. I hope his opinion of me is something different to that of the "Echo" boy who said to his pal as I passed … "look look, there is the fellow who wanted to shoot the —— Bishop of Cork". Moylan presented his memoir to the Bureau of Military History in 1953.

10   Magner *op. cit.,* pp. 241–242: 1981 interview with Pádraigh Breathnach, Private Secretary to Seán Moylan 1951–1954.

11   Jack Lynch, *op. cit.*

12   Magner *op. cit.,* p. 244.

13   McMahon, Bryan, *The Master* (Poolbeg Press, Dublin, 1992) p. 30

14   *Sunday Press*, 8 November 1953.

15   Keogh *op. cit.,* p. 66.

16   *Ibid.,* p. 67.

17   Dáil Debates, vol. 145, col. 947–951, 23 April 1954, Adjournment Debate – Punishment of Industrial Schoolboy.

18   Ryan Commission [Commission to Inquire into Child Abuse], *Report on Child Abuse*, 2009, vol. 1, ch. 7, pp. 122–123.

19   Moylan, Richard *op. cit.*

20 *Irish Press*, Thursday 28 March 1957.
21 Moylan family papers held by the author.
22 *Ibid.*
23 Dáil Debates, vol. 161, col. 1500–1508, 16 May 1957, Nomination of Member of Government – Motion of Approval.
24 *Ibid.*
25 Moylan family papers held by the author.
26 *Ibid.*
27 Moylan family papers held by the author.
28 *Kerryman*, Saturday 23 November 1957.
29 *Ibid.*
30 *Back Badge*, December 1957, p. 266.
31 *The Irish Times*, Saturday 30 March 1957.
32 Bureau of Military History Witness Statement No. 838 (Moylan Witness Statement) p. 162.

Appendix I: Martin Savage – A Memory

1 Páidín O'Keeffe TD, was elected to the First Dáil in 1918.
2 Irish Transport and General Workers' Union.
3 Martin Savage died on 19 December 1919, aged twenty-one.

Appendix II: Transcript of Voice Recording for the BMH

1 William Butler Yeats, 'Easter 1916'.

BIBLIOGRAPHY

Primary Sources

17th Lancers Regimental Diary

Census 1911

Dáil Debates

Dublin City Library and Archive

Hampshire Regimental Museum, Winchester, War Diary of the Second Battalion of the Hampshires

House of Commons Hansard (*The Official Report of Parliamentary Debates*)

Incorporated Council of Law Reporting for Ireland, Law Library, Four Courts, Dublin (1921)

Military Archives, Cathal Brugha Barracks, Dublin

Moylan, Richard, unfinished biography of Seán Moylan, n.d.

Moylan, Seán, correspondence to Jim Riordan written from New York 1924, courtesy Fr J. J. Ó Ríordáin CSsR

Moylan, Seán, correspondence with Mollie Murphy, courtesy Mrs Katty Sheahan, Newmarket

Moylan family papers held by the author

Murphy, George, Archive of Second World War Memories gathered by the BBC (Reference: A1927307 2003)

National Archives, Kew

National Archives of Ireland

National Library of Ireland (O'Donoghue papers, McGarrity papers)

6th Division Record of the Rebellion, Strickland papers, Imperial War Museum, London

Soldiers of Gloucestershire Museum, Gloucester (diary of Lieutenant R. M. Grazebrook; memoir of Captain A. H. Richards)

Strickland, Major General E. P. (Diary 1920), Imperial War Museum, London

University College Dublin Archive Department (Mulcahy papers, Fitzgerald papers, Moss Twomey papers, Fianna Fáil archive)

Voice recording: Seán Moylan to Bureau Military History, 14 December 1950, No. V.R.7

Voice recording: Peig O'Brien (née Moylan) n.d.

Bureau of Military History, 1913–1921, Witness Statements

Barrett, Annie	Document No. 1133
Cashman, James	Document No. 1270
Condon, Laurence	Document No. 859
Cronin, Tim J.	Document No. 1134
Flynn, Dan	Document No. 1240
Guiney, Dan	Document No. 1347
Harold, Owen	Document No. 991
Meaney, Con	Document No. 787
Moylan, Seán	Document Nos 505 & 838
Murphy, Jeremiah, Michael Courtney and Denis Mulchinock	Document No. 744
O'Brien, Patrick	Document No. 764
O'Connell, John (Jack)	Document No. 1211
O'Higgins, Patrick	Document No. 1467
Power, George	Document No. 451
Reardon, William	Document No. 1185
Willis, Richard and John Bolster	Document No. 808

Newspapers

Cork Examiner, Freeman's Journal, Irish Bulletin, Irish Independent, Irish Press, The Irish Times, Limerick War News, Kerryman, Mayo News, The Nation, New York Times, People (Wexford), *Southern Star, Sunday Independent, Sunday Press, The Times* (London)

Periodicals and Reports

Back Badge, Journal of the Gloucestershire Regiment

Capuchin Annual, The, 1968, pp. 182–211

Carbery's Annual 1940 (Carbery Publications, Dublin 1940)

Guy's Cork Almanac 1914 (Guy & Co. Ltd, Cork, 1914)

History Ireland, 2003, vol. 11, no. 1, p. 6

Irish Arts Review, 1984, vol. 1, no. 1, pp. 26–29

Lillywhite's Gazette, Queen's Lancashire Regimental Museum

Official Report, Debate on the Treaty Between Great Britain and Ireland (Stationery Office, Dublin, n.d.)

Ryan Commission [Commission to Inquire into Child Abuse], *Report on Child Abuse*, 2009, vol. 1, ch. 7

Moylan Commission, *Report of Inter-Departmental Committee on Seasonal Migration to Great Britain 1937–1938*

Secondary Sources

Abbott, Richard, *Police Casualties in Ireland 1919–1922* (Mercier Press, Cork, 2000)

Allen, D. H., *A History of Newmarket* (Cork Historical Guides Committee, 1973)

Barry, Tom, *Guerrilla Days in Ireland* (Mercier Press, Cork, 1955)

Barry, Tom, *The Reality of the Anglo-Irish War 1920–21 in West Cork. Refutations, Corrections and Comments on Liam Deasy's Towards Ireland Free* (Anvil Press, Tralee, 1974)

Béaslaí, Piaras, *Michael Collins and the Making of a New Ireland*, vol. II (The Talbot Press, Dublin, 1926)

Bowen, Elizabeth, *Bowen's Court* (Longmans, London, 1964)

Brennan, Michael, *The War in Clare, 1911–1921, Personal Memoirs of the Irish War of Independence* (Four Courts Press and Irish Academic Press, Dublin, 1980)

Burrows, J. W., *Essex Units in the War 1914–1919, Volume 1: The First Battalion* (John H. Burrows, Southend, 1927)

Callwell, C. E., *Field Marshal Sir Henry Wilson, Volume 2: His Life and Diaries* (Cassell & Co., London, 1927)

Coogan, Tim Pat, *The IRA: A History* (Fontana, London, 1982)

Coogan, Tim Pat, *Michael Collins: a Biography* (Hutchinson, London, 1990)

Cronin, Seán, *The McGarrity Papers* (Clan na Gael, New York, 1992)

Deasy, Liam, *Brother against Brother* (Mercier Press, Cork, 1998)

Deasy, Liam, *Towards Ireland Free* (Mercier Press, Dublin and Cork, 1973)

Doyle, Tom, *The Civil War in Kerry* (Mercier Press, Cork, 2008)

Dwyer, T. Ryle, *Tans, Terror and Troubles. Kerry's Real Fighting Story* (Mercier Press, Cork, 2001)

GAA Committee, *Our Proud Heritage, The History of Kilmallock GAA from 1884–1976* (The Kerryman Ltd, Tralee, 1977)

Gaughan, J. Anthony, *Memoirs of Constable Jeremiah Mee, RIC* (Anvil Books, Dublin, 1975)

Griffith, Kenneth and O'Grady, Timothy, *Curious Journey. An Oral History of Ireland's Unfinished Revolution* (Hutchinson, London, 1982)

Hart, Peter, *The IRA and Its Enemies: Violence & Community in Cork 1916–1923* (Clarendon Press, Oxford, 1998)

Hart, Peter, *The IRA at War 1916–23* (Oxford University Press, Oxford, 2005)

Hogan, David, *The Four Glorious Years* (Irish Press Ltd, Dublin, 1953)

Hopkinson, Michael (ed.), *The Last Days of Dublin Castle: The Diaries of Mark Sturgis* (Irish Academic Press, Dublin, 1999)

Hopkinson, Michael, *Green against Green, The Irish Civil War* (Gill & Macmillan, Dublin, 2004)

Hopkinson, Michael, *The Irish War of Independence* (Gill & Macmillan, Dublin, 2004)

Jeffrey, Keith, *Field Marshal Sir Henry Wilson, a Political Soldier* (Oxford University Press, Oxford, 2008)

Jones, Thomas (ed. Keith Middlemas), *Whitehall Diary. Volume III (1918–1925)* (Oxford University Press, London, 1971)

Kearns, Kevin C., *Dublin Tenement Life, An Oral History* (Gill & Macmillan, Dublin, 1994)

Kennedy, Seán, *They Loved Dear Old Ireland* (private printing, 1974)

Keogh, Dermot, O'Shea, Finbarr and Quinlan, Carmel (eds), *The Lost Decade: Ireland in the 1950s* (Mercier Press, Cork, 2004)

Longford, Earl of and O'Neill, Thomas P., *Éamon de Valera* (Hutchinson, London, 1970)

Lynch, Michael, *Behold Aherlow: The Glen from Bansha to Galbally* (Rectory Press, Portlaw, 2002)

Macardle, Dorothy, *The Irish Republic* (Corgi, London, 1968)

Macready, General Sir Nevil, *Annals of an Active Life*, vol. 2 (Hutchinson, London, 1924)

MacSwiney Brugha, Máire, *History's Daughter* (O'Brien Press, Dublin, 2005)

Magner, Eileen, 'Seán Moylan: Some Aspects of His Parliamentary Career 1932–1948', 1982 MA Thesis, Ref: DM1588, Boole Library, University College Cork

McMahon, Bryan, *The Master* (Poolbeg Press, Dublin, 1992)

Meagher, Jim, *The War of Independence in North Cork. The Story of Charleville No. 2 Cork Brigade* (Charleville and District Historical and Archaeological Society, Charleville, 2004)

Mitchel, John, *Jail Journal* (University Press of Ireland, 1982)

Montgomery, Bernard Law, First Viscount Montgomery of Alamein, *The Memoirs of Field-Marshal Montgomery* (Collins, London, 1958)

O'Casey, Seán, *Autobiographies, Volume II: Inishfallen, Fare Thee Well* (Macmillan, London, 1981)

O'Connor, Frank, *Guests of the Nation* (Poolbeg Press, Dublin, 1985)

O'Connor, Seamus, *Tomorrow Was Another Day* (ROC Publications, Dublin, 1987)

O'Donnell, Peadar, *The Bothy Fire and All That* (Irish People Publications, Dublin, 1937)

O'Donnell, Peadar, *The Gates Flew Open* (Mercier Press, Cork, 1965)

O'Donoghue, Florence, *No Other Law* (Irish Press Ltd, Dublin, 1954)

O'Keefe Institute, *Newmarket Court 1725–1994* (Duhallow Heritage Project, Duhallow, 1994)

O'Malley, Ernie, *On Another Man's Wound* (Rich & Cowan Ltd, London, 1937)

O'Malley, Ernie, *The Singing Flame* (Anvil Books, Dublin, 1997)

O'Neill, Tom, *The Battle of Clonmult, the IRA's Worst Defeat* (Nonsuch Publishing, Dublin, 2006)

Ó Ríordáin, J. J., *Kiskeam Cousins* (private printing, 1989)

Ó Ríordáin, J. J., *Kiskeam versus The Empire* (The Kerryman Ltd, Tralee 1985)

Rebel Cork's Fighting Story from 1916 to the Truce with Britain (Anvil Books, Tralee, 1960)

Ryan, Meda, *The Day Michael Collins Was Shot* (Poolbeg, Dublin, 1989)

Ryan, Meda, *The Real Chief, Liam Lynch* (Mercier Press, Cork, 2005)

Ryan, Meda, *Tom Barry, IRA Freedom Fighter* (Mercier Press, Cork, 2005)

Self, Robert C. (ed.), *The Austen Chamberlain Diary Letters: The Correspondence of Sir Austen Chamberlain with His Sisters Hilda and Ida (1916–1937)* (Cambridge University Press, Cambridge, 1995)

Seoighe, Mainchin, *The Story of Kilmallock* (Kilmallock Historical Society, Kilmallock, 1987)

Shea, Patrick, *Voices and the Sound of Drums* (Blackstaff Press, Belfast, 1981)

Townshend, Charles, *The British Campaign in Ireland 1919–1921* (Oxford University Press, London, 1975)

Valiulis, Maryann Gialanella, *Portrait of a Revolutionary, General Richard Mulcahy and the Founding of the Irish Free State* (Irish Academic Press, Dublin, 1992)

INDEX

A

Adams, Richard 15, 16
Aiken, Frank 14, 203, 216, 222
Aldworth, Lady Mary 248
Allen, John 96, 143, 144, 156, 157
Allman, Fr Myles 219
Andrews, Todd 203

B

Barrett, Annie 109, 124
Barrett, Dick 199, 204
Barrett, Frank 177, 203
Barrett, Michael 186
Barrett, Robert 33
Barry, Kevin 69, 158
Barry, Tom 70, 76, 107, 108, 113, 114,
    116, 156, 180, 216, 266
Barter, Denis 140, 144
Barton, Robert 194
Béaslaí, Piaras 37, 269
Beckett, Martin 34
Benn, Captain W. 151, 152, 153
Bennett (Mallow station) 88
Birkenhead, Lord 170, 174
Blake, District Inspector C. A. 71
Boland, Harry 184
Bolster, Jack 60, 71
Bonar Law, Andrew 32
Bourke, J. F., BL 143, 146
Bourke, Jim 240
Bowen, Elizabeth 191
Boylan, Seán 183
Boynes, Constable Joseph 110
Breen, Dan 35, 183, 192, 203, 216,
    218, 221, 222, 265
Breen, Timothy 140, 144
Brennan, Michael 53, 55, 76
Brown, Constable Walter 118
Brown, Margaret 269
Browne, Dan 238
Brugha, Cathal 186, 204
Bryan Brown, Eileen (née Moylan)
    217, 227
Buckley, David 157
Buckley, Ned 266
Byrne, Inspector General Joseph 36
Byrne, Robert 33

C

Cameron, Brig. General 156
Carter, Constable Edward 89
Casement, Roger 29
Casey, Patrick 133, 156
Cashman, James (Jimmy) 73, 83, 103,
    174, 238
Chamberlain, Austen 170
Childers, Erskine 195, 204
Churchill, Winston 51, 170, 174, 175,
    179, 185, 239, 240
Clancy, Maurice 137
Clancy, Paddy 48, 49, 50, 58, 59, 117,
    205
Clapp, Constable William 118
Clarke, Harry 247
Clarke, James 108, 157
Clarke, Tom 32
Clifford, Patrick (Appeal to Lords)
    154, 157
Colivet, M. P. 194
Collins, Johnny 161
Collins, Michael 36, 161, 175, 183,
    184, 185, 186, 192, 204, 217, 227
Condon, Laurence 48
Condon, Timothy 30
Conlon, Sergeant 25, 30
Connolly, General (Nat. Army) 189
Connolly, James 32

Connolly, Tim 79
Conroy, Con 160, 161, 162
Cooney, Andy 200
Cope, A. W. (Assistant Under Secretary) 170
Corbett, Ernest 53
Corkery, Dan 216
Cork Examiner 21, 76, 116, 192
Cornwallis, Captain, 71
Cosgrave, William 21, 221
Costello, M. J. 266
Cowan, Peadar 255, 256, 257
Craik, Sir H. 51
Cronin, Michael Mockie 239
Cronin, Michael T. 239
Cronin, Pat 137
Cronin, Tim 74, 82, 84, 196, 239
Crowley, Daniel 108
Crowley, Patrick 89
Crowley, Tim 69
Crozier, General F. P. 91
Culhane, Seán 186
Cullen, Tom 58
Culloty, Paddy 239
Culloty, Seán 239
Cumann na mBan 34, 176, 215
Cumann na nGaedheal 205, 217
Cumming, Brigadier General H. R. 97, 99, 103, 104, 105, 120
Curran, John Philpot 18
Curran, Sarah 18
Curtin, John B. 48, 55
Curzon, Lord 41

D

Dáil Éireann 27, 28, 29, 34, 35, 38, 45, 135, 155, 163, 166, 168, 169, 174, 175, 179, 181, 183, 184, 185, 194, 195, 218, 222, 223, 224, 226, 227, 230, 235, 245, 247, 249, 255, 259, 260, 263
Daly, Mike 211
Danford, Col 47, 49, 50, 51, 52, 55
Deasy, Liam 63, 93, 113, 177, 180, 186, 189, 190, 192, 201
Deasy, William 108
Dennehy, Michael 166

Dennehy, Thomas 108
Derrig, Thomas 186, 258
Despard, Charlotte 76
De Valera, Éamon 14, 21, 118, 163, 166, 174, 180, 185, 188, 191, 192, 205, 210, 211, 216, 217, 218, 219, 220, 221, 223, 233, 234, 240, 242, 247, 248, 252, 258, 263, 265
Devitt, Patrick 88
Devlin, Kevin 252, 253
Dillon, James 219
Doherty, Joe 27
Donegan, Batt 259
Doyle, Tom 191
Drew, Edward 213
Dunn, Captain John 16
Dwyer, Michael 270
Dyne, Constable Robert 118

E

Egan, John 155
Elton, Constable William 107
Emmet, Robert 135
Enright, Carmel (née Moylan) 217, 227
Enright, Michael 35

F

Farrelly, Patrick 195
Fehily, Jeremiah 79
Fianna Fáil 191, 216, 217, 218, 219, 221, 223, 224, 235, 250, 251, 252, 259, 260
Finn, Seán 113, 131
Finnegan, Luke 40
Fitzgerald, Michael 47, 59, 69, 203
Flanagan, John 20
Flood, Cedric 245
Flynn, Con 93
Flynn, Dan 24, 70, 73, 91, 123, 134, 211
Foley, Jim 158
Foran, Thomas 37, 268
Foxcroft, Captain, Charles 45
Freeman's Journal 20, 195
French, Lord Lieutenant J. 38, 76, 269

G

GAA 20, 21, 258
Gaelic League 14, 18, 21, 34
Galvin, Dan 18
Galvin, Denis 104, 163, 205
Gaynor, Seán 203
GHQ 50, 58, 59, 105, 113, 114, 125, 175
Gibbs, Sergeant 60, 141, 155, 157
Ginnell, Laurence 194
Grazebrook, Lieutenant R. M. 120, 121, 123, 124, 125, 129, 130, 131, 133, 134, 135, 137, 140, 152, 162
Greenwood, Sir Hamar 72, 151, 152, 153
Griffin, Constable 89
Griffin, Father Michael 69
Griffith, Arthur 25, 174, 180
Guiney, Dan 73, 83, 211

H

Hales, Seán 160, 161, 163, 183, 184, 199
Hales, Tom 22, 56, 57, 177
Hannah, Sergeant KC 155
Harold, Hugh 168
Harold, Owen 140, 144
Harrison, Constable Arthur 120
Harrison, John 205
Harrison, Nora 205
Hart, Peter 179, 180
Harte, Pat 56, 57
Hawkins, James 242
Hayes, General, (Nat. Army) 189
Healy, Constable 40
Healy, Seán 82
Hegarty, Seán 22, 112, 164
Herlihy, David 107
Herlihy, Donal 90
Herlihy, Michael 90
Higgins, Joe 230
Higginson, Brigadier General 79
Hillier, Constable Alfred 118
Hogan, Seán 35, 36, 173
Holmes, Gen. D. C. 84, 85, 86, 94, 153
Hopkinson, Michael 65, 164

Horan, Andy 95
Hornibrook, Thomas 178, 179
Hudson, Colonel 63, 89
Hunt, District Inspector Michael 35, 43
Hurley, Diarmaid 147
Hurley, Kathleen 242

I

IRA 40, 42, 43, 44, 48, 52, 54, 55, 56, 65, 74, 78, 79, 83, 86, 98, 100, 107, 108, 111, 112, 114, 118, 120, 122, 123, 128, 133, 134, 137, 142, 144, 153, 154, 157, 161, 167, 174, 178, 180, 183, 185, 196, 202, 207, 208, 210, 211, 218, 220, 222, 223, 233, 235, 238, 239, 268, 269
Irish Independent 191
Irish Press 217
Irish Times, The 52, 190, 196, 242, 244

J

Jones, John 238
Jones, Lieutenant H. G. 30

K

Kavanagh, Seán na Cóta 18, 255
Keane, Thomas 155, 156
Kearney, Peter 222
Keating, Seán 168, 232, 233, 235, 236, 237, 238, 239, 240, 252
Kelleher, Michael J. 90
Kennedy, Seán 91
Kent, Kitty and Mary 242
Kerins, Charlie 223, 224
Kiely, Roger 223, 237, 240, 249
Kiely, Tim 162
Kiely, Timothy 107
Kilfeather, T. P. 263
Kilroy, Michael 186
King, Capt. W. H. 87
King, Mrs 87, 88, 105

L

Leader, Miss 103
Leahy, Brigadier 199

Leahy, Michael 164
Lemass, Seán 216, 229
Lenihan, Corney 211
Limerick Leader 20
Lindsay, Mrs Mary 96, 108, 157
Lloyd George, Sir David 44, 60, 62, 66, 86, 138, 163, 170, 171
Longboat, Tom 20
Lucas, General 46, 47, 48, 49, 50, 51, 52, 53, 54, 55, 56, 116, 151
Lynch, Jack 250, 252
Lynch, Liam 14, 36, 37, 42, 47, 48, 49, 50, 57, 58, 60, 66, 67, 71, 100, 101, 106, 112, 113, 114, 131, 165, 177, 184, 186, 187, 188, 192, 196, 199, 200, 203, 204
Lynch, Paddy 173
Lynch, Seán 173
Lyons, John 96, 156
Lysaght, Amy 191

M

Macardle, Dorothy 167, 194
MacBride, Maud Gonne 76
MacBride, Seán 260
MacCurtain, Tomás 22, 34, 37, 40, 269
MacEoin, Seán 163, 184
MacGonigal, Maurice 233
MacNeill, Eoin 258
Macready, General Sir Nevil 51, 52, 65, 75, 86, 104, 105, 137, 147, 155, 156, 167, 179, 185
MacSwiney, Mary 194, 210
MacSwiney, Terence 22, 40, 57, 59, 69, 208
Magner, Canon Thomas J. 69
Magner, Eileen 252
Maher, Paddy 158
Maligny, Lieutenant 104
Markievicz, Constance 210, 211
Martin, Mrs 164
McAuliffe, Garrett 113
McAuliffe, Patrick 263
McAuliffe, William 87
McCarthy, Dan 50
McCarthy, Daniel 140, 144

McCarthy, Eugene 166
McCarthy, Paddy 60, 70, 71, 205
McCarthy, Tim 96, 156
McCartie, Madge 211
McCormack, Constable Thomas 118
McCreery, Lieutenant 71
McDermott, Captain 194
McDonald, Constable John 110
McDonnell, Constable James 29
McGarrity, Joe 199, 200, 203, 205, 206, 208, 209, 210, 230, 235
McGrath, Pa 250
McGuinness, Joe 21, 184
McGuire, Tom 177
McKelvey, Joe 177, 186, 199, 204
McNamara, Tom 80, 238
McQuillan, Jack 263
McSweeney, Donal 223
Meaney, Con 90, 99
Mee, Constable Jeremiah 43, 44
Mellows, Liam 171, 177, 184, 186, 199, 204
Meredith, Arthur KC 144
Mitchel, John 159
Moloney, John 107
Montgomery, Field Marshal Bernard Law 246
Moore, Maurice 120, 156
Morgan, Joe 107
Morris, John 197
Moylan, Annri 21
Moylan, Con 78, 117, 186, 200
Moylan, Daniel 19
Moylan, Gret 18, 238
Moylan, Joe 18, 19, 22, 53, 163
Moylan, Kate 21
Moylan, Liam 70, 82, 102, 200
Moylan, Mamie 18, 50, 163, 211, 239, 240, 248
Moylan, Mary 217
Moylan, Mary Noonan 20
Moylan, Maud 21
Moylan, Ned 18, 22, 23, 57, 260
Moylan, Nora (mother) 16, 18, 19, 21, 92, 162, 247, 248
Moylan, Richard (father) 17, 19
Moylan, Rick 217, 221, 251
Moyles, Constable 84

Moynihan, Thady 239
Mulcahy, Richard 175, 177, 183, 184, 194, 258
Mulcahy, Thomas 120, 156
Mullane, Daniel 88
Mullane, Denis 237
Mullane, Jeremiah 108
Murphy, Annie (Shamrock House) 168
Murphy, Constable Michael 36
Murphy, Cornelius (Con) 81, 86, 89, 117, 139, 156
Murphy, Daniel 108
Murphy, Danny Martin 23
Murphy, Fintan 58
Murphy, General W. 190
Murphy, George 241
Murphy, Humphrey 113, 183
Murphy, Jack Henry 196, 197
Murphy, John 140, 144, 195
Murphy, John (Newmarket) 173
Murphy, Joseph (died on hunger strike 25 Oct 1920) 69
Murphy, K. T. 125, 163
Murphy, Mary 174
Murphy, Matthew 249
Murphy, Mollie 125
Murphy, Nancy 238
Murphy, Nora 168, 173, 174, 197, 199, 205, 207, 208, 234
Murphy, Tim 76
Murray, Pa 204

N

New York Times 40, 50, 97, 189
Nisbet, Lieut Col F. C. 120, 135
Noonan, (Liscarroll) 62
Nunan, Seán 117, 166
Nyhan, John (Flyer) 222

O

O'Brien, Constable 33
O'Brien, Dan 128, 137, 139, 156, 157, 158
O'Brien, Dr Bishop of Kerry 216
O'Brien, John 57
O'Brien, Ned 35

O'Brien, Paddy 22, 60, 67, 92, 93, 100, 101, 128, 166
O'Brien, Peig (née Moylan) 207, 208, 217
O'Brien, Thomas 96, 156
O'Callaghan, Daniel 96, 156
O'Callaghan, Kathleen 194
O'Callaghan, Kevin 260
O'Callaghan, Stephanie (née Moylan) 216, 217, 260
O'Casey, Seán 65
O'Connell, Comdt Jack 59
O'Connell, Jack (Glantane) 50
O'Connell, Michael 166
O'Connell, Patrick 29, 50
O'Connor, Constable, Patrick 89
O'Connor, Joe 177
O'Connor, Lieut Paddy 202
O'Connor, Pat 202
O'Connor, Rory 177, 184, 186, 199, 204
O'Donnell, Peadar 177, 186, 210, 228, 229
O'Donoghue, Florence (Florrie) 37, 51, 76, 105, 113, 114, 131, 177, 183, 192, 201
O'Duffy, Eoin 183, 184, 192, 220
O'Dwyer, Seamus 184
O'Hegarty, Diarmud 184
O'Hegarty, Seán 177, 183
O'Higgins, Kevin 195
O'Higgins, Paddy 94
O'Keefe, Pat 121, 178
O'Keeffe, Dan 258
O'Keeffe, Ellen 249
O'Keeffe, Páidín 27, 37, 38, 268
O'Kelly, J. J. 194
O'Kelly, Seán T. 180, 194, 234
O'Mahoney, Patrick 96, 156
O'Mahoney, Seán 194
O'Mahony, Baby 93
Ó Máille, Pádraic 184
O'Malley, Ernie 14, 59, 60, 67, 71, 113, 175, 177, 186, 187, 189, 220, 260, 261
O'Neill, Annie 69
O'Neill, Michael 178, 179
O'Regan, John 128

O'Reilly, Charlie 37, 108, 117, 205
O'Sullivan, Gearóid 183, 184
O'Sullivan, John L. 160
O'Sullivan, Michael 108, 238
O'Sullivan, Paddy 120, 156
O'Sullivan, Tadhg 110

P

Percival, Major A. E. 56
Phelan, Constable James 118
Philpot, Jeremiah 195
Pickett, Patrick 16, 17
Plunkett, Count 21, 194
Powell, Mr Justice 144
Power, George 48, 49, 50, 60, 68, 93, 113, 115, 116

Q

Quinn, Ellen 69

R

Raleigh, Batt 15, 16, 17, 42
Raleigh, Maggie 19
Raleigh, Mary 17
Raleigh, Ned 15
Reardon, William 40
Reece, CSM 168
Reynolds, Inspector C. 202
RIC 17, 18, 22, 23, 25, 28, 29, 30, 31, 33, 36, 38, 39, 40, 42, 43, 44, 45, 46, 54, 58, 64, 65, 66, 69, 72, 73, 76, 83, 84, 85, 89, 106, 107, 108, 109, 118, 123, 124, 130, 133, 147, 148, 153, 154, 178, 211, 220, 269
Richards, Captain A. H. 122, 168
Riordan, Constable John 36
Riordan, Dr (Boherbue) 111
Riordan, Jim 73, 82, 111, 117, 118, 119, 174, 193, 201, 205, 211, 238, 239
Riordan, Johnny 132, 134
Riordan, Maurice 202
Robinson, Seamus 174, 177, 184, 216
Roche, Tom 70
Rocke, Constable 40
Ronayne, Patrick 120, 156

Ruttledge, P. J. 177, 184, 186, 194, 216
Ryan, Meda 180
Rynne, Patrick 30, 32

S

Savage, Martin 38, 264, 268, 269, 270
Scanlon, Jim 35
Scannell, Jerry 24
Scott, Michael 232
Scully, Timothy 40
Shannon family (Carlow) 243
Shea, Sergeant Ambrose 108
Sheehan, Canon 276
Shields, Dan 106, 107, 117, 124
Simms, Dr Otto 180
Sinn Féin 21, 22, 23, 27, 28, 30, 31, 35, 38, 45, 57, 66, 88, 118, 135, 140, 163, 208, 210, 216, 235, 239, 249
Slattery, Maurice 105
Smith, Constable William 120
Smith, Major Compton 120, 157
Smyth, Divisional Commissioner G. B. F. 44, 56, 85
Smyth, Patrick 36
Somerville, Michael 268
Southern Star 225
Spooner, Joseph 195
Squibs, Private 157
Stack, Austin 194, 203, 210
Strickland, Maj. Gen. E. P. 47, 51, 53, 54, 59, 98, 99, 100, 104, 114, 137, 144, 146, 156, 170
Sullivan, Barry, solicitor 140, 141, 142, 143, 144, 147, 155
Sullivan, Con 211
Sullivan, Dominic 164
Sullivan, Michael (Appeal to Lords) 154, 157
Sullivan, Mick 108, 110
Sullivan, Tobias 42, 44, 94
Sunday Independent 263
Sunday Press 252
Sweeney, Danny 118, 119
Sweeney, Morgan 76

T

Taaffe, Volunteer 126, 127, 128
Taylor, Constable William 89
Temple, Officer Bertie 131
Thompson, Captain 69
Times, The 38, 54
Tobin, Liam 58
Tone, Theobald Wolfe 135, 143
Townshend, General Charles 32
Traynor, Oscar 216
Treacy, Seán 35
Tudor, Major General H. Hugh 44, 91
Twomey, Edward 107
Twomey, Moss 186, 200
Tyrell, Col 47, 51

V

Vaughan, Dan 80, 81, 82
Verling, Algie 41

W

Wallace, Peter 35
Waters, Edward 107
Watkins, Constable Samuel 118
Webb, Constable John 120
Whelan, Pax 113, 186, 189
White, Paddy 264, 278
Will, Alexander 56
Williamson, Sir A. 51
Willis, Dick 59, 60, 71
Wilson, Field Marshal Sir Henry 62, 65, 66, 185
Wood, Albert, KC 142, 143, 144, 146, 168, 175, 235, 247
Woodcock, Constable Headley 118
Woodward, Constable George 110